Rauf Denktaş

A PRIVATE PORTRAIT

GW00385210

Yvonne Çerkez

*The authorised biography of the Turkish
Cypriot president who defied the world
to create a homeland for his people*

Rauf Denktaş

A PRIVATE PORTRAIT

Dearest June & John,
Thank you for your love &
support. Enjoy the book!
        Much love,   August 2014
                Bonnie xx

First published in Northern Cyprus 2014
This edition printed by
Okman Printing Limited

©2014 by YVONNE ÇERKEZ

All rights reserved. No part of this publication may be
reproduced, stored in a retrieval system, or transmitted
in any form or by any means, electronic, mechanical,
photocopying, recording or otherwise, without the
prior permission of the copyright holder

YVONNE ÇERKEZ
has asserted the moral right to be identified as the
author of this work. A catalogue reference is available
from the British Library

Cover Design: Livingmagazine, North Cyprus.

ISBN 978-0-9930153-0-4

For Brett

CONTENTS

PREFACE

LORD MAGINNIS OF DRUMGLASS

ALMOST exactly a year before Rauf Denktaş died on Friday, January 13, 2012, two weeks short of his 88th birthday, I had the honour — with the support of many distinguished signatories in Britain and Northern Cyprus — of nominating him for the Nobel Peace Prize. I believe the Prologue to that 28-page citation can also properly serve today as a fitting introduction to this welcome book about a man who by any measure was one of the outstanding statesmen of his age. *It read:*

'IN order to understand why the nomination of Rauf Denktaş is not merely a casual gesture but a serious proposal of genuine merit, we who support that must first set out the reasons why the accepted international view of what is generally called 'the Cyprus problem' is false, and that the island is divided not because of the intervention of the Turkish military in 1974, but because of what happened in the eleven years before that. In so doing, it will become clear why Rauf Denktaş, in his unwavering defence of the human rights and dignity of his people, is deserving of recognition. It is not an exaggeration to say that without his stand for freedom over the past half-century it is probable that today there would be no Turkish Cypriot community in Cyprus. A people would have vanished.

What happened in Cyprus between the foundation

of the Republic in 1960 and the Turkish intervention in 1974 is a period which the Greek Cypriot political class has successfully persuaded the world to forget, and to believe instead that but for the Turkish intervention the island would be a haven of peace and tranquillity. It is by presenting that intervention as the source of all the island's problems that the Greek Cypriots have succeeded in bringing about the long-standing international embargo on Turkish Cypriot trade, sport, and communications — though, of course, the Turkish Cypriots themselves have committed no wrong, if wrong there be, save perhaps that of surviving.

It is also the reason why, again successfully, the Greek Cypriots have been able to present Rauf Denktaş as an obstacle to their 'peaceful resolution' of the divisions between North and south Cyprus, and to damn him as 'intransigent' — the pariah founder and long-time president of an 'illegal state'. Yet all objective consideration demonstrates that the opposite is true. It is precisely because of his refusal to surrender or to compromise his people, and to provide them with the human rights and dignity that attend the rule of law and democratic governance, that the Turkish Cypriot community, though besieged, remains in being. And far from obstacle, it is Rauf Denktaş who has consistently put forward constructive proposals for a settlement, accepting the necessary compromises inherent therein — only to have each rejected in turn by the Greek Cypriots. Although, because of the Turkish intervention, the mass killings which preceded it are no more, the fact of that slaughter remains, even if the international community prefers not to remember it. For Rauf Denktaş, however, it is reason enough to recall that often inconvenient adage that those who forgot their history are at risk of repeating it.

Thus, for his lifelong battle for the rights and dignity of his people, and for his constant search for a peace that would endure, we hereby present this nomination of Rauf Denktaş for the Nobel Peace Prize 2011.

Would such an award be controversial? Indeed it would be, for in effect it would be a rebuke to the United Nations and the European Union that in choosing to forget the attempted genocide of the Turkish Cypriot people before 1974, and their compliance in the continued maintenance of economic sanctions against them at the behest of the Greek Cypriots, notwithstanding their own promises in 2004 to end them, they have wilfully denied the Turkish Cypriot people their human rights and dignity. Such a rebuke is long overdue.'

ALTHOUGH in the event the 2011 Prize was awarded jointly to three women for their struggle for women's rights, nonetheless Rauf Denktaş more than deserved his own nomination for his lifelong struggle for Turkish Cypriot rights, as this absorbing book amply demonstrates. The story of his long life is also the story of his unflinching determination to defend the freedom of his people through the darkest of years, but this compelling portrait of the man is also a timely reminder of how and why he came to found Northern Cyprus as an independent state. It is a legacy for which the Turkish Cypriots, and indeed for all those who support their cause, should ever — and will ever —remain grateful.

PROLOGUE

RAUF Raif Denktaş sits comfortably in his armchair with his beloved dog, Boncuk, lounging faithfully at his feet. Dressed simply in khaki slacks and a button down T-shirt, the former President gestures for us to join him. The general tone of the living room is light and spacious but with a homely appeal. There are no elaborate adornments or note-worthy reminders of his Presidency —just a smattering of family photos lining the various tables and shelves. The once-impressive girth, now reduced considerably by age, is visibly relaxed. His demeanour appears that of a doting grandfather enjoying a leisurely retirement as he reaches down to reassure an increasingly worried Boncuk of a promised walk. His expressive face, obstinately defying his 86 years, reveals a mischievous nature with a roguish glint playing about his eyes.

A bemused smile trails across his face as he waits patiently for the inevitable question of Cyprus that has dominated his life. He reaches for his tea and sips at it thoughtfully. The smile playing on his lips suddenly breaks into an infectious laugh as he begins to recount a conference he once attended involving the Archbishop Makarios.

"It was during the negotiations for the 1960 Constitution at the Government House," he explains. "Julian Amery was in charge and I received a message from Dr. Küçük that they were struggling and I was to join them immediately at the Constitutional table. I was already briefed and aware of the problems because Makarios had delayed the signing of the agreement by several months.

"Makarios was refusing to sign giving his reasons that he was in conflict with the British bases. He was arguing that from the British bases the agreement states only pens or pencils can be freely imported to the Republic and he was complaining: 'you are now trying to import ball points! Ball points are not included so you cannot do it!' Amery was losing his head and saying 'what are you doing?!' Makarios was repeating 'sorry but I am honouring what is written' and the whole thing was just grinding to a halt again. At this point I went in and was given the floor.

'Archbishop' I said, 'what are you doing? You have already delayed the signing of this agreement by nine months and you see that delaying it will not kill it; you'll have to sign it. So what are we going to do about this little matter?'

"He says to me, 'On which side are you talking from Mr. Denktaş?' implying that I was helping the British. 'Look,' I said, 'there is a Turkish Cypriot side, a Greek Cypriot side and opposite us the British side. I am sitting with the Turkish Cypriots. The Turkish Cypriots also have an interest in a quick finish of this agreement. Please, don't delay it.'

"The atmosphere was very tense and Amery, who clearly had had enough, told us all to take a break and so we walked out into the garden. I, naturally, was in the company of Dr. Küçük when Makarios approached us. 'So, Mr. Denktaş, about these divorce cases,' he said. 'The Church looks at these cases where the claim is the girl is not a virgin at the time of marriage. We are having a great deal of difficulty with this problem; it's the constant excuse that is brought before us and we're really sick and tired of it! How do you deal with these cases?'

"Well, it's my nature to be naughty so I told him: 'it's not such a problem for us as our girls' skirts are longer than yours!' His face was a picture but he laughed and then told us a dirty joke about a *Hoca* (Muslim cleric); we laughed and I fired back with three dirty jokes about a Priest."

He laughs heartily at the memory; his face creased with mirth and harbouring no signs of resentment for what was to become the ill-fated legacy of the meeting.

The final denouement of the long-waited Constitution, that had been an accumulation of nine long, arduous months, should have guaranteed the Turkish Cypriots' rights. Instead, the effort to retain a working partnership under the Constitution ended — almost abruptly as it had begun. The ensuing bitter struggle that resulted from the Constitution's failure rendered a period of disruption that reached fanatical and violent heights. The very core and identity of the Turkish Cypriots was under threat and seemingly without a future. Amidst the uncertainty, a leader emerged and thus began Denktaş' journey to achieve justice for the Turkish Cypriots he affectionately refers to as 'my people.'

PART I

Early Life

CHAPTER ONE
A Born Lawyer

Rauf Raif Denktaş was born during the early hours of January 27th, 1924 in Paphos, Cyprus. He was the sixth child and fourth son for his 40-year-old father Hussein Mehmet Raif *Bey** and 38-year-old mother, Emine *Hanım***. However, Rauf's arrival was unable to complete a family portrait of a growing close-knit family with small children vying for their parents' attention. The eldest child, first son Cahit, was already a 23-year-old and studying away from home training to be a doctor. The next, his brother Ertuğrul, just a few years younger, was also studying abroad. Two children, a boy and a girl, had followed Cahit and Ertuğrul but died in infancy. The closest child in age to Rauf was his seven-year-old sister, Neriman. Unsurprisingly Rauf's two surviving elder brothers and sister, absorbed in their own growing worlds, viewed the new arrival from a distance.

Although there were varying age differences between the children, Rauf was a welcome addition to the family. Having lost two small children, his father expressed his relief on hearing the robust screams of an obviously healthy new baby that lay nestled in his wife's arms. In honour of his arrival, the young infant was given the preferred name of his father, Raif, included in his own title.

*Bey is a mode of address for adult males and deemed a polite formality. In English it is the equivalent of 'Mr'. **Hanım is a similar mode of address for adult females and in English is the equivalent of 'Mrs/Ms/Madam'.

Rauf's appearance into the fold had incurred great expectations: it was hoped he would help to heal the wounds of a grieving family shattered by tragedy and encourage them to move on past the deaths of the two children that had been lost. An enduring family legend passed down through the generations claims that as well-wishers and relatives clustered around the newborn, Rauf's maternal grandmother held the infant aloft for the children to admire. "Look," she teased, "his little finger is red. You know this means he will grow up to be a very important person." Rauf's sister Neriman then peered up at the infant; her face wrinkled with disapproval, as she promptly declared, "he doesn't *look* very important." Observant onlookers noted that proud patriarch, Raif *Bey*, surveyed his family with quiet delight and appeared to have already decided his youngest child would make a vital difference for the family.

Despite Rauf's place in the family he would virtually grow up an only child and into a world very different from his elder siblings: his eldest brother had been born in 1901 to a father who was barely 17 and a mother who had been a 15-year-old child-bride. At that time, expectations for the young couple were limited to prospects that included little more than a life of modest security.

The ancestry of the Denktaş family* was steeped in the traditions of a farming background. Working and living off the land as a family embodied the Turkish Cypriot way of life in the late 19th century and early 20th century. The British were able to lease the island from the Ottomans in 1878 before having the opportunity of declaring it a colony in 1925. Thereafter the British became the ruling class and

---

* The family name was changed to Denktaş when the British, after establishing the island as a Crown Colony in 1925, introduced the use of surnames. Before this change was made, a father's forename was commonly used to determine family connections.

in a position to implement many changes that would benefit the indigenous community. However, the British presence on the island was not without its complications.

Whilst the Greek Cypriot community was considered by the British to be skilled Levantine traders, the Turkish Cypriots were often seen as simple, contented farmers. The conflicting attitudes of the British towards the Cypriot inhabitants would serve as an enduring legacy for Raif *Bey* and his family. His father, Şeherli Mehmet, seeking a better life than manual labour, left his family farm to become a young *Zaptiye* (policeman) during Ottoman rule. Şeherli *Bey* was a determined character and disagreed with the family view that he was in servitude to the Ottomans; rather he believed the changes were a stepping-stone for a more prosperous career and life.

Unfortunately, Şeherli *Bey's* new career would be short-lived. The arrival of the British meant that several changes were introduced including the insistence that members of the police force all be literate. Şeherli *Bey* was only able to sign his name and reluctantly had to resign his position. With the security that came with his police career now removed, the proud patriarch was left with little choice other than to resort to toiling his meagre land to eke out a living. The affect on him was belittling as he was manoeuvred back into a farming career but also left him feeling that he had to defend his position as an illiterate.

As a consequence of his experience with the British stance on having only educated civil servants, Şeherli *Bey* refused to accept that a police force could operate successfully only with a literate group of men; he believed that a masculine task force, such as the police, only required experience and physical strength. Şeherli *Bey* had an exceptional and retentive memory of events and history that he maintained

18

was all that was needed to succeed and would often undermine the need for education and literacy skills.

His son Raif, emboldened with a pioneering spirit and good work ethic, had decided on a different life and refused to be an emblematic part of the Turkish Cypriot farmers' life. Unlike his father, from an early age Raif *Bey* recognised the power of knowledge and immersed himself in books and their educational value — a legacy he was to pass on to his own children.

Despite being hindered by his father's beliefs and scorn, he taught himself to read and write in Turkish, Greek and English and later, in his mature years, put himself through school to learn law. Armed with a thirst for knowledge and a pursuit of respectability, Raif *Bey* had every intention of raising himself up from the confines of a working class environment and the trappings of menial farm labour.

IT was perhaps with a sense of irony that Raif *Bey* chose the one career that that his own father had been judged unfit to pursue: the police. At barely sixteen, Raif *Bey* presented himself to the local constabulary and applied to join their ranks. He was too young but audaciously claiming to be two years older, and being tall for his age, he managed to pass himself off as an ideal candidate. His determination and diligence were rewarded and he secured a respectable position as a policeman in the community working for the British. Although Raif *Bey* was young and inexperienced he took his duties seriously and quickly established himself as a hard-working defender of the local villages and their goods and properties.

His rise through the ranks was almost inevitable because of his commitment and the risks he was prepared to undertake. As an unmarried junior policeman he was often posted to the far-reaching and rural areas of Cyprus that were deemed a drain on resources due to the lesser level of criminal activity compared to its city counterparts. However, in these rural areas farmers suffered a particular blight — the practice of live-stock rustling. Whilst serving in the Karpaz area, situated at the easternmost peninsular of Cyprus, Raif *Bey's* zealousness of bringing these would-be raiders to book almost got him killed. He had befriended, and frequently helped, a Greek Cypriot farmer, called Yango, who was constantly targeted by raiders for his livestock. Yango had got wind of a plot to eliminate the young policeman in an effort to continue their robbery unhindered and warned Raif *Bey* in advance. The young policeman not only deftly avoided their murderous intentions but successfully apprehended the criminals bringing their criminal career to a halt. Yango and Raif became lifelong friends and, despite the turbulent political storms that ensued later to severely test their friendship, managed to remain so.

Raif *Bey's* exemplary record and commitment to enforce justice did not go unnoticed by the British authorities. He was young, keen and intelligent with multi-lingual abilities and a coveted law degree, obtained from an overseas correspondence course.

By his late 20s, and now married with children, he was honoured with the position of a junior judge, and demonstrated the same commitment to uphold the law as he had during his time as a law enforcer. Raif *Bey's* tenacity and self-deprecating manner very quickly earned him the reputation of a respected judge in the Paphos district. Cases brought before him were not quickly dismissed and always considered with patience and a willingness to listen. His rural roots had been of an advantage, enabling him to better understand problems and in turn make fair judgements. With his stoical approach and reputation for fair-mindedness, Raif *Bey* found himself a much sought-after figure in the community. Often his own home would be besieged by visitors with the ulterior motive of seeking to solicit his advice. Whether it was appeasing disgruntled neighbours or settling disputes at home, Raif *Bey's* easy manner and ability to offer an unbiased opinion made him the ideal arbitrator.

"Father was always sorting out squabbles, especially at home," Rauf recalled. "When Atatürk* started to become ill, daily bulletins were being issued. We didn't have a radio but one day he brought home a HMV radio because my father wanted to listen to the bulletins. Immediately both my grandmothers, who were living with us at the time, rose up in arms saying, 'this heathen instrument! It will affect the prosperity of the house!' It was a new invention and they were both terrified of it and refused to go near it. Instead, they made a lot of noise with their crying and wailing and made clear their intentions to throw the thing out. Father simply walked over to the radio, switched it on and tuned it to an Egyptian station that was broadcasting the call to prayer. They immediately sat down, covered their heads and began to pray in earnest. And that was how my father settled that affair. He never said a word and both grandmothers were tamed and loved that radio!"

The calming influence of Raif *Bey* would often serve as a buffer for his children growing up in the midst of a busy household, which was beginning to include extended

---

* Mustafa Kemal Atatürk (born 19 May 1881 died 10 November 1938) is a revered figure in Turkey and credited with founding modern day Turkey after the collapse of the Ottoman Empire. On 29 October 1923 the Republic of Turkey was established and Atatürk became its first President.

family members. His affable nature and even-temper quietly guided the family and instilled stability as well as much needed respite from family conflicts.

The source of strife would often loom in the shape of Emine. She was of small stature but imposing in her personality. At a time when women usually occupied a more subservient role in the family, Emine *Hanım* was less inclined to conform to her societal status. She was not afraid to voice her opinions to her husband (which she did frequently) if she disagreed with his decisions. She possessed a strong will and asserted herself as the household's disciplinarian keeping a firm hand raised loftily above the head of her brood.

Emine and Raif's respective grandmothers had instigated their marriage, wisely recognising the shy young policeman would benefit from the confident Emine *Hanım*— although Emine had to be convinced of Raif's intentions and suitability as a prospective husband.

Emine *Hanım*'s stubbornness was legendary and her displeasure at being told she was to be married at the tender age of fifteen without her consent, as was the custom, sent her hurtling to her bedroom and finding refuge beneath her bed. In an unusual display of assertiveness, Raif *Bey* pulled her from her sanctuary and assured the unhappy Emine that he would honour and respect her at all times. Emine, encouraged by Raif's calm temperament and good nature, acquiesced and the twosome were married and became a successful partnership.

As she matured Emine *Hanım*'s vivacious nature complemented Raif *Bey*'s quiet reserve and she was known as a gracious host particularly when entertaining Raif *Bey*'s many visiting colleagues. As the popular wife of Judge Raif (as he became commonly known) she had a status of her own that she took seriously and was a loyal and keen supporter of her husband's growing interest and activism in local politics.

With the family amicably settled into domesticity, Judge Raif's seniority and career flourished affording him a modest income and the family a comfortable life style, accepting of a middle-class status. Always with a book to hand, Judge Raif placed great emphasis on education and impressed this upon all of his children. He sent his two elder sons, Cahit and Ertuğrul, to be educated privately in İstanbul, Turkey and his daughter was expected to follow in her brothers' footsteps a year or two later. He would visit his children once a year in Turkey and took an avid interest in their studies as well as the opportunity to visit friends.

One planned excursion by Judge Raif created tension between himself and his wife who had decided that she should accompany her husband. At the time Rauf was just seventeen months old and Emine *Hanım* was six months pregnant with their fifth child. Judge Raif immediately vetoed the idea and insisted that she stayed home until after the birth of their child. Emine *Hanım* expressed her upset to relatives, complaining bitterly about her husband's refusal of allowing her to travel with him. She went on to take drastic and unorthodox measures to assure her place by her husband's side in Turkey. Her decision was to have dire consequences.

By 1925, a year after Rauf's birth, a new period of change and discovery was being ushered in. Turkey had formed a Republic and people were adjusting to new ideas and reforms. Unfortunately most Turkish Cypriot leaders were out of touch with the process of modernisation that was taking place in Turkey at the time: Atatürk's religious, social and legal reforms were slow to reach Cyprus and Judge

Raif was keenly aware of this and the ramifications this had for the Turkish Cypriot community. He had watched the changes with great interest and was eager to go to Turkey as it afforded him the opportunity to embroil himself in political discourse with his colleagues there and inform other like-minded Cypriots on his return. Meanwhile, Emine *Hanım* prepared herself for another trip entirely.

Emine *Hanım* felt that if she was not pregnant Raif would change his mind about her accompanying him to İstanbul. Soliciting the help of a sympathetic neighbour, she embarked on a dangerous mission to eradicate her problem. She made the decision to have an abortion and sought out the local midwife who conducted a disturbing business side-line as a practitioner in the art of 'losing unwanted babies'. An arrangement was made and Emine *Hanım* secretly left the house to meet with her 'abortionist'. On arrival at her house, the midwife, who had so often given nature a helping hand with the delivery of babies prepared to 'operate' and bring about an end to Emine's dilemma.

After the procedure, Emine *Hanım* returned home and waited for nature to bring closure to her torment. The conflicting emotions that she undoubtedly experienced would have been unbearable but possibly she had been driven in her misguided attempts to be at her husband's side, rationalising that this was a sacrifice to be endured. However, she was certainly aware Judge Raif would never have agreed to such a procedure and had allowed her own desperate needs to override his authority which prevented her from making an informed decision.

Whilst Emine *Hanım* spent many angst-ridden moments contemplating her actions, it wasn't long before she felt the familiar stirring of contractions induced by the attempted abortion. The pain was excruciating and it forced her into her bed from which she was never to leave. Judge Raif, worried by his wife's sudden illness and concern for his unborn child, cancelled his trip and stayed by her side.

The untrained 'midwife', who had so willingly agreed to the operation, was, as many were at the time, ignorant of proper aseptic techniques. The procedure was not only illegal but also rarely practised — even by trained physicians. Antibiotics were not manufactured until the late 1930s and early 1940s and lack of access to blood transfusions, with the added risk of blood type compatibility not as yet understood, increased the chances of mortality. Emine *Hanım* was to become another casualty of ignorance and her fate was sealed. A flurry of activity at Emine's bedside by doctors called in to determine the cause of her illness revealed gangrene was apparent in one of her legs causing irrevocable damage to her ailing body. Amputation of the leg was diagnosed and considered to be the only course of action as the infection threatened to spread and end with her inevitable death.

Typically, Emine *Hanım*'s stubbornness surfaced as she dismissed any attempts to amputate her leg. Judge Raif had employed the best medical care available to him at the time in an attempt to allay any fears that Emine *Hanım* may have felt about the surgery, but she could not be persuaded and remained steadfast in her refusal. Desperate pleas from her husband and family fell on deaf ears. Fully aware that her decision would result in certain death, Emine *Hanım* retreated into silence. Her seemingly determined resignation may have been motivated by guilt — she had confessed all to her husband, but never enlightened him, or any other member of the family, on the reasons for surrendering herself so capriciously to death. Judge Raif, although confused, felt powerless. His experiences as a judge may have weighed heavily when considering the rights of his wife to refuse or accept medical aid; but in any case, he decided he had no other recourse but to respect his wife's wishes and could not enforce the medical procedure.

A last photograph of them together, taken just days before her death, paints a bleak and sad picture: both Emine *Hanım* and Judge Raif solemnly face the camera — her eyes blackened with fatigue as he sits forlornly beside her, one hand gently resting on her arm. Emine *Hanım* appears to be aware that her time is drawing to a close from her choice of apparel. She shrouds herself in the traditional *çarşaf* dress* chosen specifically in the mourning colour of black. The intrusive camera-lens shares the pained couple's last moments together and captures the stark clarity of Emine's impending death. Rauf was considered too young to understand his mother's illness and was prevented from visiting her bedside. The photograph was to become his only tragic reminder of his mother's last days.

Emine *Hanım* was buried in accordance with Muslim traditions at a small cemetery in Paphos. Judge Raif and his children were once again plunged into turmoil as another two lives were enlisted in the family's grieving history.

For the eighteen-month-old Rauf, however, life became a chaotic affair tainted with bitter-sweet experiences. He suddenly found himself inundated with female attention as aunts, grandmothers and elder cousins descended upon the house to support Judge Raif and his young children. The house became awash with a sea of female voices and the bustling of competing women. Two young girls, employed as maids in an effort to aid the household, were also thrown

---

* *Çarşaf* translates literally as 'bed sheet' in English and is a dress that completely covers the body. Worn by females only, it is usually black in colour and was a common mode of dress in parts of the Ottoman Empire.

into the array. In the midst of it all Judge Raif sat in quiet despair, appearing to be drowning in the furore, making no attempt to silence the house. The children, sensitive to their father's anguish, learnt to tip-toe around him and tacitly agree never to mention their mother in his presence.

Whilst Rauf had the attention of older female relatives, the loss of his mother and a solution to quell his searching questions as to her sudden disappearance needed to be managed. An answer was found in the shape of a kitten that he instantly fell in love with and she became the object of his affections and constant companion. As Rauf now had a focus for his attentions so too did Judge Raif eventually learn to manage his grief through his youngest child.

Recognising the bewildered plight of his youngest child, who had so eagerly transferred his affections to a cat, Judge Raif adopted the dual role of mother and father in earnest. Young Rauf was showered with attention and deposited firmly in the centre of his father's world. He became known as the 'little companion' and dutifully escorted his father wherever he went. The twosome became a familiar sight in the local coffee shops — the renowned forum for local men to banter and expound their political opinions. It was Rauf's first induction into the world of politics and he soaked up the atmosphere from his privileged position at the forefront, perched on his father's knee.

Unsurprisingly, Rauf became a very articulate two-year-old. His world littered with adults, he was only aware of other children when his elder siblings came home from school on holiday. By now his maternal grandparents had moved into the family home and Rauf found himself another adult best friend and confidante in the shape of his grandfather. When the presence of his father was lacking, Rauf's grandfather often took over the role of teacher and mentor.

Slowly life returned to normal after Emine *Hanım's* loss and when Rauf was two-and-a-half years old, a fresh start for the family was promised when Judge Raif was transferred to Nicosia. Everything was packed up including the young Rauf onto moving lorries. As the convoy of lorries trundled along the dusty tracks, Rauf remembered his beloved cat and anxiously enquired after her. Seated on his grandmother's lap in the front seat, Rauf became agitated when his queries were met with silence. The commotion that ensued from his tears prompted his grandmother to reassure him that the cat was on one of the other vehicles and would be waiting for him at the other end.

Despite his tender age, Rauf remains convinced that the incident was his first memory and the moment was particularly poignant as it was also to become his first 'exposure to adult deception'. The cat was not waiting for him in Nicosia and the distraught Rauf was inconsolable. However, Judge Raif quickly alleviated Rauf's distress by presenting him with a puppy. The puppy was promptly named Rex and Rauf's lifelong friendship with animals began along with his guarded awareness that people could not always be trusted to tell the truth.

Nicosia, as the capital of Cyprus, was a thriving place of commerce and social activity. The town itself was a labyrinth of sprawling buildings each homed in a street trailing to another. Clusters of tall, window shuttered houses lined the dusty streets, furnished with scores of playing children darting in and out of the busy throng of daily life. Rauf's new home was situated in the central part of town (now known as Atatürk Square) and boasted a large courtyard, complete with a flowing fountain and pond.

The rooms were spacious and Judge Raif wasted no time in creating a study filling it with volumes of books that the young Rauf delighted in lingering over in the hope of emulating his father's reading prowess. The nearby courthouse allowed Judge Raif easy access to attend court and a social life to engage in at the many coffee shops. A new life without Emine, for Judge Raif, was beginning to emerge as he became immersed in his new post and occupied by the energetic environment.

However, the bustle and excitement of Nicosia was lost on young Rauf as his protective father had confined him to the custody of his grandparents. Rauf's days were mostly whiled away playing with his dog, Rex, and the menagerie of animals that were beginning to occupy the house at his insistence. Trips to the park were accompanied by his grandfather and evenings were spent in his father's company as Judge Raif patiently listened to the small boy's chatter and latest escapade involving his beloved Rex; Judge Raif, in turn, would coach the by now three-year-old Rauf in the complexities of reading and writing, maths and history.

Whilst Rauf's childhood was not isolated, Judge Raif saw the necessity for his son to be in school and have the opportunity to socialise with other children. Rauf was therefore enrolled in the local kindergarten — much to his displeasure. Like most small children the experience of being away from home, albeit for a few short hours, was a painful wrench. He objected to being taken away from the familiar surroundings of home and, most of all, his numerous pets.

His first day at school was a traumatic affair as he was prised from his father's legs and deposited unceremoniously in the classroom alive with the clamour of three-year-olds jostling for attention. The precocious Rauf struggled to find anything in common with the other children and felt awkward: he was quite unused to the heaving sounds and behaviour of so many children in one place. Always more comfortable in the company of adults, Rauf fixed his sights on the young music teacher.

Rauf's interest in the young teacher was apparent from the beginning and he probably wasn't alone in his view. She was employed to teach her young charges songs to which the children would all enthusiastically join in. Often she would complete the lesson with her own songs accompanying the singing with her violin. Immediately the children were captivated by the soothing tones from the stringed instrument. The result would have a calming and very powerful effect — particularly for the young Rauf as he marvelled at her ability to enrapture and quieten noisy children. Later, the adult Rauf was able to recall, with several chuckles, his infatuation with the young teacher:

"She was beautiful and I decided at all of three years that I was in love with her. Every night when my father asked me about my day, I told him about my music teacher and how lovely she was. I was consumed by her, I really was. Eventually my father had enough and decided to visit the school and meet this teacher for himself. I can't be sure, but after his visit, I think he fell in love with her too!"

Despite his young age Rauf exhibited the early signs of being wholly committed to his beliefs and the relationships he formed. Whether it was declaring his ardent love for a teacher or caring for the stray pets that he was accumulating, he could not be dissuaded otherwise in his intentions. Judge Raif conceded that his youngest child needed nurturing but also had a need to nurture others. His elder children demonstrated the same qualities with their chosen studies: all studied and eventually entered in to the field of medicine. Rauf himself had declared his own intentions to be a veterinarian (although he was often influenced after a

Saturday visit to the cinema by the thought of becoming a cowboy or Tarzan). Judge Raif knew he had to pay serious thought to Rauf's future.

Cyprus was facing tumultuous times and Judge Raif had been astute in recognising the difficulties with which young Turkish Cypriots were being confronted. He feared that too many young Turkish Cypriots fortunate enough to receive further education often took their skills abroad where the economy and prospects were more enticing. His eldest son, Cahit, had sent apologetic letters home telling him of his wishes to remain in Turkey to practise medicine. Despite Judge Raif's pleading that young, skilled Turkish Cypriots were needed at home to contribute to the community, Cahit remained adamant. He cajoled his father by insisting that he would be practising in the poorest regions of Turkey, where hygiene, medicine and education were lacking — far more so than in Cyprus. Judge Raif relented but remained ardent in his view that the Turkish Cypriot community needed reforms and, more importantly, skilled young people to implement them.

One by one, letters from Rauf's siblings outlining their intentions to remain in Turkey found their way into Judge Raif's exasperated hands. Concerned that his youngest child would also grow up and succumb to the lure of Turkey, he had to consider how best to encourage Rauf to remain in Cyprus and be a productive member of a dwindling educated Turkish Cypriot community.

Judge Raif had always fostered the idea that the young Rauf would follow in his judiciary footsteps but now he became ever more determined. He set about instructing his youngest child in the hopes he would become a lawyer.

Rauf's dying mother, Emine Hanım, and father Raif Bey,
circa 1925

Family portrait with Rauf, *second from left, bottom row,*
circa 1926. The seat without a family member purposefully
left empty to acknowledge Emine Hanım's absence

Rauf with
father Judge
Raif Bey
and sister
Neriman.

Judge Raif, now
in Western dress,
with his two
younger children,
Neriman and
Rauf, circa 1930

CHAPTER TWO

Trouble Ahead

IN 1931, Judge Raif made the decision to send Rauf to be schooled in İstanbul, Turkey like his siblings before him. It was a decision that may in part have been influenced by the growing tensions that were seeping through Cyprus at the time. The Greek Cypriot community was agitating for *enosis**— union with Greece. The underground rumblings of dissension by the Greek Cypriot community, which had been apparent since the beginning of British rule, were beginning to bubble to the surface, finally reaching a bloody climax that, in just one week, saw the Government House destroyed, several deaths and resulted in harsh punishments meted out to Greek and Turkish Cypriots alike irrespective of their involvement.

When Britain began its rule on the island in 1878, they virtually ignored the previous administrations of allowing the indigenous communities to be in control of their own affairs. Their Ottoman predecessors had been tolerant and accepting of religious and cultural diversities. As a result, Turkish and Greek Cypriots had successfully managed their own communities and economic affairs and had even been allowed to elect their own representatives in Council.

Enosis (meaning 'union' in Greek) refers to the movement of various Greek communities that live outside of Greece, for incorporation of the regions they inhabit, to the Greek state.

By contrast, British administration dominated all affairs and, more importantly, Turkish and Greek Cypriots no longer had their own representatives in the new Council. Unsurprisingly, hostilities grew towards the British who appeared unaware or did not contemplate the threat seriously.

Tensions finally peaked in October, 1931 under the administrative rule of the then Governor, Sir Ronald Storrs. Storrs was a 'classically trained administrator' fluent in Greek but chiefly concerned with implementing his own lofty ideals onto the island. With rigorous determination Storrs set about developing the island, recognising its potential as a tourist destination. However, despite his best efforts to raise Cyprus' profile, Storrs had little time for the local inhabitants. He often expressed his disapproval and disappointment at the Greek Cypriot lack of knowledge and regard for what he deemed as their rich, classical heritage. The Greek Cypriot community was equally disappointed with the Governor who they had hoped would affiliate himself with them and their cause to achieve *enosis.*

Seizing on the opportunity of an indifferent Governor and administration, the Greek Cypriot population demanded the immediate removal of the British rule from the island and unification with Greece. The demands were punctuated with a week of rioting and violence erupted in several districts led by the priests and Bishops of the Orthodox Church. The swelling crowds that formed were incited by speeches from the Church leaders, inflamed with nationalism and the desire for *enosis.* Greek flags were hoisted as British and Turkish flags were torn down.

The actions of a divisive community would have a profound effect on the seven-year-old Rauf. As he walked with his grandfather, he witnessed flags being desecrated and attempted to sum up later the feelings it evoked in an interview: "My Grandfather told me, as we watched with sadness our flag being burned in the street: 'one day you will see the Turkish flag again. It won't happen in my time, but you will see it in yours.' He was absolutely right."

Eventually Britain sent her forces to the island to restore order. They succeeded in containing the riots and bringing about public peace, although the threat of *enosis* was never quelled.

The young Rauf was able to feel safe largely due to the assurances his father and grandfather gave him. They, like most of the Turkish Cypriot population, felt that the presence of the British was all that was necessary to maintain peace on the island and prevent *enosis;* in the event that the British left, Turkey would be there. Despite this, Judge Raif took his own precautions and sent his youngest son to the Feyziati boarding school in İstanbul — a safe distance away from possible trouble.

Having made his way to İstanbul, a nervous Rauf was pleased to be met by a familiar face on arrival — his eldest brother, Cahit. Cahit was now a married man and happily settled in Turkey but felt that the young boy could benefit from some advice derived from his own experiences of having been schooled in Turkey. In grave tones a concerned Cahit advised Rauf 'not to tell anyone that you come from Cyprus' explaining that Cyprus was only known in Turkey for its donkeys; furthermore, he counselled, if Rauf was to tell the other children he came from Cyprus he would be immediately labelled as one. He urged the wide-eyed and impressionable Rauf to claim he came from Ankara instead.

Rauf accepted his older brother's counsel and tried to prepare for his first day. Although initially feeling excited and full of adventure it did not quite go as well as he had planned. As soon as he was left in the large, imposing school hall the overwhelmed youngster promptly burst into tears. A young girl, who had been eyeing the small boy with curiosity, approached him and asked the reason for his tears. Rauf was bereft without his protective father and blurted out to an amused girl, not much older than him, that he had been left alone and missed his father terribly. More accustomed to sympathy and gentle coaxing, Rauf was surprised by the girl's sharp retort. She pronounced him 'a little fool' and stated she had little time for his self-pity. Her anger gathered momentum as she explained her own position as an orphan, left by an uncle to fend for herself, and concluding that he should 'stop being a baby'.

Rauf surmised later that the girl was not only without an immediate family but also very ill. She had no hair and ashen features; traits that suggested she was almost certainly a cancer victim. She was also conspicuous in her frequent absences from lessons and never saw the end of the school year. Rauf realised much later how difficult it must have been for the girl to feel compassion for his paltry problems.

However, meeting the rest of his classmates he fared little better in their affections. As the children surged on the newcomer with ardent questions, he remembered his brother's advice and, fearing being ridiculed, dutifully repeated it. "I was very popular," he recalled, "until they asked me how I had travelled from Ankara. By boat I told them proudly!" Fortunately for Rauf there was a teacher on hand to dispel the sniggering children. The teacher then gently explained to Rauf that Ankara was inland and therefore it was not possible to come by boat but, more importantly, he should not be afraid to admit where he came from — a lesson that Rauf took to heart and vowed never to feel ashamed of again.

Rauf's school days in İstanbul were short-lived and he was returned home within the year. Judge Raif offered the reason that he could not afford to continue paying Rauf's school fees. The economy had suffered in Cyprus, as it had globally, after the Wall Street crash of 1929 and continued to have far-reaching consequences. The 1930s were economically depressed and the Cyprus pound had fallen dramatically from ten Turkish Lira to just eight. The British sought to weather the financial storm in Cyprus with a new budget (devised by Storrs) that mainly fell on the local population with imposed taxes.

The locals, who largely lived off their lands and already had difficulties with debts accrued to maintain their farms, now found themselves with increased taxes (this in part had also instigated the riots in 1931; the new budget devised by the British caused the Greek members of the Legislative Council to resign in protest). Judge Raif, who had been paid in pounds, now had to review his finances and consider the cost of having four children living and studying in Turkey. However, he continued financially to support Rauf's three elder siblings' education in Turkey and it is more likely Rauf's recall to Cyprus was a result of Judge Raif missing his 'little companion'.

Rauf was delighted to be returned home and wasted no time reacquainting himself with his precious animals and the familiar surroundings of home. An exuberant Rauf raced to the water fountain situated in the courtyard and launched himself into it and began to splash about happily and throw water in every direction. Whilst he enjoyed playing in the coolness of the water he failed to spot Judge Raif arrive home from work. Confronted with the sight of his young son wading in water up past his chest, Judge Raif was enraged and bellowed at his son demanding to know what he was doing.   Caught unaware, Rauf could only stutter 'nothing' as an explanation to his father. The adult Rauf recalls this as the first and only time he saw his father so angry and with a raised hand as if to smack him. In retrospect, Rauf believes his father's angry response had more to do with the fact that his short answer of "nothing" was tantamount to a lie as he was clearly swimming in the forbidden fountain in plain sight. Judge Raif was of the opinion that if Rauf was up to mischief he must defend or own up to his actions and not resort to denying any involvement.

Judge Raif's wrath was quickly alleviated but his need to teach Rauf important lessons and life skills never abated and were apparent in everything he did with the young boy. As well as encouraging his son to be honest and always stand by his convictions, he also wanted Rauf not to falter at the first or even last obstacle he may face in life.

As a child, Rauf and his family would spend holidays in the village of Karaman (also known as Karmi). Judge Raif was a nature lover and a favourite pastime would be to take long walks on hilly trails often with Rauf in tow. Occasionally they would come across stretches of clumped shrubbery that Judge Raif would leap enthusiastically over. If he saw Rauf faltering and hesitating to make the same jump he would offer Rauf a moral dilemma: "suppose I am in trouble on the other side — you will not come to my aid? Jump! You can do it!" Rauf was fearful of scratching his legs but nevertheless would follow his father without ever questioning him. Although Rauf did accept he was learning more than just how to jump over offending shrubbery.

The village Rauf and his family stayed in housed a thriving mixture of villagers comprising of Greek and Turkish Cypriots. Rauf remembers the village as having a friendly atmosphere and good neighbourly relations between the different communities. The summers spent there also proved to be an eventful time for Rauf. Judge Raif insisted on more than just teaching Rauf principles, he also expected his son to carry out physical chores for his neighbours. 'Life is not all joy and holiday' he would reprimand his son. Each morning, Rauf was sent to work for a Greek Cypriot neighbour toiling in the fields picking onions or other produce. He would be paid sixpence for his labours which he discovered later was given to the 'employer' by his father to be paid to Rauf. One hour a day was also devoted to Greek lessons administered by Judge Raif himself before he was finally allowed to swim and enjoy the sunshine.

In 1939, Rauf was able to learn a lot more from his father by simply observing his actions. Judge Raif was selected to receive an MBE (Member of the Most Excellent Order of the British Empire); however, the nomination placed Judge Raif in a precarious position. A selected few only were presented with the prestigious award but it was an accolade that roused mixed feelings in the community. It held connotations of treachery for some who were still feeling the bitterness of British rule and the restrictions that had been imposed on Cypriots after the 1931 riots.

Judge Raif's identity was in constant conflict as a Turkish Cypriot leader in the community and as an official of the Court dispensing justice on behalf of the British and now he appeared to be forced to make a distinctive choice between the two. His dilemma of whether to accept the medal was further compounded by the fact that his colonial masters wanted him to wear a fez for the occasion — despite being aware that in 1925 the fez had been prohibited in Atatürk's new Turkey; it was also made clear to him that a hat of any other description would be unacceptable. The reason for British insistence on Judge Raif wearing the fez is not clear. However, it appears that the British not only enjoyed the bright dress of the national Turkish costume but also felt it to be proper and in accordance with societal hierarchy. Turkish house servants, at the height of colonialism, in British employ were expected to wear their embroidered colourful waist coats, *Şalvar* trousers* and of course the fez. Greek Cypriots in service, by contrast, were encouraged to anglicise their attire to appear more like their British employers. Judge Raif, as a civil servant, also dressed appropriately in a suit and tie, as was expected of him, but the addition of a fez at such an auspicious ceremony would have been a reminder of his social status amongst the British.

Keenly aware of his responsibilities to both his employers and community, Judge Raif found himself under pressure and facing an uncertain future. The stark choice he was given meant he could either offend the principles of Atatürk, whom he greatly admired, or his British superiors thereby blighting his career and only form of income. A compromise was reached when Judge Raif attended the ceremony in the scorching sun bareheaded. The young Rauf was also in attendance at the ceremony, proud of his father's ability to negotiate his way through a complex minefield with his principles intact.

After the excitement of summer, Rauf was sent to the English School of Nicosia in Cyprus to continue his education. It was a reputable school founded in 1900 by the flamboyant character Canon Frank Darvall Newham. His teaching principles, which remained consistent and still evident when Rauf arrived there in 1931, were influential and unusual in equal parts. Canon Newham advocated

---

* *Şalvar* are traditional trousers worn by Turkish men and are part of folk costume in Turkey.

41

cultural and social diversity and the all-boys' school reflected this in abundance. Children of several nationalities were housed at the school including Armenians, Maronites and English as well as Turkish and Greek Cypriots. Despite its reputation of having a good ethnic and social mixture, the school placed great emphasis on English teaching methods and English standards. The presiding headmaster was usually a classically-trained British teacher and a graduate from a distinctive university — Rauf's headmaster, Mr. Simms, was no exception and typified the ideals originally introduced to the school by Canon Newham.

Although the boys had varied backgrounds, they were encouraged to integrate and view one another as equals and with respect. They were taught and spoken to solely in English giving them a language in common and enabling them to communicate with each other. The method was generally successful and at times worked well to form cohesion in spite of some of the obvious differences noted by the teaching staff (the Turkish Cypriot boys were considered to be less advanced and lacking in experience). Rauf, however, managed to avoid the generalised opinions and even gained a certain amount of popularity and notoriety amongst the boys. This was in part due to his coveted status as 'the boy who had schooled in İstanbul'.

An overseas education, and the son of a prominent judge, gave him an air of sophistication that set him apart from the other boys. He was best remembered by his childhood friends as a notorious prankster and well-liked — although Rauf dismissed this and jokingly referred to the fact he was the prestigious owner of his own bicycle as the most likeliest cause for his popularity. In any event, it was clear Rauf had settled much better at a school based in Cyprus and quickly became a leader amongst his peers as well as earning the regard of his teachers. The Headmaster, Mr. Simms, was particularly fond of Rauf and encouraged the budding amateur in his hobby of photography. Rauf's first camera was a small Japanese model given to him by his father on his tenth birthday and of which he took great care.

Noting how diligent Rauf was with his camera, Mr. Simms entrusted his own camera to Rauf for the purpose of taking photographs of a picnic outing that had been arranged for the school boys. Rauf wasn't used to Mr. Simms' more expensive model with its intricate design and struggled to open it. Rauf vividly remembers the experience:

"I, being the expert of course, broke the camera! He [Mr. Simms] discovered it was broken when he went home. So, the next day there was a very angry headmaster demanding to know what the hell I had done with his camera! I said I tried to open it and I couldn't, when of course I had broken the camera by trying to force it open. My father was furious and took the camera to be repaired when I finally admitted to him what I had done."

Mr. Simms' patience was to be tested several times over the years by Rauf but it appears that Rauf's charm always heralded him a safe passage through.

Despite his congenial personality and the tender years of the children at school, Rauf also remembers a tenacious relationship with the Greek Cypriot boys. "You were friendly, but you couldn't be close," he recalls. "There was always a distance between us. They had their views and we had ours." The 'distance' was a sad reflection of the tensions created by the adult community causing the children to squabble as they were exposed to their parents' views. The children were constantly being reminded of their cultural backgrounds and differences in nationalities and religion which in turn spilled out on to the playground. After the riots in 1931, the British attempted to remove the threat of *enosis* and discourage nationalist behaviour by removing all flags, except for the British, and banning public demonstrations and meetings. The issue of *enosis,* however, remained steadfast in young Greek Cypriot minds — and proud nationalist thoughts of being Turkish in Turkish Cypriots. Later, in Rauf's teenage years, the squabbles in the playground would become bloody scuffles as the young men fought to preserve their views.

The fighting and arguing became commonplace between the Turkish and Greek Cypriot boys creating divides and factions amongst the boys whilst those without a Cypriot identity occupied a neutral zone.

As a teenager, Rauf was a stocky boy and noted for his fearless attitude and readiness to leap into action. He would vigorously defend his right to be a Turkish Cypriot and refused to be insulted or accept jibes from the Greek Cypriot boys about his nationality; he would also extend his defence to the protection of other Turkish Cypriot boys. Often he was called upon by his fellow compatriots to help them when trouble loomed in the shape of a physical altercation. He would hold down the offender until he apologised with the result that he became the boys' champion. Very few Greek Cypriot boys enjoyed the humiliating experience of being pinned down and made to recant their words, so they eventually gave up taunting Rauf and kept their distance.

Rauf was also an articulate teenager and would frequently take the arguments into the debating arena of the school. Although the debating subjects were not nationalist topics, which were strictly forbidden, the Turkish and Greek Cypriot boys would divide themselves into opposing camps so as to have the opportunity to score points against one another. One particular debate was the subject of God versus

Science and the competition became heated with Rauf's team, on the side of God, seemingly losing. Whilst Rauf attempted to gain ground during the closing argument, a sparrow began tapping furiously on the window pane loud enough to capture the audience's attention. Demonstrating an ability to think quickly and improvise, Rauf challenged the opposition to explain the sparrow's appearance and odd behaviour. "If your science can produce this sparrow and its desire to be heard, I will concede," he announced with confidence. The fortuitous moment proved successful for Rauf's team as no one could explain the sudden arrival of the sparrow and the debate was won.

Rauf's debating topic in defence of God was considered an interesting choice as he had never demonstrated any strong religious views. It was his need to gain any advantage possible over his Greek Cypriot peers that provided his incentive. At every possible opportunity Rauf placed himself in direct opposition to the Greek Cypriot boys in an attempt to define their differences. However, the teenage boys were not always able to prove how dissimilar they were.

Irrespective of their opposing views and arguments, the boys all appeared to be in unison when it came to the subject of girls. Rauf's teenage years, along with most of his peers in the late 1930s, were spent admiring the female form as a forbidden fruit that was to be desired from afar. For Rauf, the times were remembered as frustrating with limited contact with the opposite sex: "you just watched, you loved from a distance and you loved very badly," he mused. "Everybody knew who was with so-and-so; for example, Hasan's girlfriend: they had no contact but he would say, 'I passed her house last night, twice, and the light was on and I'm sure she saw me.' We would reply: 'mine rode past on her bicycle and she looked at me...'"

It was an innocent time where the boys would indulge in their respective fantasies about the object of their desires but were not able to converse with their 'girlfriends' or have any physical contact.

Rauf was luckier than most. At the tender age of fourteen he experienced his first kiss from an unlikely source. A school-trip to Bedford in England had been arranged giving the young men an eagerly anticipated opportunity to mix socially with the opposite sex without the oppressive frowning of furrowed brows from their Cypriot chaperones. It was an exciting time that allowed the boys to enjoy a variety of activities including school dances, which promised the rare experience of being able to engage in some forbidden 'hand holding.' A farewell school dance at the end of the boys' holiday signalled the end of any romances and the chance for blushing teenagers to kiss their beaus goodbye.

Clearly a charming young man, Rauf caught the eye of a few girls and was looking forward to the prospect of making his farewells but was surprised when a young teacher in her early twenties asked him to dance. He duly obliged the young teacher her request and politely danced with her. At the end of the dance, the young woman took the initiative to steal a kiss from the surprised fourteen-year-old Rauf. Although shocked, Rauf relished his first real kiss and had a story to tell on his return to Cyprus.

HOWEVER, back on home soil, Rauf's holiday romance quickly faded into obscurity and was replaced by his growing awareness of the lack of status — politically and socially, that Turkish Cypriots had in the community. Rauf was not alone in his concerns but he also had to contend with the unsettling resentment that was apparent amongst his Greek

Cypriot peers at school: children chiding each other in the playground had been usurped by frustrated teenagers with a political awareness of their social environment and the urge to insult. Rauf exhibited early signs of political shrewdness by taking his counter-arguments and defences to the public stage and a wider audience. At just sixteen, he embarked on a literary recourse to express his own frustrations and began writing profusely to local press outlets to air his concerns on the subject of Turkish Cypriots and drawing attention to their plight as citizens without an identity. Rauf was no longer concerned with teenage dramas at school and more interested in becoming an advocate for the rights of Turkish Cypriots.

Encouraged by his father, Rauf's early writing material was beginning to gather momentum and garner the attention of other like-minded Turkish Cypriots. Despite his youthful years, Rauf was writing prolifically and with a maturity normally reserved for a more experienced writer. He wrote, both in prose and poetry, expressing the sentiments of Turkish Cypriots without a voice. In his last year at school the influential Turkish language newspaper, *Halkın Sesi*, was published and Rauf naturally submitted articles for the newspaper's publications. He caught the attention of the proprietor, Dr. Fazıl Küçük*, who recognised the young man's writing talents and, more importantly, his sincere resolve and commitment to the Turkish cause which coincided with his own.

Halkın Sesi publicly argued the need for Turkish Cypriots to take a stand and fight for a recognised existence which

*Dr. Fazıl Küçük (1906-1984) was, and remains to date, a well-known figure amongst Turkish Cypriots. He was an active campaigner for Turkish Cypriot rights and elected as the Turkish Cypriot choice for community leader later becoming the first Vice-President of the newly-formed Republic of Cyprus in 1960.

was slowly being submerged. Reforms within the Turkish culture were also being advocated and encouraged: changes to existing marriage laws, education and civil rights were in need of modernisation — all of which Rauf agreed were necessary to be amended.

As a reformist and outspoken member of the Turkish Cypriot community, Dr. Küçük was a formidable character. He was extremely popular and took up the position of leader and representative of the Turkish community and sought to make political changes to a flawed system. Rauf's own association with Dr. Küçük was initially based on mutual respect as fellow writers intent on highlighting the issues of Turkish Cypriots and attempting to procure a more secure status for their compatriots.

However, Judge Raif's untimely death at the age of 57 (although official records place him at the age of 59 his earlier pretence of giving himself an additional two years meant that he had to perpetuate the lie throughout his career) propelled Rauf further into the political realm and he became more ardent about the cause that his father was so passionate about. Under the tutelage and protective wing of Dr. Küçük, the twosome struck up a professional relationship that flourished and spanned several decades. Dr. Küçük and Rauf became political allies intent on saving Turkish Cypriots and their very existence that eventually changed the face of Cyprus.

Rauf during his teenage years. At the time he was writing profusely to local press outlets to air his concerns on the subject of Turkish Cypriots and their plight

Government House, Nicosia, before Greek Cypriot rioters' protest against Colonial Rule and after on 21st October, 1931

CHAPTER THREE

London Calling

1941 marked the end of Rauf's childhood as his school year came to a close, but, more poignantly, the death of Judge Raif. Ultimately, Judge Raif had been Rauf's closest confidante and the single most influential person in his life — Rauf's political awakening and foray into the world of Turkish Cypriot social affairs had always been discussed with his father. The discussions were an established routine between father and son and were ongoing up until Judge Raif's death.

Judge Raif, although instrumental in helping Rauf to navigate through the intricacies of Cyprus' politics, hoped his legacy would extend to more than Rauf becoming better informed. He also wanted to instil in Rauf the importance of becoming an active member of the law profession. The dedicated Judge had maintained an almost obsessive stance on the necessity to have educated Turkish Cypriots remaining on home soil. His opinions stemmed from the idea that knowledgeable citizens would not only advocate amendments to the law but also be in a position to challenge and produce effective changes beneficial for the Turkish Cypriot community.

Sadly, Judge Raif's demise had resulted from his own intentions to make a difference in his work related to helping Turkish Cypriots being abused by a defective system. In

1939, he had been appointed the vice-President of the Debt Settlement Board established by the British in order to save the villagers in the grasp of unsavoury usurers. The British government had become aware of Turkish Cypriot lands being acquired in an effort to reduce Turkish Cypriot land ownership. Turkish Cypriot farmers and land owners became vulnerable targets for their properties as they attempted to make ends meet in a hard pressed economy.

Often land owners were forced to borrow amounts against their lands from unscrupulous financiers with the ulterior motive of taking the land. Borrowed amounts would be at steep interest rates with lands offered as sureties. Each year when the debts were not able to be met, the terms of repayments would be doubled and then trebled as well as accruing grossly inflated interest charges. The Turkish Cypriot land owners would then find themselves at the mercy of the loan sharks. It became tantamount to extortion as lands were lost and forcibly handed over to usurers as repayment.

Judge Raif and the soon to be Attorney General, Stelios Pavlides, as the President of the Debt Settlement Board, would visit the villages where applications had been made to claim the land. Disgruntled loan operatives and concerned land owners, unwilling to submit their lands, would present their cases to Judge Raif and Pavlides in something akin to a village court. Judge Raif and his colleague would then decide on a fair and appropriate amount to be repaid which often resulted in the interest charges being considered unacceptable thereby saving the lands of the owners.

The constant tours of the villages took its toll on Judge Raif and he caught a cold that progressed to bronchitis. The infection quickly spread over a course of six weeks affecting his heart and leaving him in a weakened state. Every

Saturday, at the end of the school week, Rauf would rush to his father's side and engage him in conversation, often provoking debates in an attempt to keep his father mentally alert. Rauf hoped that his constant flow of chatter would stimulate his father, as it had always been inclined to do so before, thus ensuring a speedy recovery.

Rauf became painfully aware on his last visit that his father was not in any condition to converse coherently and his frail body not able to withstand any physical exertion. Eventually Judge Raif's debilitated state prevented him from giving any type of response and uncharacteristically Judge Raif's interest in Rauf began to wane. He showed no interest in the young man once his 'little companion' —which devastated Rauf. Leaving a gaunt figure behind him, Rauf made the journey back to school carrying the ominous feeling with him that he would not see his father alive again. Within two hours of returning to school he received a frantic call from a friend of his father's urging him to return to the family home as his father had 'just a few hours left'. Rauf raced frantically back to his father's bedside but was too late.

Judge Raif had worked tirelessly for both his community and the British government and his loss had a profound effect. The *Cyprus Gazette* was a government issue that kept meticulous records as a matter for public record by the British since their occupation as administrators on the island back in 1878. Although the publication made for banal reading with its endless lists, it recorded Judge Raif's death, on 10th October 1941, paying careful attention to his rank and achievements. Later publications from various sources, including Greek Cypriot, also made mention of his death and appeared to recognise his abilities labelling him a 'fair man' whilst mourning his loss and contributions.

For Rauf, a deeper chasm opened as he was now bereft of a supportive father and a unique source of wisdom. Judge Raif had not been a traditional father in the sense of assuming total authority with his family. Unlike most Turkish Cypriot fathers, Judge Raif had not insisted on a patriarchal stance in which to govern his children. He retained an objective attitude when dealing with his children's life choices and encouraged them in their ambitions — even when he disagreed with their choices. In Rauf, he imbued him with a sense of confidence and gave him the security to feel free to challenge decisions as well as pursue what he felt was right.

However, Rauf had relied heavily on his father's guidance and understanding of things beyond his experience. He had felt strongly about becoming a pilot despite being aware that his father preferred him to enter in to the law profession. Within a week of Judge Raif dying, Rauf decided that he would follow the advice of his father and become a lawyer.

Rauf knew he was taking on a daunting task without his father to guide and usher him through the doors normally closed to a novice. He was assured by his father's friends and colleagues at Judge Raif's funeral that he 'need not worry' and that in a few short months of finishing school he would be guaranteed a job and be 'taken care of.' Rauf was to discover that in the sentiments of death, rash promises were usually made and rarely kept.

Rauf trawled the courts and law offices seeking out Judge Raif's friends hoping to take up the promised opportunities of employment and gain work experience with a view to becoming a lawyer. Each office door he knocked on was met with the same response: 'if only you had come here a few weeks earlier; we did have a vacancy but the post has now been filled.' Rauf would give his polite thanks and quietly move on — all too aware that every visit would end with the same result. Rauf's naivety quickly abated as he came to realise that he would not be considered on the basis of being Judge Raif's son. He had nothing more than his determination to offer but decided he had more pressing needs at hand.

Although Rauf had pinned his career hopes on becoming a lawyer, he was soon to realise that he also lacked the financial means as well as a mentor. Judge Raif's estate had been small and not enough to support Rauf; it was also 1942 during WW2 and shortages and hardships commonplace. He did, however, leave school having done exceptionally well in all his courses and boasted good language skills in Greek and English as well as his own native Turkish.

He was offered a job as a translator with his uncle, the registrar Mehmet Tevfik *Bey*, at the courts in Nicosia, which he eagerly accepted. He did not spend long at the courts as, like his father before him, Rauf's good work ethic and language skills came to the attention of the British — this time the British Army, whose Anti-aircraft Regiment was based in Cyprus during wartime to protect the Sovereign bases on the island. Rauf was approached and asked to work for the regiment as an aide with duties specifically designed to interpret for the officers in any general field.

Rauf was deemed a civilian but was obliged to wear a sergeant's uniform allowing him free access through the military bases to complete his duties as a translator. The sergeant's uniform was not without its compensations. The NAAFI store* was one such perk restricted to army

---

*NAAFI, the Navy, Army and Air Force Institutes, was created by the British in 1921 as a much needed service for servicemen and their families. As well as selling goods in its shops and providing services to meet the needs of its servicemen, the NAAFI still exists and has recreational services such as restaurants and bars etc open to all serving on military bases.

personnel only, allowing soldiers to buy goods at affordable prices and not usually available to the general public. Rauf had taken advantage of the items available at the store but had been charitable enough to share his good fortune with his family. The astonishment of an aunt impressed by the bounty of groceries he brought home prompted Rauf to repeat the story several times later in life both as a cautionary tale of the hardships suffered and for amusement:

"She was surprised at how I was able to get my hands on such luxury items and asked me where I got them from. 'NAAFI' I told her. 'Oh, what a nice man,' she said. 'Invite him for lunch.' That was the laugh in the house for some months!"

The merriment would quickly dissipate as Rauf's experience of working with the British army soured. Just a few short months later Rauf witnessed the savage beating of a Greek Cypriot man by a handful of British sergeants. The Greek Cypriot, like Rauf, was a civilian required to wear a uniform and working at the base. The reason for the harsh punishment being meted out was never made apparent and appeared to be an unprovoked attack. A complaint was filed and Rauf attended the Court Martial as a witness. Just one of the offenders was brought to trial and he was acquitted.

The other casualty of the sorry trial was Rauf. His unwillingness to give anything other than a truthful account of the events earned him the cold shoulder of the British Army. He was asked to leave their employ and found himself looking for anther job. Once again, with the help of his uncle, Rauf returned to the courts. He was employed as a clerk in the courts of Famagusta and relished being in the midst of court dramas. However, it soon became apparent to the ambitious young Rauf that being a clerk only saw him on the peripheral of court life and he wanted to be fully immersed. Learning from his previous experiences and failed attempts to procure help, Rauf resorted to an encyclopaedia to determine how best to becoming a lawyer. Finding that he should write to the Inns in England, he dashed off a letter to Lincoln's Inn.

Rauf's best efforts to get a letter to England were almost thwarted. It was war time so airmail was suspended meaning that postal services were consigned to the laborious process of travelling by land or sea. The services were further hampered by letters being removed from their envelopes, examined thoroughly and photographed by military authorities before being approved and dispatched. The lengthy process meant that mail could take several months before arriving and returning to its intended destination. Nevertheless, the coveted letter cleared all the hurdles and within three months the official application forms from Lincoln's Inn were received by Rauf.

The comprehensive list of requirements included three character references — two of which had to come from barristers. Rauf felt discouraged at the prospect of once again having to seek the support of his father's friends at the courts; so far his efforts to enlist their help had been fruitless. However, he reasoned that seeking recommendations was not the same as asking for employment.

He arranged an appointment with a friend of his father's, the only Turkish Cypriot High Court Judge, Halit *Bey*, and strode forcefully to his office. Bolstered with confidence, he explained to Judge Halit his purpose and hoped that as the son of Judge Raif, he would be considered an ideal candidate for study at the prestigious Lincoln's Inn. Judge Halit surveyed the young Rauf with a practised eye before calmly refusing his request. Rauf was then politely dismissed but not before he was given a stinging explanation.

"I'll never forget what he said to me", recalled Rauf. "He told me: 'my dear boy, I knew your father very well and I respected him very much but this is the first time I've seen you. I don't know who you are, what you are, and, as such, how can I give you a recommendation?' I left his office in virtual tears."

Humiliated and his resolve shredded under the glare of Judge Halit, Rauf stood in the corridor of the courts. By chance the director of the Land Registry, an Armenian friend of his father's, was passing. After listening to the forlorn Rauf's tale he promptly gave him a letter of recommendation, stamped with his own qualifications that also revealed he was a barrister. The second recommendation was a glowing reference obtained from a willing Greek Cypriot barrister, Mr. Indianos, who had also known Rauf's father.

Unsurprisingly, a daunting shadow was cast over Rauf's opinion of Judge Halit. "For a long time I had this disrespect for Judge Halit," pondered the older, wiser Rauf. "How could he do that to me? I asked myself. Then when I became somebody in Cyprus and people I didn't know, complete strangers, came to me for recommendations, I knew the man's reaction was absolutely right. Yes, I might have been the son of Judge Raif, but he didn't know me."

Although Rauf coped with the rejection from Judge Halit, he was not prepared for the denial he received from his school. Believing that his former teacher and mentor, Mr. Simms, would not pose any obstacles, Rauf wrote to him with his request. Mr. Simms' response was to write back insisting on a private meeting.

Standing in front of Mr. Simms' imposing desk, Rauf retreated to his childhood as he found himself being admonished and berated for his choices. Mr. Simms' formidable voice was raised levelly at Rauf, arguing that war time was not conducive to study and how was Rauf 'expected to learn anything in London during these dangerous times?'

Undoubtedly Mr. Simms' outburst stemmed simply from his paternal concerns for the young fatherless Rauf. However, Mr. Simms had a struggling Turkish class of boys on his hands who were below school standards. He convinced Rauf to stay within the confines of a relatively safe Cyprus and help with the failing class, slyly offering the bribe of writing the recommendation at the end of the school year.

Rauf accepted the terms, fully aware that Simms had every intention of encouraging Rauf to take up the challenge of teaching and leave behind him the dream of becoming a lawyer. With the negotiations settled, and each agreeing tacitly to the other's terms, Rauf prepared himself to become a teacher.

Rauf was immediately charged with the responsibility of the boarding house and realised quickly that the unruly boys lacked discipline. The onus fell on Rauf's young shoulders to teach the boys the rudiments of daily life and the importance of hygiene. Unfortunately for Rauf not all the boys took kindly to a teacher who was barely much older than themselves.

Menial tasks such as cleaning lavatories and keeping the dormitories clean and presentable were considered demeaning by some of the boys. Rauf would lead by example in an effort to prove to his young charges that everybody was responsible. The boys eventually relented, encouraged by Rauf's willingness to share the burdens; one boy, however, remained defiant and every tact employed by Rauf to persuade him to share the duties of his peers fell on deaf ears.

The young maverick who had consistently rebuffed Rauf's authority was a Greek Cypriot boy from a wealthy family. He was adamant that he should be exempt from cleaning the dormitory, insisting that his parents paid for his education and not for his services as a cleaner. Rauf, having exhausted every effort to cajole the boy into line, reported him to Mr. Simms.

Rauf stood with the boy and his parent in the office and was stunned into a silent stupor by Mr. Simms' reproach. As an angry mother confronted Mr. Simms on his policy of expecting the boys to take responsibility for cleaning duties, she was met with a terse response: "do you want us to make a man of your boy?" when the mother replied in the affirmative, Mr. Simms raised himself from his desk, glowered at the woman, uttering that she should then 'leave him to us' before bidding her a curt good day.

Rauf returned to the boarding house and felt a quiet discomfort. He had not relished the humiliation of the mother and sought to make amends. Whilst he acknowledged Mr. Simms' bombastic approach achieved results, Rauf had a fine appreciation of humour that he realised could be far more effective. He befriended the boys and enjoyed a jape or two that endeared him to them, eventually earning their respect and compliance.

Although Rauf had been willing the school term of nine months to pass quickly so that he could then begin law school, he admitted in a letter to his brother that he had enjoyed his time there. In the missive sent home he regaled in some of the exploits of the students but had been more impressed by some memorable moments of improvisations performed by less than perfect teachers.

Each morning the school would be gathered for morning prayers with a short sermon delivered by Mr. Simms. The

Muslim boys were not expected to recite the prayers but traditions dictated the prayers be translated by their Turkish teacher, Necat *Bey*, with the boys offering their solemn *Amen* at the end. Unfortunately for Necat *Bey*, on one particular gathered assembly, he had forgotten his paper with the translated prayers. Pulling an auspicious piece of paper from his pocket, he cleared his throat and announced with great reverence: "well boys, as you know our head teacher here does not speak our language, so I'll just blather on for a bit about the weather and when I stop talking, you all know what to say." "*Amen!*" chorused the boys enthusiastically at the appropriate pause.

Rauf's nine-month term had not been wholly unproductive and certainly pleased Mr. Simms. He successfully brought the flagging Turkish boys' results up to standard and became an asset to the school. It was then that he presented himself to Mr. Simms and reminded him of his promise of a reference for his law school aspirations. Mr. Simms, impressed by Rauf's fledgling year as a teacher, confessed he had in mind a teaching profession earmarked for him. Rauf, fearing another lost year and opportunity, remained firm reiterating he felt compelled to become a lawyer as his father had wanted.

Mr. Simms was an uncompromising individual but a man who abided by a 'gentleman's agreement'. He honoured his verbal agreement with Rauf, sealed with a handshake, and wrote an eloquent reference expounding Rauf's merits. To further prove his commitment, he arranged for Rauf's written applications to be submitted to the British Council that had appointed a Committee to approve and fund scholarships overseas.

The Committee board Rauf was to attend comprised a variety of councillors including a Greek and Turkish Cypriot member. Mr. Simms was aware the residing Turkish Cypriot member had been disapproving of Judge Raif and unlikely to offer a scholarship to Rauf. The biased member held the view that Judge Raif had been a poor example of a Nationalist; he felt that a pro-British supporter could not also claim to be an ardent Atatürk admirer and have Turkish Cypriot interests at heart. However, the ambitious Turkish Cypriot member was also a member of the Executive Council and frequently was absent at meetings with the Governor in Troodos. Mr. Simms instigated Rauf's interview to occur on the same day allowing a fair and impartial hearing. The acting member designated to appear in the absence was a congenial man who Mr. Simms felt sure would accept Rauf for a scholarship. That day several young ambitious students earned the privilege to study overseas including Rauf and his friend, Hasan, to study for the Bar in England.

An excited Rauf rushed to inform family members of his success. Instead of receiving congratulatory well wishes, he was met with a cold shrug of indifference. The family's feelings were revealed in a letter from his eldest brother who echoed the family sentiments. Cahit made clear that Rauf was not to leave Cyprus and trek to war-torn London and, as an added threat, claimed he would disown him should he venture to the shores of England.

Rauf, having overcome so many trials to achieve his goal, refused to succumb to the emotional blackmail and booked his passage on the boat that would leave Famagusta and dock in England. London was calling and Rauf was ready.

CHAPTER FOUR
Make Study Not War

Rauf's intentions to leave Cyprus in 1944 during wartime had naturally aroused the attentions of his family and friends. As a close-knit Cypriot community it was important to be given the opportunity to offer a departing member of their fold advice and farewells; and, as was expected of him, Rauf embarked on a hectic round of visits to receive their concerns. Despite the severe misgivings and dire warnings he was subjected to, all wanted to embrace Rauf before he left.

It was during the course of these numerous visits, Rauf found himself being encouraged to visit the headmistress, Kadriye *Hanım*, of the local elementary school who had a revered reputation — as a coffee-cup reader. As the lady in question was a good family friend Rauf agreed to pay his respects.

Approaching the headmistress' open front door, Rauf was greeted with the distinctive aroma of Turkish coffee being brewed and knew he had been expected. Not being of a superstitious nature but wishing to appear polite, he drained the proffered coffee cup and dutifully handed the dregs over to be read. With great aplomb Kadriye *Hanım* announced Rauf would achieve his goal of becoming a lawyer but only after experiencing three difficulties on his way to England. With a dismissive air and wry smile that signalled the end of the reading, she then casually informed him he would be married on his return.

Rauf's last visit the following day, before boarding the boat at Famagusta port, was to the more immediate members of his family: his father's brother, Tevfik *Bey* and his wife and children. After receiving their own solemn reproaches at his abandoning Cyprus for the more dangerous shores of England, the atmosphere lightened and Rauf was treated as an honoured guest.

Whilst Rauf enjoyed the home-made *böreks* (traditional Turkish pastries) and the hospitality of his kin he became aware of his second cousin, Aydın, shyly loitering in the doorway and smiled encouragingly at her. A timely elbowed nudge from his aunt prompted his uncle quickly to his feet to shepherd Rauf out the courtyard garden.

As the two sat beneath a lemon tree, sheltering from the midday sun, Rauf's uncle began an awkward conversation of how Rauf must not succumb to any temptations that the lure of London might offer. Rauf squirmed uncomfortably but met his uncle's glare with meek and embarrassed nods to assure his uncle he would behave appropriately. Rauf continued to nod vigorously at his uncle's prompts but he joked later it wasn't just a lecture he received; it had also been a clever bid to extract a promise of marriage. "Before I knew it," recalled Rauf, "I was semi-officially engaged to my uncle's granddaughter, Aydın!"

A family joke had apparently gathered momentum and become a serious matter for Rauf's uncle. At the time of Aydın's birth, Rauf had been just nine-years-old. His paternal grandmother (and Aydın's great-grandmother) had placed the new-born Aydın in the arms of a bewildered Rauf and, to the amusement of everyone, declared, 'Rauf, meet your fiancée!'

Arranged marriages were a common occurrence amongst Cypriots and it was not unusual for distant cousins to be married off. Often with the matriarch of the family supervising proceedings, prospective brides and grooms would be vetted with families discussing the possibility of an impending marriage before consent would be given. Rauf's uncle had the hindsight to see that Aydın and Rauf would make a suitable match when Aydın became of age and also an assurance that Rauf would return home once his promise to marry was elicited.

Rauf, perceptively, realised that the impending nuptials had been contrived amongst his family and friends but agreed that after his schooling and when he was financially able, he would marry Aydın. He left the house for Famagusta port with the warnings of his family ringing in his ears that he was now a 'promised man' and to behave accordingly.

Arriving at Famagusta port, Rauf was greeted with a heady sight of colour and noise from the eclectic groups of people gathered. The port was a major source for travel and commerce and had a long-standing reputation for receiving esteemed colonial visitors. It also had a small fishing port attached to it for the local fisherman who traded their wares with enthusiastic voices vying to be heard over their rivals. Soldiers in their distinctive uniforms were interspersed as the port did its civic duty and transferred them to and fro. An excited Rauf made his way through the throng of people clutching his ticket in readiness and approached the departures area.

Once the customs and passport representatives had been satisfied, Rauf headed for the ship to board it. As he began his ascent on the gangway he was suddenly confronted by a drunken soldier staggering towards him. The soldier was flanked by two bemused British policeman who had the dubious task of escorting him off the ship. A crowd had also formed to watch the spectacle and enjoy the entertaining antics of the soldier as he lurched backwards and forwards.

However, the policemen's smiles, along with the crowd's, quickly vanished when the soldier produced a knife and began waving it furiously. A precarious dance erupted between the policemen and soldier as they did their best to avoid each other, whilst Rauf unwittingly found himself in their midst. Deftly sidestepping the trio, Rauf narrowly missed the soldier's knife as he thrashed it about indiscriminately. Scuttling up the gangway Rauf reminded himself of the 'three difficulties' that had been forecast and decided he had at least overcome one of them.

Once all the passengers had been settled on board, the ship heaved itself from the port with Rauf and a small group of friends also bound for study in England. With relative ease, the ship silently made its way to Cairo for a ten-day stopover before a pre-arranged transfer to Alexandria.

In Cairo, Rauf and his companions were placed in the *Semiramis Hotel* and had little else to do other than wander the dusty streets. As the group roamed aimlessly, they stumbled upon a run-down street where a large sign above an apartment stood out claiming that the occupant could read fortunes.

The bored young students decided to take up the sign's invite although all claimed not to believe in fortune-telling.

Entering the shabby establishment a self-titled 'professor' invited them to sit in his waiting room and suggested the giggling friends read his visitors' book which boasted several important clients who had sought his services. Rauf sifted through and was impressed to see an entry from the Prime Minister of Great Britain, Winston Churchill dated 1941.

The entry was a reminder that during the 1900s Churchill

had visited the fortune teller and was told he would become Prime Minister and lead his people out of a great disaster. Churchill's 1941 entry stated he was indeed Prime Minister and hoping the rest of the Professor's prediction would come true. Rauf was affected by the claim and agreed to have his fortune read.

The professor took Rauf's palm and tracing the lines with his finger explained to him he would have six children but, more importantly, become a founder of a State. Rauf and his friends were amused by the grand statement and left the professor's apartment laughing. Throughout the day, Rauf was at the mercy of his friends who teased him incessantly about his incredible future. Although he didn't mind being teased, Rauf never forgot the prediction and would often repeat it later.

Eventually Rauf and his companions were transferred to Alexandria and the waiting ship. The lengthy sojourn in Egypt had been to enable the military to form a convoy to escort the liner en route to its final destination – Liverpool. It was a necessary precaution as the Mediterranean region, which had a long history as a passage for trade and travel, had become a treacherous area for sea farers during the war saturated years; now a significant route for vital supplies being ferried by the military, saw a war being waged at sea. A campaign to disrupt the supply route meant that the sea had been lined with explosives coupled with the added threat of Germany's infamous U-boats terrorising the sea beneath the surface.

Surrounded by several warships, the passenger ship eventually left the port of Alexandria and began its tense journey. The nervous atmosphere amongst Rauf and his fellow travellers during the perilous time was prevalent and heightened by a seemingly unnatural violent swell of the sea causing the ship to frequently soar upwards. Occasionally a muffled booming sound would accompany the motion and filter up to the passengers' ears causing concern and mild panic.

Rauf knew a few of the soldiers on board and sought them out to try and determine the cause of the erratic motions of the ship. The soldiers appeared quite unperturbed as they explained depth charges were being released periodically by the accompanying military ships to ward off possible U-boats in the vicinity. The explanation did little to calm Rauf who returned to his group of friends deciding the information was best kept to himself whilst fervently praying the threat was being allayed.

The arduous journey finally came to a halt 24 days later as Liverpool docks loomed into sight. Rauf and his companions disembarked and were directed to Lime Street station to catch the train to London. Dishevelled, and with wrangled nerves after the fraught boat journey, they made their way to the *Red Court Hotel* in Holborn hoping for a less excitable evening.

As they sat in the hotel's restaurant recovering from their ordeal at sea, a sudden eerie silence descended on the room; within seconds the wail of a siren permeated throughout the hotel to announce itself and the threat of a bomb raid.

Rauf and his company stood up in fearful silence, rooted to the spot, unsure of what to do. A young man with a wooden leg had caught sight of the terrified group and limped over to them yelling there was nothing to be afraid of whilst hurling a defiant 'you only die once' as a comforter. The amputee was a young war veteran and herded the group onto a balcony in an attempt to initiate them into the rigours and trials of London being bombed.

Waving expansively at the inky blackness of London

before him, the young man advised 'when the flames of the flying bombs were visible, there is no fear.' However, they were cautioned when the flames were no longer visible it meant the engines had stopped running and that was the time to 'get down on the floor' as it meant the bombs were about to rain down.

Rauf and his friends watched and waited in nervous anticipation as they witnessed rockets with flaming tails stride across the sky. Suddenly, the lights were doused leaving London in total blackness and Rauf, taking the experienced veteran's advice to heart, launched himself from the balcony with the intention of finding secure ground to lie down on.

Fortunately for Rauf, the balcony had only been a few feet above ground. He conceded later he was lucky not to have broken his neck 'never mind being killed by flying Nazi bombs!'

Rauf's induction to the flying bombs that were showering London and the stoical response of the British was a revelation for him. Despite the terrible injuries being inflicted on the face of Britain's capital, Rauf marvelled at how the residents of London refused to succumb to self-pity. "The daily routine of clearing bomb damage and assessing loss of lives and property had become a way of life for these people," remarked Rauf, in a reflection of his war experiences.

He quickly became accustomed to the practical 'daily routine' Londoners had adopted but never ceased to be amazed by their unique resolve. Often Rauf would find himself a member of London's swollen congregation sheltering in one of London's underground tube stations praying for an end to the bomb raids. There he also encountered the cheerful resistance of the British public as they waited out the threat. Once the all-clear alarm pealed through the tunnels, Rauf would watch in awe as people picked up their hurriedly-snatched belongings and trooped outside to resume their daily lives amongst the carnage.

Rauf's home comforts were also interrupted by war. Within a week of being in London lodgings were arranged in Orpington, Kent by the British Council for both him and a fellow study colleague, Ahmet Zaim. The two young men found the address and stood back to admire the house with the pretty front garden and its carefully planted borders of roses. The typically suburban semi-detached and its neighbouring houses had a quiet demeanour suggesting elderly and reserved occupants.

The front door was opened and Rauf and Ahmet's suspicions were confirmed as a mature gentleman greeted them each with a stiff handshake. After the formal introductions of the landlord, Mr. Bloss and his wife, were made, the young men were shown to their bedrooms. As Rauf was the older of the two Mr. Bloss had thought it prudent to allocate the larger bedroom to him. Ahmet's protestations that he was paying the same amount of rent provoked a glowering stare from Mr. Bloss. Rauf, keen to defuse the situation, promptly granted Ahmet the larger room claiming he would be quite content in the small box room.

Later that evening, after a sedate dinner and stilted conversation with the Bloss's, Ahmet cheerfully retired to bed and Rauf prepared to do the same. After organising the small space as best as he could, Rauf settled down to sleep. A few hours later the stillness of the night was shattered by the unmistakeable sound of an explosion erupting, shaking the house and its sleeping occupants awake.

A startled Rauf checked himself and his surroundings — relieved to discover nothing was amiss or broken, when he heard the plaintive wails of Ahmet calling to him. "Rauf, I'm dead!" declared Ahmet in English for the benefit of his landlords. Confused, Rauf faltered for a moment just as Mr. Bloss yelled: "as you are shouting, you are not dead! Now, shut up and go back to sleep! We'll see what's what in the morning."

Rauf crept stealthily to Ahmet's room, fearing he would be held responsible for disrupting Mr. Bloss's sleep further with the tread of his footsteps. Setting foot in Ahmet's prized room Rauf was confronted with the sight of his friend in bed lying beneath a few fragments of rubble. The explosion, caused by a bomb landing nearby, had dislodged parts of the ceiling. The effect had been discomforting for Ahmet but had otherwise left him completely unscathed. Ahmet, having recovered from his 'untimely death', swiftly offered to exchange rooms with Rauf. "I couldn't believe it," chuckled Rauf, recalling the memory. "After all the fuss he made to get the room. Naturally, I refused."

London, in just one week, had made an indelible impression on Rauf. He had been exposed to the rigours of war and an appreciation of British humour in the face of adversity. However, Rauf was keen to start studying at the prestigious Lincoln's Inn. Unfortunately the British government had other plans for him. Rauf received papers notifying him he had been conscripted into the British army. Rauf was furious at being confronted with yet another setback hindering his studies. He marched straight to the British Council and confronted the first suit-clad official he came across. "If you wanted a British soldier, why didn't you just say so?" demanded the exasperated Rauf. The official rolled his eyeballs in complicity and explained to Rauf this occurred frequently and promised to sort it out.

The British Council did intervene and a decision was

made by the civil defence leading to a compromise: Rauf could attend school but he was 'drafted' to firewatch duty twice a week from the roof tops of the Inn. He would not be alone as an elderly barrister called Mr. Cole would be on duty with him on each of the nights. Despite the challenge of remaining awake, and attending classes the next day, Rauf relished the opportunity to spend long periods engaged in discourse with an experienced barrister.

On Rauf's first night, perched from the lofty heights of the Inn, Mr. Cole entered and gave a cursory nod in Rauf's direction. Rauf offered a polite 'good evening' but received no response from his aloof companion. Undeterred, Rauf attempted to draw the barrister into conversation but was met with a stony wall of silence. Each vigil ended as the night began: in awkward silence as Mr. Cole refused to be drawn into dialogue with Rauf. A nearby explosion on one particular night shattered the library windows but still did not encourage the resolutely silent man to utter a single syllable towards Rauf.

Rauf later discovered from another barrister that Mr. Cole's eccentric behaviour derived from never having been formally introduced. It appeared Mr. Cole considered it poor etiquette to engage in conversation with a complete stranger. Fortunately for the reticent barrister, the twice-weekly rooftop encounter passed without any spectacular events occurring allowing him the grace of never having to confer with Rauf.

Having acquainted himself with some of the more conservative members of the Inn and their reserved natures, Rauf threw himself into the more demanding challenge ahead — gaining his credentials to practise law. He spent all of his available time in the Inn's library or at the nearby High Court following trials. In addition to utilising his spare-time productively, he saved his money to buy extra reading material and acquired a sizeable library of his own. His diligence paid off and he received excellent marks in his first year securing him another year's scholarship from the British Council.

The summer break did not see Rauf become idle either. He attended classes in Scotland at St Andrews University and, back in London, psychology classes for a short period. He was intent on soaking up as much useful information as he could to enhance his law studies. To counter the strenuous study programme the British Council had arranged for him to spend a week on a farm in Surrey. Rauf perversely had written on his original application he was interested in farming and horse riding without having any aptitude or inclination for either. The British Council took him at his word and sent him to a farm owned by an ex-naval commander.

The farmer, wishing to accommodate his young guest, had organised a week of activities revolving around farming life. He was also the proud owner of a stable of prized horses and Rauf was to be treated to a long hack with him on the lead horse. Rauf found himself faced with a brute standing 17 hands high and gingerly clambered aboard. Once mounted, the horse proceeded to walk in confused circles at Rauf's hapless instructions. Dismounting quickly, Rauf confessed to never having 'ridden anything superior to a Cyprus donkey.'

The following summer Rauf decided to spend his time more productively. He signed up for a seminar on child crime which also procured him a 15-day placement at a young offenders' institute. It would have a profound affect on Rauf and helped shape his views on how young offenders were dealt with in Cyprus. In later years he would often point to the British model for dealing with young criminals. During the British administration, young offenders were housed in a reform school situated in Morphou (now known as Güzelyurt). The institute was eventually closed leaving young criminals to the mercy of adult prisons.

"Now we have teenage boys of 15 and 16 in jail with adult murderers. Instead of being reformed, they come out hardened criminals," claimed Rauf during one of his campaigns to see a reform school reinstated in Cyprus.

Rauf's willingness to learn from the British was a trait he inherited from his late father. Judge Raif had always admired British values which had produced a democratic society. He had also hoped the British role in Cyprus would be influential and supportive of the Turkish Cypriot community (although Judge Raif was keen to point out to Rauf the importance of learning from both the mistakes and successes of the British models).

RAUF, during his London years, had kept a watchful eye on the political turmoil of Cyprus. He read with interest news articles written by Turkish Cypriots — many of whom were friends of Judge Raif's — expressing concerns at the changing face of Cyprus.

He had already established a relationship with Dr. Küçük, the founder of the influential Turkish newspaper, *Halkın Sesi*, as a young student in Cyprus and had continued writing for the paper from abroad. His input to the paper increased dramatically as tensions began to rise causing him to write fervently echoing the sentiments and concerns of Turkish Cypriots everywhere.

In 1945, exiled Greek Cypriot leaders, after the riots of 1931, returned to Cyprus and their calls for *enosis* were once again reverberating through the Cypriot communities. Rauf wrote in protest, reminding the readership of the threat of *enosis* and encouraged Turkish Cypriots to stand firm. Occasionally he would write in poetic form with verses lauding the virtues and rights of Turkish Cypriots; the common theme would inevitably be for Turkish Cypriots to unite in their struggle against perpetrators intent on removing them from their homeland.

With his writing, Rauf was gaining a following and a certain amount of notoriety back in Cyprus. His old friend and mentor, Mr. Simms, was concerned enough to send Rauf a veiled message indicating that his 'friends back home' were not pleased and provoked by his outpour and scorn for *enosis* and Rauf was possibly endangering his return. Undeterred, Rauf wrote under several pseudonyms although it was widely acknowledged he was the probable author of the penmanship.

Whilst trouble was stirring at home, 1945 brought peacetime in England as WW2 in Europe finally came to an end. Germany had capitulated and Nuremberg prepared to bring war criminals to trial; meanwhile, London prepared for celebrations. Street parties were in abundance and throngs of people gathered in and around London's famous landmarks to celebrate the end of war. Rauf was in Piccadilly Circus and witnessed strangers hugging and kissing with abandon. He later recalled in his memoirs the 'crazy atmosphere of irresponsible wake, as if people weren't celebrating but were flapping to drown'. However, the youthful Rauf also admitted the frenzied emotions of a normally reserved nation would lead to the opportunity of kissing a few girls!

At the end of a long night, and still without a kiss, Rauf headed for Charing Cross. The early-morning trains had yet to run leaving him and several other exhausted revellers stranded. Rauf took the first initiative and lay on the ground to sleep. He awoke a short while later to find a pretty blond with her head nestled on his arm sleeping soundly. Before he could congratulate himself on his good fortune, he noticed her large sailor boyfriend watching the pair intently. "Shall we change watch?" Rauf politely ventured. Nodding in agreement, the sailor neatly transferred her head to his own lap and Rauf discreetly removed himself.

The previous night's celebrations of peace and freedom had also liberated Rauf's wallet as he was to discover. Without the two-shilling fare, Rauf was perplexed and did not relish the thought of walking 13 miles to Orpington. Slumped on a bench, feeling dejected, Rauf found his downcast gaze confronted with a pair of neatly-polished brogues. Filled with curiosity he looked up and came face-to-face with an elderly Englishman. The sight of the forlorn Rauf at such a wonderful time had prompted the man's concern. Rauf explained he had been the victim of a pickpocket during the celebrations and now was without his fare to return home. The gallant gentleman pressed two shillings into Rauf's hand, waving Rauf's offer to pay him back aside, stating 'anything can happen during peacetime.'

A jubilant Rauf wended his way back to Orpington with renewed vigour. He had survived the war — and peace. His confidence had grown from his experiences and he felt encouraged. With less than two years left to complete his studies, his success was assured along with his return to his native homeland.

**Lincoln's Inn, London, the Inn of Court where Rauf was
called to the Bar**

**Rauf, in his wig and gown as a new barrister-at-law and a
contemporary signed photo of him sent to his older brother
Cahit**

CHAPTER FIVE
Trials

By his final year of study the 23-year-old Rauf had left Orpington and moved to the more desirable Kensington Gardens in London. He had outgrown the Bloss's small, comfortable house but his decision was not based on the lure of a more attractive postcode. The relocation to London meant Rauf was in closer proximity to Lincoln's Inn which gave him the opportunity to spend longer periods of study at the Inn's library. The final examinations were looming and Rauf retreated into isolation as he spent all of his available time poring over law books and attending the local courts following cases.

His self-imposed exile into the realm of study came as no surprise to those who knew him. It was an indication of his fervent desire to succeed; even after completing the finals, the impending results were causing a deep-seated anxiety for Rauf who fretted about their outcome.

However, Rauf's agitations were not entirely from his concerns regarding his academic performance. His contact with Cyprus, through his writing, had not wavered and his last few months as an undergraduate in London were marred by his concerns for the ongoing political situation tearing at Cyprus' seams. The war was over and Europe, along with the rest of the world, was slowly recovering;

Cyprus' wounds, however, were far from healed as the threat of *enosis* had been reignited and the two communities were once again engaged in their own inter-communal battle.

Fortunately for Rauf, his new roommate, Fazıl Plümer, was a fellow Turkish Cypriot compatriot and shared Rauf's passion and concerns for Cyprus. He was also older than Rauf by ten years and his maturity and experience were influential on Rauf. Although a law graduate from Ankara, Turkey, Fazıl was unable to practise on home soil as, under British administration, lawyers needed to be a graduate of English law. Fazıl, like Rauf, was completing a law degree at Lincoln's Inn but his previous experience of law study and timely presence in London offered Rauf support and at times a welcome distraction from the rigours of study.

In Fazıl, Rauf had discovered a companion he could relate to. The twosome would frequently talk long into the night discussing the issues affecting their homeland and an everlasting bond was forged that lasted until Fazıl's death in 2001. Rauf had also felt able to confide in the older man his personal fears and hopes including his intentions to return home on completion of his law study and becoming a 'powerful lawyer and reporter' as his father had hoped.

For Rauf, failure was a dismal prospect as his career and the opportunity to contribute to changes for Cyprus depended on his success of passing the bar. His fears were unwarranted as his call to the bar was announced in typical grand style at the Inn. In 1947, he became an official member of the British bar earning himself the prestigious right to call himself a Barrister at Law.

Rauf had not been a typical student and rarely visited the bars, preferring instead to immerse himself in study. At the time of the graduation his attitude had remained unchanged. Whilst the rest of his peers revelled, or commiserated, their successes and failures, Rauf chose to forgo the end of term celebrations. He was eager to return home and instead made preparations for the homeward bound journey.

During his time in England he had amassed a vast library of books that rivalled his father's own large collection. The heavy shipment of books meant an extra payment of 15 pounds — a princely sum of money equivalent to an average worker's salary for an entire month. Rauf's tenacious nature and his avid love of literature meant he refused to leave his books behind, placing himself in debt by borrowing the money to ensure their safe return. Regardless of the setback this may have incurred for Rauf, he and his precious cargo finally arrived at Famagusta port in March 1947.

His uncle, Mehmet Tevfik, was there to greet him along with the rest of his family. Despite their previous admonishments and disapproval of his travelling to London at such a hazardous time Rauf was shepherded to the family home to celebrate his achievement and homecoming. There was more to celebrate as his uncle coyly reminded him of his promise to marry his granddaughter, Aydın. The homecoming party shifted to an engagement party and Rauf came face to face with his fiancée.

The shy young girl Rauf last saw had been replaced by an attractive and mature-looking 15-year-old. Aydın had inherited her father's genes possessing striking blue eyes and a mane of blonde hair that swept passed her shoulders. When reintroduced to Rauf she greeted him warmly exuding an air of confidence. It was deemed acceptable for young women to be married at 15, but, despite being impressed by Aydın's maturity, Rauf was adamant the marriage should be stalled until Aydın came of age at 18. The family agreed with the added proviso they were at least to be an officially engaged couple.

Rauf's insistence on a prolonged engagement was in part to protect Aydın from being a 'child bride'. He had always expressed concerns with how family law in Cyprus viewed the rights of women; a divorced woman not only faced the stigma of divorce but also financial difficulties as she was rarely granted access to her husband's property. His opinion extended to that of young women who entered into marriage contracts without realising the stakes — often not having the emotional maturity or education to understand the implications of marriage and how their rights would be affected if the marriage failed. There was more, as Rauf reminded the family, he needed to establish himself as a lawyer with an income and be in a position to support a wife.

BEFORE he was able to assert himself as a lawyer, Rauf recognised he had limited support. Making important connections were essential in the law fraternity — particularly for Turkish Cypriots with little or no experience. He wisely reached out to another man that had once been a friend of his father's and now his own; a man that Rauf knew was able to make a difference to his life as well as all Turkish Cypriots: Dr. Fazıl Küçük.

He arrived at Dr. Küçük's clinic and was received with a welcoming broad smile. Küçük was a renowned heavy smoker and delighted to see Rauf had taken up the habit. Küçük derived a great deal of pleasure from smoking and Rauf was struck at how he would 'draw lovingly on a cigarette', often punctuating an important point with a sharp exhale of smoke. The pair smoked compulsively in between visiting patients as Küçük wasted no time enlightening Rauf on the situation that was troubling Cyprus.

Cyprus was once again caught up in political turmoil which had been aggravated with the return of exiled church leaders announcing their intentions to continue working on the cause for *enosis*. With an angry finger stabbing at the air Küçük further claimed the British administration might suddenly bequeath Cyprus to Greece. He informed Rauf he was in contact with Turkey via the ambassadors but unhappy with the progress he was making in getting Turkey to understand the gravity of the situation.

Taking a long draw on his cigarette and exhaling slowly, Küçük looked levelly at Rauf and assured the young man his presence back on the island would be helpful. Echoing the sentiments of Rauf's father Küçük stated Cyprus desperately needed young, dynamic Turkish Cypriot professionals in exalted government positions.

Rauf was shrewdly aware Küçük had a pre-determined plan for him the moment he had walked through the clinic's door. Rauf was just 23 but Küçük recognised his keen intelligence and ambition — coupled with the fact that he was the son of the well-respected late Judge Raif. He suggested Rauf entered the forthcoming elections for the municipality — a move which would alter Rauf's path and propel him into politics.

Rauf, aware of Küçük's fiery nature, gently declined. "I knew what he was asking of me," Rauf recalled later, "but I really wanted to get my practice off the ground and didn't want to be pushed into politics."

The young man sat opposite the intimidating doctor and countered that his purpose would be better served rallying people to support Küçük's party. He reminded Küçük that he was not without his opponents within the Turkish Cypriot community itself. Those strongly opposed to Küçük were known as the pro-Evkaf group or pro-British government, and felt that Küçük's policies were going to disrupt the country.

Rauf believed he could aid Küçük by uniting the community and encouraging them to understand and support Küçük's policies. It was a not too transparent attempt by Rauf at appeasing the doctor. He had deliberately played on Dr. Küçük's insecurities for he was known by Rauf to be a man frequently concerned about who was 'on his side'. Küçük was satisfied with the compromise and Rauf left the clinic an accepted part of Dr. Küçük's Nationalist group.

Rauf hadn't got the support he was hoping to get as the meeting had been dominated by Dr. Küçük's interest in Rauf becoming an active member of his party; although he felt sure that having Dr. Küçük listed as a friend could only aid his ambitions as a lawyer. Filled with determination, Rauf continued on his way to Atatürk Square in Nicosia with the intentions of finding an office and beginning his life as a lawyer.

After the war, the popular square had resumed trading with renewed vigour. Shops had reopened and prospered leaving little room for advocates' offices. Rauf, unable to find affordable office space, did, however, find a lawyer prepared to offer him a partnership — at least until Rauf was able to find offices of his own. A Greek Cypriot lawyer, Antonis C. Indianos, with a respected reputation, had the foresight to see the benefits of taking on a new and young Turkish Cypriot lawyer.

Indianos was working on a large case that he was in danger of losing and due in court the same day he took Rauf on. After being hurriedly briefed the excited novice lawyer accompanied Indianos to the court. Indianos introduced Rauf to the presiding judge, Vasiliyadis, and made an exaggerated point of referring to Rauf's new qualifications as a Barrister-at-Law and his very first appearance in court that day as a lawyer; he then informed the judge his clients would be changing their plea to one of guilty on the advice of his new colleague, Rauf.

Judge Vasiliyadis listened intently with a bemused smile before formally accepting the guilty plea. He sentenced the accused to a heavy fine and warned them their lenient sentence was due to Rauf's appearance in court. Before an astonished Rauf could understand the reasoning for the judge's statement, Judge Vasiliyadis issued a stark warning and explanation to the accused. For the benefit of the packed courtroom, the judge announced it was the tradition in court on a lawyer's first day to avoid heavy sentencing. He felt the accused were thoroughly deserving of a jail sentence but was abiding by traditions. He then promptly congratulated Indianos on his expedient thinking to change the plea and his audacious nature to remind the court of its traditions!

Rauf's first appearance in legal circles had not made quite the impact he had hoped for but he was now at least established and practising. It wasn't long before he was approached with an offer to operate from his own offices by İbrahim Yahya, a man well-known to lawyers, and a wily old character who had been a lawyer's clerk and secretary at various times but mainly operated as a go-between procuring clients for lawyers. He had heard Rauf was looking for his own offices and made a subtle offer to Rauf. He proposed Rauf used his own offices and paid the utilities whilst he sought out clients for Rauf to represent — for a nominal fee.

Rauf's very first client was presented to him soon after taking up residence in offices under his own name by the ever-resourceful İbrahım. A Greek Cypriot prostitute had

had a disagreement with her Turkish Cypriot pimp and the two had parted company. Rauf listened without prejudice as the disgruntled woman complained she had not taken her mattress. He assured her the mattress could be retrieved but was startled by her vehement response. "She made it absolutely clear she didn't want the mattress due to the 'wear and tear'" recalled Rauf, laughing heartily at the memory.

Apparently the woman's intentions were to sue her former pimp for compensation which would amount to a new mattress. She produced the stamp duty and two shillings for Rauf's services. The two shillings were her own rate and Rauf looked down incredulously at the money sitting on his desk aware he could not accept the immoral earnings.

İbrahim, on the other hand, had no such qualms about the origins of the money. He scooped up the money unabashedly and replaced it with his own whilst reminding the young lawyer that 'money is money'. Although the newly-qualified Rauf couldn't disagree with İbrahim's logic he was crestfallen. He had envisaged for himself a far more glamorous role as a lawyer; that of a 'high flyer' — an image which swiftly took a nose-dive in front of İbrahim in his small office.

Rauf still lodged the case and as it was being deliberated he was fortunate enough to be able to welcome another new lawyer into the folds of his office. Oktay Feridun had only just returned from England as a law graduate and like Rauf eager to earn his credentials as a lawyer. Rauf wasted no time exploiting the young, keen graduate and promptly handed the case of the prostitute's dispute with her pimp over to him. With a wave of his hand, Rauf dismissed Oktay's troubled look explaining the case was 'a blessed case as it is the office's first case' and sent Oktay off to court.

Rauf's newly-established practice was thriving due in part to İbrahim supplying a steady stream of clients. However,

Rauf's own credentials were also winning him favour. Turkish Cypriot lawyers numbered very few and news of a practising Turkish Cypriot lawyer in the community sent waves. He also had the distinction of being Judge Raif's son which allocated him a firm place in the hearts of the community who had not forgotten his father's sense of justice and eagerness to help those in trouble.

Whilst Rauf was kept busy as a lawyer, Dr. Küçük stepped up his political aims to defend the rights of the Turkish Cypriots and the resistance of *enosis* which saw him prepared to go head-to-head against the British administration. Küçük had several supporters and was a popular figure amongst Turkish Cypriots but was an outspoken individual — often offending his own allies. His policies were not entirely palatable to many Turkish Cypriots who were chiefly concerned with losing the British from the island, believing that British support underpinned the safety of the Turkish Cypriots.

Küçük, as Rauf had pointed out to him, had his opponents within the Turkish Cypriot community. As a result of Rauf's observations, Küçük leaned heavily on Rauf's reputation and standing in the community as the son of Judge Raif and an up-and-coming lawyer for support. He would often require Rauf 'to be seen' at various meetings and rallies by his side. Although Rauf had no intentions of joining party politics he supported Küçük's endeavours whole-heartedly and was amenable to lend his presence when called upon. On one such occasion Rauf gave a rousing speech in support of Küçük to a gathered crowd and was received with explosive applause rivalling Küçük's own powerful orations.

Despite Rauf's insistence on keeping a distance from politics his association with political affairs increased at Küçük's prodding. His involvement was extended from simply writing in Küçük's newspaper to joining committees and preparing reports for government use, most notably working with the consultative assembly to establish a constitution for self-government.

IN November 1947, within months of Rauf's return to Cyprus, the British held their first meeting of the Cyprus Consultative Assembly. Under the chairmanship of Mr. Chief Justice Jackson, and with the then British governor, Lord Winster, presiding, Turkish Cypriot's entered a five-man committee, of which Rauf was a member, to represent their interests. Discussions got under way to agree on writing the constitution that would benefit both communities. Less than a year later the assembly was dissolved by the British.

The short-lived exercise was a result of dissension amongst the Greek Cypriot committees. Bowing to pressure from the church, which claimed the measures proposed would be the death knell of *enosis*, the remaining Greek Cypriot committees walked out.

The resulting closure of the assembly left Rauf incensed. He was nominated by his own committee members to approach the chairman and air their views and dissatisfaction. Rauf didn't need any encouragement and made an eloquent statement to Mr. Chief Justice Jackson citing the losses to Turkish Cypriots, given their willingness to participate and their continued backing for the assembly.

The breakdown of the constitutional assembly was a turning point for Rauf. He recognised the need to be more than a supportive bystander and took a pro-active stance to aid Turkish Cypriots whilst keeping a tenacious distance from internal politics.

Rauf became a member of several committees formed as a

result of the failure of the assembly but was concerned by the disjointed factions appearing amongst his own community. He would consistently voice the need for unity and was thrilled by the newly-formed Turkish Trade Commission in 1948. The purpose of the committee, headed by Judge Zeka *Bey*, was to visit all the district villages and towns and determine the needs and views of each.

Rauf found himself in a role which had been similar to his father's several years earlier: he was to gather the information and write a report which also gave him the opportunity to meet with the community leaders. The young lawyer, Oktay Feridun, who had been handed Rauf's first office case, was also involved as he was elected the commission's secretary. The two earnest lawyers collated the information and the report was finally published on the 20th January 1949. Signed by Judge Zeka *Bey*, the report was then presented to Lord Winster. Based on the contents of the report legislation was expected to be passed by the Attorney General's office. Rauf felt Turkish Cypriots could finally enjoy social and economic prosperity and prepared to return to the practice he had neglected for several months.

Unfortunately in the Attorney General's office there were no Turkish Cypriot personnel — its own evidence of a bias against them. The problem was solved quickly by Judge Zeka *Bey* and Dr. Küçük who pressed Rauf into service again. The two men together encouraged Rauf to apply for a new vacancy created under the job description of Junior Crown Counsel. Although Rauf needed some convincing, Judge Zeka *Bey* and Küçük knew that depositing him in the Attorney General's office would ensure new laws derived from the submitted report would have a chance of being passed.

Rauf considered the ramifications of working at the

Attorney General's office: the salary wasn't as lucrative as his earning potential from his private practice; the prospect of being responsible for Turkish laws (and any potential failure) wasn't appealing to him either. Engaged to be wed the same year he decided it would be prudent to discuss the proposal with his fiancée.

Unlike her father, Aydın did not ask after Rauf's salary. She threw her weight behind the Attorney's office believing Rauf, as a civil servant, would be working a regular nine-to-five job and be at home in the evenings.

With Aydın satisfied Rauf applied and got the job with little difficulty. He reasoned he would spend three years in the Attorney General's office gaining experience that could only enhance his career — an argument that was also substantiated by Dr. Küçük. Knowing there would be some economic hardship for Rauf, Küçük attempted to soften the blow by claiming Rauf would only need two or three years to complete the laws then would be able to return to his practice.

RAUF started work at the Attorney General's office in June 1948 and quickly became a newsworthy item amongst his peers. Few Turkish Cypriots occupied offices within the civil service and in the Attorney General's office there were virtually none save for a few elderly civil servants, with unimportant positions, close to retirement. The Turkish Trade Commission's report had outlined its concerns of the disproportionate Turk-Greek balance in government posts prompting the British Administration to respond.

Rauf's position as Junior Crown Counsel reflected the concerns as it was a newly-created post that had been opened to Turkish Cypriot candidates. For the Turkish

Cypriot community, a young lawyer of their own joining such officious ranks instilled a sense of pride and earned satisfied commendations from the community leaders. A quirk of fate also saw Rauf assisting the son of retired Attorney General Pavlides — who his father, Judge Raif, had been an assistant to during his role as Vice-President of the Debt Committee. Paskalis Pavlides, held the senior position and Rauf was expected to report to his office each day with his cases for briefing by Paskalis.

The two lawyers knew each from the lawyers' circuit and had a wary appreciation of each other but would frequently disagree on how cases should be handled. Rauf felt Paskalis had an over-zealous attitude as a prosecutor and would habitually condemn in his own mind each suspect guilty as charged. He later wrote a thinly-disguised contemptuous account of Paskalis in his memoirs:

"...he [Paskalis] would work very hard and stubbornly...in order to ensure that the suspect would go down. Acquittal of the suspect was considered to be an insult to his personality and [he] would be upset for days after. Especially when it came to capital punishment."

Paskalis had an exemplary record as a virtually unbeaten prosecutor although Rauf was one of the few not to be impressed. He claimed Paskalis' success was in part due to his negligence of overlooking any evidence that might cast doubt over the suspect's guilt. According to Rauf, Paskalis would often accept without question testimonies and statements regardless of how flimsy they appeared.

Rauf opted for a more balanced approach and insisted on scrutinising each case with a careful eye before forging ahead. He was often motivated to question evidence — particularly when it appeared 'water-tight'. He was not adverse to summoning investigating officers, subjecting them to his own line of questioning, to satisfy himself a guilty verdict was in order. Rauf's diligence and compassion towards the accused was borne out of his reluctance to send a man to the gallows. He believed hanging was a 'primitive' exercise that 'does not suit mankind'. Paskalis, on the other hand, was an avid supporter of capital punishment. Cases of extreme crimes presented to him were inevitably concluded with him demanding the maximum sentence — the death penalty.

Fully aware of Paskalis' stance on capital punishment, Rauf resorted to not seeking Paskalis' opinions on any cases that came to him directly. In doing so he avoided Paskalis' input and was able to mete out his own independent way of handling the case and thus avoiding the death penalty wherever he felt was possible.

Dealing with Paskalis became a daily occurrence and a fixture of Rauf's job but the allotted government income had also raised some concerns that nearly saw Rauf leave. During his time at the Attorney General's office Rauf's salary had been drastically reduced. His assigned income from the office amounted to approximately 30 Cyprus pounds which was in vast contrast to his earnings from his private practice that exceeded more than five times the amount. The considerable loss in earnings to him would have a measured affect on his future as a man intending to become a husband.

Fortuitously his good friend and confidante from England, Fazıl Plümer, had returned to Cyprus and spared the fate of having to establish offices for himself. Rauf handed his private practice to a grateful Fazıl with his client base and in return received a share of the practice's earnings. The extra income supplemented Rauf's earnings which alleviated his concerns as a young man due to be wed.

Despite his youth and limited experience, Rauf had the reputation at the Attorney General's office as a fair-minded individual that did not hamper his skills as a prosecutor; in fact, he became a powerful prosecutor known for his prowess in the court room and determination to procure justice. Dr. Küçük had been right in his assessment that Rauf would gain experience and distinction from his career with the Attorney General's office.

However, Rauf's biggest trial was about to begin as he prepared for marriage.

CHAPTER SIX
Marriage And Politics

By early 1949, just two short years since his return from studying in England, Rauf had managed to climb remarkable career heights. Although only 25, he held an enviable position in an esteemed establishment as a prosecutor for the Attorney General's office. His initial reluctance to take up the post left many in doubt as to how genuine his protestations were as Rauf appeared to accept the benefits of his coveted position. His career within the civil service offered him job security and a springboard to elevate his status in society. Employment at the Attorney's office had also encouraged his peers to view him in a different light giving him his own individual identity: he was thought of less as simply Judge Raif's son, emerging more as a lawyer in his own right.

When Dr. Küçük and Judge Zeka *Bey* first approached Rauf he insisted that he felt disparaged, and ruefully claimed in an interview several decades later that his 'stupidity took over' when he had applied for and got the job. However, the younger Rauf was clearly bolstered by the benefits of his job. He felt secure enough within weeks of starting at the Attorney's office to wed his fiancée.

Aydın had turned 18 the same year and Rauf honoured his engagement promises to marry her without further delay. Their wedding nuptials were set for that summer on the 17th July. Rauf was determined to offer his bride-to-be security on their wedding day that other prospective brides were commonly denied. Influenced by his father's horror stories of women divorced on a whim and thrown onto the street with no recourse, Rauf made alarming changes to his wedding vows.

Local traditions dictated an amount of money should be offered by the groom in his vows and then recorded and signed for by him. The purpose was supposedly to secure the bride's future should her husband die or in the event of a divorce. A nominal amount of between 10-20 pounds was usually considered as doing 'justice' to a discarded wife. Rauf, keen to break the traditions, created a stir, and his male elders to grumble, when he announced he was offering the staggering sum of £200 for his wife. He went further still when he insisted his bride also have the right to divorce him.

Divorce was considered a man's prerogative and it was unheard of to allow women the same right. The *Hoca* (Muslim cleric) marrying the pair managed to smile benignly at Rauf's generosity and continued conducting the ceremony with just the faint trace of an arched eyebrow. Whilst signing the agreements, the *Hoca* gently reminded Rauf that 'life was too long and one never knows what might happen in the future'.

Rauf was not deterred by the *Hoca's* friendly warning and happily placed his signature next to Aydın's. His signature was meant as a challenge to the partisan views and represented an important reform.

Family Law needed strong revisions that would improve women's rights and still had not been amended at the time of Rauf's wedding, much to his annoyance. Although Rauf had strong opinions, the subject of modernising Family Law appeared to divide a community wishing to progress but retain its patriarchal benefits. The resistance to reform had mainly come from an influential community leadership that firmly rejected all attempts at adjustments to the existing Family Law.

Years earlier, Judge Raif and his colleague Judge Halit had submitted a report to the British administration calling for changes to be made. The British Administration had accepted the report but later bowed to the objections of the then community leaders and the report, along with Judge Raif's hopes to modernise Family Law, was dismissed.

Rauf was chastised by several men at his wedding reception the following day but vehemently defended his decision to allow his bride to enjoy the same privileges of marriage as he would. He followed up his commitment to revise Family Law later in the same year when the Turkish Trade Commission's report was submitted also advising changes. The responsibility for preparing the legislation, which would bring about Modern Family Law, fell on Rauf's shoulders. For Rauf, the undertaking had sentimental value as he was in a position to bring into fruition reforms that had been of importance to his father.

RAUF was sincere in his commitment and had a mature approach, as well as a healthy respect for the institution of marriage, but he was never destined to be considered a romantic husband. In an informal interview in 2011, Aydın revealed during their courting days that Rauf had once presented her with an expensive box of chocolates. The chocolates were a rare luxury for Aydın and she had been impressed that he had managed to get his hands on a box as they were not usually seen on the shelves at the market-place.

Relishing the thought of eating the much sought-after chocolates, Aydın opened the box expectantly but was surprised to see empty spaces dotting the tray where chocolates should have been. Apparently Rauf had taken the liberty of selecting his favourite ones and eating them before passing the remainder of the chocolates on to her. As Aydın recalled the story to gales of laughter, her husband looked on with a bemused shrug of his shoulders, unperturbed and still seemingly at a loss to understand the slight.

Rauf may have had his failings as a suitor but he was intent on being a good husband and provider for his new family. Rauf and Aydın's marriage reflected the typical marriage unit of the late 1940s with its clearly defined roles: Rauf worked as the sole provider whilst Aydın harboured no career desires and was content to stay at home and keep house. Rauf was comfortable with the *status quo* within the household and attributes the arrangement to the longevity of his marriage.

Although Rauf rarely made public statements about his wife, in private he would frequently praise Aydın for her patience and acceptance of his work which often removed him from the family home. He retained the belief the family were able to avoid the casualty of divorce because Aydın became the erect backbone of the family unit. This was achieved, he felt, by Aydın staying at home and not wishing to court a career or publicity of her own, preferring very much to remain in the background and view the family as her main occupation.

Several years after his position as President in the TRNC had come to an end, Rauf felt more comfortable in discussing his personal opinions on his peers' marriages. He held a scathing view of his successors' wives suggesting they 'meddled' with their husbands' politics and was grateful to Aydın who had allowed him to remain focused on his work.

Rauf's view on marriage may be deemed old fashioned by contemporary standards but he did attempt to incorporate some modern values in the early years of his marriage. Uncharacteristically for a Turkish Cypriot male in the 1940s, Rauf was keen to explore the kitchen and impress his young wife with his own culinary skills.

The newly-weds' first visitor invited to dinner was Judge Zeka and Rauf insisted on cooking for the three of them. Aydın was gently brushed to the side and could only look on helplessly as Rauf cheerfully prepared over five kilos of freshly peeled potatoes and a slab of meat heftily weighing in at almost two kilos. The gargantuan feast was then crammed into the oven for roasting as Rauf busied himself with making rice and giving no thought to vegetables or salad for a side dish.

Rauf's efforts, when it was eventually served to Judge Zeka, resembled soup and was virtually inedible as the meat was undercooked. Judge Zeka demonstrated immense tolerance for the young couple by eating the meal and claiming 'it tasted very nice'. He then went on to regale the embarrassed pair with similar mishaps from his own marriage during its early days.

Aydın was horrified but Rauf's *faux pas* may have encouraged the tone for their marriage. Aydın promptly gained control of the kitchen along with all other household chores which always caused Rauf to smile wryly and insist his wife 'prefers to cook for me and doesn't like me in the kitchen'.

Having settled their domestic differences early, Rauf and Aydın planned to have several children with Rauf claiming they had set the number for at least six. Their first child, a boy, arrived on 26th January 1951, a day before Rauf's own birthday. Rauf was overjoyed and named his first-born after his father. Raif Rauf Denktaş was quickly followed by a brother, born on 7th May 1952, and named after his maternal grandfather, Münür.

The idyllic family unit was only marred by Aydın's burgeoning desire to have a daughter. It wasn't long before Aydın was pregnant again and despite Rauf's attempts to encourage her to enjoy the prospect of another child, Aydın fretted throughout her pregnancy. She was adamant she wanted a girl and could not be consoled by Rauf with wanting anything less. Rauf found himself confronted with Aydın on a daily basis with her fears of expecting another boy and constantly reminded his wife that a healthy child was more important.

Aydın's relief was evident when she did indeed give birth to a little girl, Dilek, on the 29th May 1955; Rauf's earlier expectations for a healthy child were not mirrored. His concerns for his child's health became a nightmarish prophetic legacy for the infant. Dilek was a beautiful little girl with a content nature and seemingly undisturbed by the boisterous environment created by her two brothers. At three months her non-responsive attitude to her mother's playful kisses and tickling suggested something might be wrong. By six months, Dilek was still unable to sit up unaided at a time when most babies were trying to roll over and crawl.

Dilek's developmental problems urged her parents to seek out medical advice only to have their worst fears confirmed. Dilek may have appeared physically healthy but it was thought her lack of progress stemmed from a neurological disorder. The extent of Dilek's neurological problems could only be ascertained by a specialist, which Cyprus lacked, leaving Aydın and Rauf confounded and distressed. The Denktaş family embarked on a round of overseas trips in search of a diagnosis and cure that included visits to hospitals in Turkey and Beirut before finally being referred to Great Ormond Street children's hospital in London.

At Great Ormond Street, Dilek was diagnosed with a rare form of brain disease and her parents were left to cope with the devastating news the child would not live beyond two years of age. An experimental operation offered a glimmer of hope for Dilek's future and the desperate parents signed the consent forms for the operation.

Unfortunately Dilek died before she was able to undergo the procedure on 12th May 1957 — just a few weeks short of her second birthday. Her parents' religious beliefs, as Muslims, meant Dilek's funeral was held within 24 hours and the child was buried at the children's cemetery within the grounds of the hospital.

Aydın and Rauf returned to Cyprus bereft of their only daughter and struggling to come to terms with their grief only to be shattered by the tragedy of losing another child four months later.

Their middle child, Münür, like his father, constantly suffered from bouts of tonsillitis and needed to have his tonsils removed. Rauf had refused to allow the child to be operated on fearing the child would not survive being given an anaesthetic. He had read a disturbing article offering unusually high statistics of children dying on the operating table as a result of adverse reactions to anaesthetics.

At the time of Münür's illness, Rauf was in İstanbul with the then Turkish Foreign Minister, Fatin Rüştü Zorlu*. Aydın, still grieving and vulnerable, was approached by Dr. Burhan

---

*Fatin Rüştü Zorlu (born 1910) was a Turkish diplomat, politician and later the deputy prime minister of Turkey (1954-1955). He was Minister of Foreign Affairs from 1957 until Turkish Armed Forces staged a coup in 1960 and ousted the government. Zorlu was arrested for 'violating the constitution' and hanged as a traitor on 16 September, 1967.

Nalbantoğlu*, a family friend, with his medical concerns that Münür needed to be operated on. Aydın had been encouraged to believe that Rauf was being over-protective and made the decision without informing her husband. The child died on the operating table becoming another unfortunate statistic that Rauf had been afraid of.

The tragedy of losing their two children within months of each other caused an insurmountable amount of pain and tension that was to affect each parent differently. Aydın was inconsolable and was plunged into depression for two years, grieving for her lost children, particularly the longed-for daughter.

The struggle for Aydın to cope signalled an important episode for their marriage as well as testing Rauf's endurance. His own experiences and memories of the painful episode became gauged by his wife's behaviour during that time which forced him to comment later that they had only merely existed whilst they 'lived and died for two years with Dilek's death'.

Whilst Aydın was able at least to express her grief, Rauf was more subdued and used work as his coping mechanism. Dilek's birth in 1955 had coincided with a terror campaign mounted by EOKA**, headed by Colonel George Grivas*** and determined to realise *enosis* through the threat of violence; by the time of Dilek and Münür's deaths in 1957,

* Dr Burhan Nalbantoğlu (1925-1981) was a founding member of the TMT, a medical doctor and served as the Minister for Health in 1969. He founded the current state hospital in Lefkosa which is named after him.

**EOKA is a Greek acronym (*Ethniki Organosis Kipriakou Agonos*) for National Organisation of Cypriot Struggle. Its purpose was to force out the British and bring about union with Greece — *enosis*. Their terrorist campaign officially began on 1st April, 1955.

*** Colonel Georgios Grivas (1898-1974) was a Cyprus-born general in the Greek army. He formed EOKA and directed its terrorist campaigns. He was known in EOKA by his code name Digenis.

the campaign was rampant leaving a murderous trail in its wake.

Initially Grivas and his followers were selective and targeted the British before turning their attentions to any non-Greek Cypriot nationalities. Determined to establish himself and eliminate the threat of the British, Grivas' efforts succeeded in creating an intense uprising. He earned a fearful reputation as a cold-bloodied killer and unleashed a reign of terror that included bold assassinations of British soldiers.*

The murders of the servicemen led to a swift response from the British administration which was determined to diminish the reputation of EOKA and bring its campaign to a halt. Any members of the group found guilty of terrorism were severely punished and frequently hanged. It was the hope that the punishment would serve as a deterrent but the British also feared releasing the terrorists back into public life to resume their activities. In a bid to make sure the desired results were achieved through the courts, the British took the precaution of handing all EOKA-related cases to Rauf. Effectively they were also making it known they had no confidence in Greek Cypriot prosecutors remaining unbiased.

The confidence shown in Rauf was an encouraging sign for his career with the Attorney General's office but his workload had increased forcing him to often stay away from home — although this didn't appear to be an issue for him. The family home had become an increasingly difficult place as Aydın struggled to cope with her depression and Rauf used the extra work as an opportunity to remove himself.

*The Cyprus Emergency (1st April 1955 – 18th April 1959), saw the EOKA led campaign by Grivas incur the loss of 371 British servicemen from the Royal Navy and Royal Marines (28), RAF (69) and the British Army (274).

Ironically the respite from home and his personal grief would be served by dealing with the murder and mayhem created by the terrorist actions of hardliners demanding *enosis*. Distancing himself from his own problems and channelling them into work became a typical trait of Rauf's, but it was not without its consequences.

AT the time of the EOKA trials Rauf received several death threats. On one occasion five bullets had been strewn in front of his office door — an undisguised threat along with the cruel reminder that before the deaths of Münür and Dilek they had been a family of five. Rauf knew there was no mistaking the intentions of the message behind the bullets: his family had become an easy target to reach and was at risk.

Rauf kept Aydın ignorant of the dangers but as a safety measure moved his family from the secluded area of Boğaz to the surrounded district of Nicosia. Renting a house next to Dr. Küçük's clinic, which was also owned by the doctor, Rauf hoped his family would appear less conspicuous in the busy town; it was closer to his work too enabling him to reach his family quickly if the necessity arose. The children had grown in number to include another son, Serdar*, and twin girls Ender and Değer, but fortunately the household managed to live in relative peace with few incidents.

Eventually Rauf was relieved of his duties as the prosecutor against EOKA. The overwhelming surge of EOKA suspects

*Serdar Denktaş (born 12th July 1959) in Nicosia, was elected to the TRNC parliament as National Unity Party MP for Nicosia in 1990. In 1992, he resigned from this party and helped form the Democratic Party. He has since held several Ministerial positions in government, including Deputy Prime Minister and Minister of Foreign Affairs.

brought to trial and the sensitive issues relating to the cases prompted the British to bring in special prosecutors and judges from England. But Rauf was still held accountable within the Greek Cypriot community for his involvement.

Long after his association with the prosecution of EOKA had finished, Rauf continued to receive intimidating threats and in the impossible situation of never being able to appease EOKA supporters who persisted in their harassment even after he volunteered to defend two known EOKA terrorists.

After the Republic was formed in 1960, legal actions against EOKA suspects were still ongoing in the courts. Languishing in jail, awaiting trial on charges of terrorism, were two Greek Cypriot brothers. According to the Chief of Gendarmerie, they had been labelled as traitors by their own community and he was determined to seek legal aid on their behalf.

It was a difficult time as the atmosphere of the communities after the British had left had become stricken with paranoia: Greek Cypriot lawyers were refusing to defend the men and certainly no Turkish Cypriot lawyer was prepared to take them on. It appeared their fate was sealed unless they could find a lawyer to represent them. Aware of the men's plight the Chief of Gendarmerie had advised the men to contact Rauf knowing his reputation for fairness and ability to remain unbiased.

Rauf had shown no interest in the case until he was informed of their predicament — that if the men could not find proper representation they would not be fairly tried. Risking his own reputation amongst the community, he agreed to defend the pair. The public uproar that ensued led Rauf to argue for his own defence. His actions were questioned and berated but Rauf publicly, and privately, stated the 'Rule of Law' was the most abiding principle. He believed if the community was to live in harmony then everyone needed to respect the principles of the law and, more importantly, have its protection regardless of their nationality.

Few echoed Rauf's sentiments where the terrorist actions of the men were concerned, but Rauf's reputation as an exemplary lawyer and his commitment to justice fortunately remained intact despite losing the case which resulted in both men being hanged.

The loss in court had impacted on Rauf but a few years earlier, prior to the case, Rauf had his own doubts about remaining a lawyer at the Attorney General's office. He had begun to question Cyprus' future under the guardianship of Britain and the stranglehold Greek Cypriots had within it. By 1957, he was concerned enough to make the decision to end his lucrative career with the Attorney General's office and instead pursue a career in politics.

Although Rauf always maintained he never set his sights on becoming a politician, his active participation in the field suggests there was never really an alternative. Rauf feared the British were going to give in to the demands of the Greek Cypriots and allow Cyprus to become annexed under the jurisdiction of or with Greece (just as Dr. Küçük had warned him previously). He had begun to suspect the British were in discussions with Greece following the release of the exiled Makarios from the Seychelles to Athens. The proposals by Lord Radcliffe in 1956 and later the Macmillan Plan, in 1958, also left him questioning British motives. All were enough to agitate him and rethink his career, believing he could better serve Cyprus as a politician than a prosecutor for the British.

At the time Rauf's suspicions were aroused he had been promoted and was due to be seconded to Hong Kong. He had already thought through his decision of leaving his prosecutor's career behind but was tempted to reconsider for the lure of overseas which would have paved the way for his promotion to QC. Reeling with uncertainty, Rauf went to see his friend and mentor, Dr. Küçük, to discuss the possibility of him leaving Cyprus. Rauf's intentions to leave the island were at best half-hearted and had coincided with important movements occurring politically along with his developing role with The Federation of Cyprus Turkish Associations. (The Federation had been formed to bring cohesion to all the dispersed factions within the Turkish Cypriot political community; it served as an important spearhead for all the associations and acted as the representative and accepted political voice for all.) The Federation, headed by Faiz Kaymak*, had clear political aims and strength in its numbers. Ideas and aims were passed through the Federation allowing the first notions of *Taksim*** to be aired which later gathered momentum with the collective.

Rauf and Dr. Küçük had spent a great deal of time together discussing ideas and the functions of the Federation which was due to dispatch a committee to New York for a conference at the request of Turkey. Rauf had been responsible for the preparation of the document intended for New York and had become very involved with the subject matter with many of the issues raised causing a great deal of concern.

It had become apparent that Makarios intended to take the Cyprus issue to the United Nations determined to have his policy of *enosis* realised. Rauf's documentation for

---

* Faiz Kaymak, (1904-1982), a teacher by profession was the founder of the Committee for Turkish Cypriot Minority Group.
** *Taksim* (Turkish for 'division') became the objective for Turkish Cypriots who supported a partition of the island between Turkish and Greek, conceived as early as 1957 by Dr. Küçük

the delegation to take to New York was intended to highlight their case with the United Nations, countering Makarios in his bid to request *enosis*.

The discussions arising from Rauf's meetings with Dr. Küçük over their thoughts on the Federation's purpose in New York had evidently increased the prospects of Rauf realising his political ambitions. When the subject of Rauf leaving for Hong Kong was broached, Dr. Küçük was blunt with his request. "What about our case?" he asked, "who will help me?"

Dr. Küçük's challenge to keep Rauf in Cyprus was met by Rauf without resistance. He was swept up by the political storms that were erupting and decided to stay, hoping his own contributions to the cause could help ease Cyprus into calmer waters.

Aydın and Rauf on their wedding day, 17th July 1949

Aydın, Rauf, and their four children Raif, Serdar and twin daughters Ender and Değer in 1961

Rauf with two of his children posing by the family
car and *above* Aydın and Rauf captured next to a
German Shepherd during an official outing

PART 2

Fighting The Cause

CHAPTER SEVEN

For The Republic

BY 1958, a disillusioned Rauf had left the Prosecutor's office after concluding that the British were no longer safe-guarding Turkish Cypriot interests and had edged closer to Dr. Küçük and his politics. His position at the Attorney General Office had become precarious as he struggled to balance his views as a civil servant for the British and a politically aware Turkish Cypriot. He had been reprimanded more than once by his superiors for 'meddling' in politics, which was deemed inappropriate for a high-ranking prosecutor serving the British Administration. Rauf, unable to ignore his gnawing suspicions of the British Administration, resigned from the Attorney General Office feeling bitterly disappointed.

Rauf's resignation meant he severed his ties with the British and could freely engage in Turkish Cypriot politics without interference. He did, however, acknowledge that his experience with the Attorney General's Office had gained him an advantage. He was aware of the legal foundations and the strategies that the British had adopted and fully intended to exploit the knowledge for the political advantage of Turkish Cypriots.

Coupled with his own orating skills at public events, Rauf was convinced he could make a difference. He had the ability to hold an audience's attention and encourage positive reactions. The speeches he had given in the past, at Dr. Küçük's request, had been received with explosive applause and there was an element of pleasure he derived from the public adulation of him. He recorded with remarkable clarity in his memoirs the first time he was called to give a public speech and expressed delight at the public's reaction:

"In the November of 1948, I spoke for the first time to the crowd that had gathered in front of the Selimiye mosque for the anti-*enosis* meeting. The speech was impromptu and I was very excited and I could feel that I had passed this excitement onto the crowds. I stepped down from the podium amongst intense applause and cheer. My father's colleagues came to embrace me. Some of them were in tears. Words like 'if your father was alive and could see you!' encouraged me even further."

Rauf was well known to the general Turkish Cypriot public and was confident of their approval of him. Despite his popularity, Rauf had to encourage the political community to endorse his stature as a political candidate. There was an established hierarchy in the community that was difficult to infiltrate. Prominent members of the political community were seasoned elders consistently elected to their posts by their peers. Rauf had the support of Dr. Küçük, who represented the community, but he knew he still needed to break the traditions of the voting policies to place himself.

An opportunity quickly presented itself in late 1957 in the form of The Federation— the all-important governing body of Turkish Cypriot politics. The leadership of the Federation was in disarray and Rauf seized the reins under controversial circumstances. His unchallenged election to the headship was easily facilitated and appears to have been acquired by a mixture of coincidence and manipulation.

A petty dispute involving Dr. Küçük and the head of the Federation, Faiz Kaymak, had turned relations between the two of them sour. Dr. Küçük's newspaper, *Halkın Sesi,* had been successfully printing both the news and information for political purposes on a printing press Faiz claimed had been donated by Turkey for the benefit of Turkish Cypriots. A disgruntled Faiz argued that Dr. Küçük was using the press as his own property and wanted the printing press to be registered with the Federation.

Tensions between the two leaders began to spiral out of control and seeped into the public domain causing the community to lose confidence in its leadership.

The fragile relationship between the public and the leadership needed to be repaired. Elections for the Federation were approaching and Dr. Küçük saw an opportunity to oust Faiz and restore unity within the rank. He threw his weight behind Rauf to be nominated as the head of the Federation and Rauf didn't protest; in fact, Rauf went to see Faiz whom he now viewed as a political opponent.

Faiz had been unchallenged before and had played an integral role within the Federation since its infancy but was now facing uncertainty as its leader. His feud with Dr. Küçük had seen his support diminish and he now had to consider the ramifications this would have on his candidacy at the forthcoming elections. Rauf's calculated visit to Faiz included tenuously reminding Faiz of the problematic relationship he had with Dr. Küçük. Rauf ventured his own opinion that 'unless Faiz could make it up with Dr. Küçük, there was no merit in him standing as a candidate'.

Rauf's brazen approach to Faiz may have been a contributing factor in Faiz's decision not to submit his candidacy. Rauf, however, did stand. On the day of the elections there were no other candidates allowing Rauf to be shoed-in unchallenged.

Many of Rauf's contemporaries have speculated on Rauf's entrance into politics with some labelling him as ambitious and arguing his motives. Dr. Küçük's son, Mehmet Küçük, appears to be a strong opponent of Rauf and categorically refutes the claims that his father was so instrumental in

Rauf's decision to become a politician. Instead he offers that Dr. Küçük regarded Rauf as a wayward son with an impetuous nature constantly needing to be reeled in. Furthermore, Rauf exhibited a penchant for leadership and was never going to be satisfied with being relegated to the background.

Mehmet Küçük supported claims that Rauf was motivated by his own desires to succeed with the ultimate goal of taking over the leadership. Vedat Çelik, the former foreign minister for the TRNC, and a long-time friend of Rauf's, retains a more rounded opinion. "We are all human," he noted in a philosophical tone during an interview, "and he [Rauf] was looking to go to the top, but he was also the right man for the job. He was the brains behind it all and had the right ideas."

The 'right ideas' were evident in Rauf's management of the Federation when he grasped control of the helm. He implemented changes and sought to boost the flagging finances of the Federation. He also introduced a radical concept that would encourage the Turkish Cypriot community to become independent and instil a sense of unity.

Rauf had noticed how his own community was virtually non-existent in industry and commerce in contrast to their Greek Cypriot counterparts. The Greek Cypriot community flourished in all areas of industry creating wealth and affluence which remained exclusive to themselves. The polarised effect on the commercially and professionally weaker Turkish Cypriots saw them dependent on their wealthier Greek Cypriot neighbours and the social divide this caused.

Rauf was horrified to witness the deference paid by Turkish Cypriots to Greek Cypriot professionals. Turkish Cypriots held the general opinion that Greek Cypriots were better educated and qualified. The consequence of their beliefs caused them to seek the service of a Greek Cypriot professional before consulting someone from their own community.

In commerce, there existed a few pockets of Turkish Cypriot-owned markets that fared no better as they were consigned to remain within a small business infrastructure without hope of expansion. Turkish Cypriot traders were relegated to buying wholesale from Greek Cypriots before selling the products back into the community. Rauf also concerned himself with the irony of how Turkish Cypriot money was funding EOKA activities as he noted dryly in his own memoirs: "EOKA was receiving taxes from the Greek Cypriots in the name of 'National Struggle Taxes.' In other words, the monies that they earn from us come back to us in the form of bullets..."

Recognising there was an urgent need to re-educate the community, Rauf set about reminding them of the Greek Cypriot desire to achieve *enosis* and the necessity for Turkish Cypriots to unify and support each other. He had been impressed by the independence of the Armenian community who had prospered commercially. Their success was solely enabled by their unity and dependence on each other.

Rauf had not forgotten an Armenian friend of his father, Bogos Efendi*, who exemplified the solidarity of the Armenian community. Bogos Efendi could often be found enjoying topical debates with his Turkish Cypriot peers at the coffee shops. On one typical day, the Armenian excused himself from the group of men to go and buy some cigarettes. A few metres away in full view there was a shop that sold his brand but he walked straight passed and continued on to an Armenian-owned market much further away. Rauf

---

*Efendi in Turkish is a title of nobility to mean Lord or Master. Colloquially it is a polite term meaning Mr or Sir and is frequently used to address adult males replacing the family last name.

was inspired by the Armenian community's loyalty often citing 'Bogos Efendi as a man who would prefer to walk for half- a-mile in order to buy a box of matches from a fellow Armenian.' He realised that if his own community adopted the same attitude as the Armenians they would become economically independent and therefore empowered. He initiated a scheme to be debated in a meeting attended by all the villages' associations and representatives to encourage Turkish Cypriots to work with each other and the Turk-to-Turk campaign was born.

The Turk-to-Turk scheme was based on a simple principle: Turkish Cypriots would only trade with or seek the professional services of another Turkish Cypriot. The success of the campaign was illustrated by the younger generation who began to filter into the trade industry that allowed a competitive Turkish market to spring up quickly. The Federation attempted to prevent exploitation with a 'watch dog' body known as the Market Control Committee. Their attempts to regulate the market were not always successful as Rauf admitted later that a few individuals did take advantage of the system for their own profiteering gains.

However, policing of the villages to ensure Turkish Cypriots only sought the professional services of their compatriots was vigorously implemented. Turkish Cypriots wishing to visit a doctor or lawyer of Greek Cypriot origin needed to obtain permission from their village Federation representative. They were rarely granted permission having the Turk-to-Turk campaign cited as a reason forcing an individual to content himself with the services of a Turkish Cypriot.

During his time as the head of the Federation, Rauf received a visit from an elderly man who complained he had been denied permission to see his Greek Cypriot doctor who treated him every year for his skin disorder. Committed to the campaign's principles, Rauf questioned why it was so important to see a Greek Cypriot doctor instead of one from his own community. The man eagerly explained his treatment was paid for every year by Makarios but worse, for him, was the fact that the Federation had also denied him permission to visit Makarios. Filled with curiosity, Rauf pressed further and insisted on knowing the nature of the man's relationship with Makarios.

Rauf listened patiently as the man explained he had saved Makarios from drowning when the priest had been a small boy. After he had been anointed as Archbishop, Makarios went to the trouble of visiting the man's village and renewing his acquaintance. A grateful Makarios had then offered to pay for treatment each year to ease the man's irritating eczema.

Rauf eventually granted the elderly man his request but couldn't resist mocking him and reminding him of his allegiances to Turkish Cypriots. He asked if the man was 'proud' of saving the person who had 'perpetrated so many bad deeds' against the Turkish Cypriots. The embarrassed villager stuttered an explanation that if he had known what Makarios would have grown up to be, he would have allowed him to drown. In a state of distress he offered to lower his trousers and show Rauf the extent of his complaint to punctuate the importance of why he needed to have treatment. Rauf, having already satisfied himself he had made his point, raised his hand in an authoritative manner and insisted the man show his irritation to Makarios instead.

The unkind behaviour Rauf demonstrated towards the elderly man was possibly a reflection of his frustrations and disappointment in his community who appeared comfortable with their ambivalence towards Greek Cypriot dominance. Rauf had focused on what he believed to be a form of social conditioning imposed on the Turkish Cypriots allowing them to accept unquestioningly the status of underclass. Removing the deeply-ingrained perceptions was challenging but Rauf persisted with the Turk-to-Turk campaign, irrespective of personal injuries and slight he might inflict, believing it to be the remedy for Turkish Cypriots.

His deep-seated belief that Turkish Cypriots needed to free themselves from their dependency on Greek Cypriots and strengthen themselves remained a cause he advocated throughout his lifetime. During his retirement, Rauf expressed his 'grave source of sadness' and blamed successive governments for not protecting the Turk-to-Turk campaign — which, in his view, played a vital role in encouraging progressive measures for Turkish Cypriots and was the 'first step to determining their own will and future.'

DESPITE being ultimately responsible for opening the borders on 23rd April 2003, allowing both communities to freely roam across the divide, Rauf questioned the need for modern-day Turkish Cypriots to seek hospital treatment and buy produce from Greek Cypriots.

Rauf's dissatisfaction stemmed from the many years of effort he had thrown behind Turkish Cypriots to secure that they were both competent and confident to obtain equal status and could self-govern without aid. He sought to arm Turkish Cypriots to ensure their safety and worked closely with the education sector to protect their future. His work with the Federation concentrated on schools and graduates — a legacy from his father who taught him education was paramount and the key to rehabilitating a society hampered by their own inferiority.

Using his knowledge of British law, Rauf went on to introduce financial methods that would promote the Federation's efforts to aid schools as well as small, impoverished villages. He was chiefly concerned with the poor standards and difficult circumstances teachers were expected to work under: their salaries were low and the school environments were lacking in materials. One financial scheme meant to boost the coffers was the introduction of the lottery, which was immediately vetoed by the British Administration. Any attempts to introduce a lottery came under scrutiny with a strict evaluation and an assortment of licences required that were designed to discourage gambling. Rauf's previous experience at the Attorney General's office was invaluable as he was aware of an earlier case where the Attorney General's office had already agreed that permission to run a lottery was not necessary for an established foundation.

Rauf went on successfully to finance many schools and enabled students from poorer areas to attend school allowing them the opportunity to have an education that would normally have bypassed them. The efforts he employed on teachers' behalf created a secure working relationship and he enjoyed a great deal of support with teachers at the forefront of many of his campaigns. Although, to his amusement, as Turkish Cypriots began to strengthen and unions were formed in later years, Rauf found himself the target of one of the first striking groups: teachers.

At the time of his involvement with Turkish Cypriot independence it was not solely limited to the Turk-to-Turk campaign and education. In the same year of taking over the Federation, Rauf became involved with an underground movement of Turkish resistance fighters. The group of fighters were known as TMT* and came out of a need to counter EOKA. Prior to the TMT there had

---

*The Turkish Resistance Organisation known as *Türk Mukavemet Teşkilatı* (TMT) was a Turkish Cypriot pro-*taksim* paramilitary organisation. It was commonly thought Rauf and Turkish military officer Rıza Vuruşkan formed the resistance group in 1958 (although its origins date back to the early 1950s) to counter the Greek Cypriot organisation, EOKA, as well as force partition of the island.

been other resistance groups, but were not considered as effective. TMT was a splinter group that had taken shape from as early as 1950. It had steadily gained strength in numbers over the years and was easily recognised from its proactive stance against EOKA. The TMT's popularity increased partly due to its ardent cry for *Taksim* (partition of the island) — a provocative notion that was beginning to gather momentum amongst the community.

For several years Rauf was seen as the founder and head of the TMT — a mantle he wore willingly to protect the identities of the real organisers. The truth behind Rauf's actual involvement in setting up TMT remains an interesting enigma that has endured years of speculation.

An interview he gave to a Greek newspaper in 1948 appears to have been the source of his being labelled as responsible for TMT's formation: when pressed by the reporter of what actions Turkish Cypriots might take should *enosis* be realised, Rauf responded with "...if it does, we shall take to the mountains and fight!" Rauf's bravado comment would consistently be used against him in later years as the basis for instigating 'terrorist' actions perpetrated by the TMT. He also became the subject of a smear campaign by the Greek Cypriot propaganda machine professing him to be the man who would ruin peace based on the same comments.

Although Rauf's input into the TMT's foundations appear vague, there is no doubt he was instrumental in making sure the organisation was effectively trained with the professional assistance of Turkey. Military operatives from Turkey were being filtered into Cyprus under the guise of bankers, businessmen and teachers. In late 1957 and early 1958, via the Federation, Rauf readily received these secret operatives and worked closely with the man installed as the commander of TMT, Colonel Rıza Vuruşkan. Rauf and the Colonel would become synonymous with TMT and its activities — Rauf as the figurehead and Colonel

Rıza Vuruşkan as the military director. The dedicated pair worked in unison to protect the interests of the Turkish Cypriot population against a militant Greek Cypriot threat. Smuggling and secreting caches of weapons was the directive issued by Turkey to aid the resistance movement and a difficult responsibility undertaken by Rauf and Vuruşkan. Both men took personal risks as they became recipients of the illicit armoury. Very often Rauf's wife would find large, heavily-laden trunks hidden underneath the children's beds to be told by her husband to ignore the offending chest as it was only filled with books.

Their combined efforts in the face of extreme dangers led to a mutual appreciation and respect for each other. After the collaborated talks had accumulated in the Constitution being drawn up*, and the birth of the Republic, Vuruşkan left the island in October 1960 to resume his duties in Turkey; but not before writing a long letter of appreciation to Rauf.

In his letter he expressed a great admiration for Rauf and noted the 'unforgettable sacrifices' performed by Rauf. Uncharacteristically for a military operative, Vuruşkan also revealed the extent of Rauf's involvement with TMT in his missive and the risks to Rauf's personal welfare: "you appeared to have drawn up some of the operations that were my responsibility thus putting yourself at risk" he wrote candidly.

The Colonel followed up his concerns and thought it prudent to warn Rauf and assure him that he would do everything he could to prevent Rauf's exposure to further danger: "...I have cancelled some of my plans that were not vital, in order to protect you from gaining further enemies..."

The 'enemies' Vuruşkan alludes to are not mentioned by name but he hints the threat is ever present despite the birth

*After the country won its independence in 1959, the Constitution of Cyprus was prepared and ratified on 16 August 1960, and was meant to act as the abiding principles for the government of Cyprus known as the Republic of Cyprus.

of the Republic. Neither Vuruşkan nor Rauf were convinced by the political developments that led to the newly-formed Constitution which was to bring into being the foundations for a new Cyprus. Vuruşkan held the steadfast belief there still remained 'growing dangers' for the Turkish Cypriot community and Rauf was the 'strongest assurance' for their future and survival.

VURUŞKAN'S pessimistic view regarding the newly-formed Republic of Cyprus was not unwarranted. Rauf had been an integral member of the committee representing Turkish Cypriots in The Cyprus Agreements and experienced first-hand the intransigency of Makarios.

Osman Örek* (later to become the Minister of Defence) had been assigned to negotiate on Turkish Cypriots' behalf in London and struggled to resolve issues with the Greek Cypriot representative. A frantic Julian Amery, the Minister of State, who was chairing the agreements, brought the meetings to Cyprus to include Dr. Küçük and Makarios in the hope of resolving the issues from London. Amery's hopes were on the verge of being dashed as Makarios continued to disrupt the meetings with petty issues forcing the delay of the signing of the agreements. (The Zurich agreements had been signed in London on February 1959 and nine months were allocated to complete the constitution and declare the Republic. Makarios had delayed the signing by a further nine months after the allotted time frame).

Amery was ready to call a break in the talks and return to England with his delegation but made a last-ditch attempt to conclude the talks by inviting Rauf to support Dr. Küçük at the table. Rauf stalked into the conference room and

---

*Osman Nuri Örek (born 1925 — died 1999) was a prominent lawyer and academic who became the first Minister of Defence upon the declaration of the Republic of Cyprus. He would later serve as Prime Minister of Northern Cyprus in 1978.

firmly reminded Makarios that the public at large had been patiently waiting for several months for the agreements to be signed. His reminder to Makarios had also insinuated that the Archbishop did not have the best interests of Cyprus in mind. The implication had not been missed by Makarios and his rejoinder was to question whose side Rauf was on. Rauf erupted and made clear his position as a Turkish Cypriot with Turkish Cypriot interests that needed to be met and demanded Makarios take note of the fact.

The tit-for-tat that ensued caused Amery to suggest a ten-minute break which allowed each side to cool down in the gardens of the Governor's residence. Without the oppressive atmosphere of the boardroom, Makarios and Rauf engaged in jokey foreplay that saw them scoring points off one another. Makarios admitted that 90 percent of divorce cases amongst Greek Cypriots were filed, by men, as a result of the bride found not to be a virgin. Rauf, renowned for his impish sense of humour, quickly retorted that Turkish Cypriots didn't have the same statistics because Turkish Cypriot girls' skirts were longer! Makarios had his own quips to offer and joked about Muslim religious leaders.

The banter went back and forth between the two but appeared to have appeased everyone involved. The meeting resumed and common ground was found leading the way for arrangements to be made for the respective sides to sign the agreements.

The laborious meetings and the constant wrangling had left their mark on several people involved. More than two decades after the Constitution was finalised and the Republic proclaimed, Rauf, in 1983, declared the Turkish Republic of North Cyprus and had been to New York to defend his decision.

On his return from New York he stopped in London to attend a dinner in his honour and there he had the occasion to meet again with Julian Amery.

121

Amery gave a sober speech reflecting his experiences of the meetings at the Governor's residence. As he droned on with formal particulars he suddenly broke with the polite rendition to make an astounding statement: "The British Government does not recognise Denktaş's declaration of his Republic", he bellowed authoritatively to his audience, "nor does it recognise him as the President of that Republic. Why should it recognise it?" Rauf was stunned into embarrassed silence by the audacious remark and recorded the moment in his memoirs as wondering 'if Amery had attended the dinner in order to insult us'. However, Amery hadn't finished. After a suitably dramatic pause, Amery continued:

"Yes, why should it recognise it? Unlike Makarios, and as in other colonies and their leaders, who ordered the killings by shooting them from behind, he [Denktaş] didn't murder British soldiers and their families!"

Rauf, having been reprieved by Amery, never forgot the moment. He realised he had not been alone in his concerns about Makarios. However, on the birth of the Republic of Cyprus in 1960, he struggled to get Turkey, and the rest of the world, to understand Makarios' intentions and the severity of the situation implied for Turkish Cypriots.

Rauf speaking at a public event during the 1950s

**British Minister of
State Julian Amery**

CHAPTER EIGHT

No Man Is An Island

The 1960 constitution finally came into fruition paving the way for Turkish Cypriots to participate in government and granted them a partnership status. Its long-awaited labours gave birth to the Republic of Cyprus on 16th August, 1960 and Turkish Cypriots were jubilant. Celebrations were in abundance as Turkish Cypriots took to the streets to rejoice and revel in their long-overdue independence. In the political sphere, politicians were congratulating each other and making preparations to enter government. Rauf, however, remained wary but consoled himself with the Communal Chambers* which formed the basis of the federative state.

Dr. Küçük, as the newly-elected vice-President of the Republic, was kept busy as he prepared to fill his quota of ministerial posts for Turkish Cypriots in the new government. His allotted amount of three ministers, compared to the seven posts designated for the Greek Cypriot administration, meant he had to consider his choices carefully. The eventual cabinet he chose consisted of Osman Örek, Dr. Niyazi Manyera and Rauf's old law-study partner, Fazıl Plümer. He had wanted Rauf in a parliamentary post but Rauf

*The Communal Chambers, established under the 1960 Constitution, were two legislative bodies, one each for the two Cypriot communities. The Greek Cypriot Chamber was abolished in 1965 and its responsibilities transferred to the House of Representatives. The Turkish Cypriot Chamber was never officially dissolved although it hasn't exercised its powers since the division of the island in 1974.

rejected a position and insisted he would prefer working within the Communal Chambers, as he felt it to be of more importance. The Communal Chambers represented the political partnership between the two communities and gave communal autonomy to each. Rauf viewed himself as the caretaker of these communal rights and intended to prioritise his work to safeguard the foundations of the Chambers.

Rauf, having convinced Dr. Küçük of his preference, was elected as the President of the Turkish Communal Chambers with little difficulty. It was hardly surprising that Rauf faced no objections to his validation as head of the Chambers: the budget for the Communal Chambers was meagre and salaries were considerably less than parliamentary duties without the same prestige. The difference in the salaries also meant Rauf struggled to find willing recruits to fill posts in the Communal Chambers as would-be politicians scrambled to find a ministerial duty.

Despite the initial problems of putting together a team, Rauf succeeded in enlisting a cabinet of worthy members for the Chambers. Their first official engagement was to receive the Turkish Ambassador, Emin Dirvana, due on the island to complete his tour of duty for a period of one year. On the first day of the new Republic, the entire cabinet was present to receive their esteemed guest arriving at Nicosia airport.

Tall, handsome, and impeccably dressed, Dirvana impressed Rauf and his colleagues as he strode forcefully across the tarmac and greeted the party with his military habit of clicking his heels sharply together as he shook hands. One member, Asım Behcet, was unable to contain himself and echoed the thought of the entire Chambers' members when he excitedly whispered in Rauf's ear that

Turkey had sent a 'wonderful Ambassador' who 'would teach Makarios a lesson.'

Whilst Rauf nodded approvingly in agreement at Asım's sentiments, it did not take him long to realise that Dirvana did not have the same regard for him. The following day, Rauf and Asım Behcet visited the Ambassador at the embassy. Rauf wasted no time in informing Dirvana of the problems surrounding Makarios and his belief the Archbishop would destroy the Agreements at the first opportunity*. Rauf also ventured his own opinions, should the agreements fall into dissolution, that *Taksim* would be the only viable solution.

Dirvana was not a man accustomed to being confronted and took Rauf's forthright approach as a personal insult to his country's integrity. He banged his fist furiously on the desk sending pens flying in all directions. As Rauf and his companion stood in mute disbelief, Dirvana roared that Turkey stood as a guarantor and Makarios had no right to destroy anything carrying her signature. He jabbed his finger in the face of a startled Rauf, adding that Turkey was to be trusted and Rauf had absolutely no right to question her intentions.

Rauf and Asım left the Ambassador's office with Dirvana's formidable voice ringing in their ears. As soon as they had retreated to a safe distance, a visibly-shaken Asım linked arms with Rauf and managed once again to translate his company's thoughts: "My God," he offered, "now the shit has hit the fan!"

Dirvana had taken an instant dislike to Rauf and his views became well-documented in several media publications.

---

*Makarios had made his position clear to the then Prime Minister of Greece, Konstantinos G. Karamanlis, his objections to the agreements before and during the London-Zurich agreements in 1959. His opposition was mainly due to the veto right of the Turkish Cypriot vice-President, Turkey's right of intervention and the stationing of Turkish and Greek armed forces on the island.

The source of his antagonism towards Rauf appeared to have been heavily influenced by his superiors in the Turkish government. Rauf's views for partitioning the island and his mistrust of Makarios were well known. The Government of Turkey, however, had considered the problem of Cyprus resolved and forewarned the Ambassador that Rauf was attempting to upset the apple cart.

Dirvana took his obligation of maintaining the *status quo* of Cyprus seriously which, in his view, meant keeping Rauf firmly in the background. Reports written by Rauf in his attempt to enlighten Turkey of evidence he had gathered proving contingencies were invariably ignored and dismissed by Dirvana, who would frequently marginalise Rauf in his own reports.

Simultaneously Dirvana was considered ineffectual by Rauf as an Ambassador. He was particularly concerned at how Dirvana was making successful leeway in tearing at the internal politics of the Turkish community. Rauf blamed Dirvana for creating tensions between himself and Dr. Küçük with his constant admonishments regarding Rauf's role in politics. Dirvana believed Dr. Küçük was allowing Rauf too much political expression which, in his opinion, was the realm of the Doctor's.

Dirvana's misgivings about Rauf were later partly responsible for a miscarriage of justice that almost had Rauf incarcerated. During his time in Cyprus, he was consistent in his reports to Turkey claiming to be successfully managing the Cyprus issue (and Rauf with it) and built up a good rapport with Makarios and his underlings. His success was enough to convince Turkey to extend his tour of duty in Cyprus by another year, which spelled more trouble for Rauf.

On 23rd January 1962, the *Bayraktar* mosque was the

subject of a terrorist attack that spawned an intricate web of deceit resulting in the murder of two young Turkish Cypriot lawyers. Relations disintegrated between the two communities as the Greek Cypriot media declared the bombing of the mosque to be the work of Turkish Cypriots. The attempt of the media was to lambast the Turkish community and suggest they were intent on upsetting the agreements for their own gains to achieve *Taksim*. Dirvana added fuel to the emotionally-charged fires declaring the Greek Cypriot Minister of Interior, Polycarpos Yorgadjis, had irrefutable proof it was the work of Turkish Cypriots.

Rauf was aghast by the claims and insisted the incident be investigated and a committee formed to determine the truth. He was one of the lawyers assigned and cross-examined Yorgadjis who stated his informants were two young Turkish Cypriot lawyers and budding journalists, Ahmet M. Gürkan and Ayhan Hikmet. As the case was unravelling in court, Gürkan and Hikmet launched the newspaper, *Cumhuriyet*, and publicly proclaimed the bombing of the mosque to be the work of Turkish Cypriots, hinting the Turkish Cypriot leadership was also culpable.

The revelations left Rauf and Dr. Küçük reeling with confusion but far worse was to come. The two unfortunate lawyers were murdered and Yorgadjis immediately contacted Dirvana to inform him Rauf and Dr. Küçük were responsible — their motives were to silence the men from exposing their part in the bombing of the mosque. He also claimed to have taped recordings with Gürkan to substantiate his claim of Rauf and Dr. Küçük's guilt.

The ominous situation had taken a sinister turn as Rauf and Dr. Küçük now faced allegations of murder. Dirvana acted swiftly and summoned the pair to his office where he made an incredible offer to both of them. The Ambassador appeared to have already decided to take Yorgadjis's word as evidence of Rauf and Dr. Küçük's guilt and wanted to 'close the matter' quietly. His suggestion was to hold a private inquiry behind closed doors with an investigative team from Turkey; should the pair be found guilty, Dirvana would have the men exiled to Turkey where they would live as guests of the country.

Both Rauf and Dr. Küçük were appalled at the suggestion and argued they had a right to a trial, which was their legal and constitutional right — a right that Dirvana appeared to be denouncing. Rauf was particularly disturbed at the thought of their good names being 'tanned' before being ejected to Turkey.

Rauf knew Dirvana had been looking to dispose of him but was astounded that Dirvana would go as far as to make such extreme sanctions based on Greek Cypriot hearsay. Rauf had his opportunity that day in Dirvana's office to express his anger and blasted the Ambassador for allowing the 'words of EOKA supporters to be trusted.' He concluded his outburst stating that 'Yorgadjis was an active terrorist' as Dirvana sat seething with rage whilst Dr. Küçük looked on nodding with agreement. The trial was to be important for the vindication of Rauf and Dr. Küçük's name but Rauf had hoped it would finally be enough to convince Dirvana of the extent Greek Cypriot tactics were capable of.

The ensuing trial succeeded in exonerating Rauf and Dr. Küçük with the help of Yorgadjis's own conversations he had recorded with one of the lawyers. Dirvana was furious at the admissions made on the tape (which actually pointed the finger at a press consultant who had not been in contact with either of the lawyers). The so-called damning tapes amounted to general hearsay with a flimsy suggestion of Rauf, or Dr. Küçük, having been out of the country to meet with a shady group in London to arrange for the mosque to be bombed. Proving Rauf and Dr. Küçük were responsible for the atrocity would have made them accountable for the murders of the lawyers too. Fortunately for Rauf he had not left the country since July 1961 and Dr. Küçük's official engagements overseas could account for his whereabouts.

The recording did, however, demonstrate the zealous attitude of Yorgadjis who repeatedly asked for confirmation Rauf was involved in the bombing of the mosque. At one point he asks in an excited manner if Gürkan has "...any information that Denktaş had these bombs planted or are you merely hazarding a guess?" A subdued Gürkan responded with, "I can't claim that Denktaş had the bombs planted..."

During the trial Yorgadjis' cross-examination by Rauf frequently ended with Yorgadjis declining to answer or claiming not to know the answer. In any case, it left Yorgadjis' credibility with Dirvana in tatters although it did nothing to endear Rauf to him or change his opinions of Cyprus. He remained staunch in his belief that Rauf and Turkish Cypriots were the cause of Cyprus' failure to live as an integrated community under a federative status. In later years he was quoted as accusing Turkish Cypriots of sparking riots and violence for their own end.

In an interview recorded for an ITV documentary, *End of Empire,* Dirvana maligned Turkish Cypriots with a damning, although unfounded, admission of Turkish Cypriot terrorist acts:

"...Turkish Cypriots burned and looted Greek shops and homes. Soon came counter-attacks and the fighting spread around the island. A friend of mine, whose name must still be kept secret, was to confess to me that he had put this little bomb in the doorway in order to create an atmosphere of tension so that people would know that the Turkish Cypriots mattered."

To Rauf's immense relief, Dirvana exited the island in late 1962 and was replaced by Mazhar Özkol. Whilst Rauf had a better relationship with the new Ambassador, Dirvana's detrimental opinion of him and the trial had caused irrevocable damage. Rauf's reputation had been tainted to such a degree, it kept him under suspicion for several years with the authorities.

The backlash Rauf endured from his ordeal defending his name and proving his innocence of murder paled by comparison to the events ignited on 21st December 1963. A Turkish Cypriot couple had returned to Nicosia late at night and resisted an unwarranted search by a Greek Cypriot patrol. The couple were fired on and brutally murdered — the man died at the scene and his female companion a few hours later in hospital. Civil unrest quickly flared as protesters gathered to express their anger. The protestations resulted in more shootings which continued throughout the day. The violence was enough to encourage leaders from both sides to appeal for calm with little success.

Rauf also took immediate action on the same day and visited a school in Nicosia to tell the over-excited teenage boys to remain calm and not endanger their community by becoming embroiled in violent protests. According to their assistant headmaster, Mr. Salih Coşar, after Rauf's impromptu visit, the boys left in good spirits, deeply moved by Rauf's speech. As they filed out of the school, a passing police car filled with Greek Cypriot policemen randomly fired into the school yard wounding two of the students.

The incidents had coincided with Makarios' attempt to amend the constitution with his thirteen-point proposal that effectively ousted Turkish Cypriots from having a

governing seat and removing their partnership status.*
Inter-communal violence had begun to rage and Rauf knew
that Turkish Cypriots faced an onslaught as he believed
the violence towards his community was a premeditated
operation to remove them by force as well as politically.
He divided his time making appeals to Turkey to intervene
whilst visiting make-shift trenches in Nicosia that had
become commonplace as a community prepared to defend
itself.

On 25th December, two days after the fatal shootings
in Nicosia, Rauf had seen enough of the trenches and the
desperation of poorly-armed Turkish Cypriots and went to
see Ambassador Mazhar Özkol. The Ambassador listened
quietly as Rauf explained he wanted to get a message to
Turkey's Prime Minister, İsmet İnönü**, before he slipped
Rauf a bit of paper. Rauf hastily scribbled a message outlining
the dire circumstances and reiterated 'the agreements had
been signed trusting in Turkey's position as our guarantor'.
He received assurances Turkey would be sending a warning
volley of Turkish jets that would fly over the ravaged area of
Nicosia.

Rauf waited on the roof tops of the embassy in
anticipation. In his enthusiasm he almost destroyed the live
radio communications cable as he attempted to hoist himself
up further. Fortunately he was pulled back before he could
destroy them and was rewarded with the unmistakable sight

*On 30th November 1963 President Makarios presented Vice-President Küçük with
his proposed amendments to the constitution. These proposals were rejected both by
Turkey and the Turkish Cypriot community.
**İsmet İnönü (born 1884 died 1973) had a successful career in the Turkish military
and earned several distinctions during his service. He later became a prominent
politician and was considered the most suitable candidate to succeed Atatürk as
President upon his death. İnönü was elected the second President of Turkey on 10th
November 1938.

and sound of two fearsome F-100 Super Sabre jets flying towards Ledra Palace.

The show of force by Turkey provided a temporary cease-fire, preventing more bloodshed for Nicosia, and instigated the 'Green Line' agreements. Both communities, along with British representatives, convened to discuss the situation at the British High Commission. Glafkos Clerides* was in attendance as a representative for the Greek Cypriots and Rauf the Turkish Cypriots. Their discussions were also based on negotiations — several hundred Turkish Cypriots had been abducted and it was Rauf's job to secure their release.

The Cypriot representatives arrived at the British High Commission and were asked to surrender any weapons at the security gate before entering the building to begin negotiations. Rauf dutifully handed over his single hand-gun and then watched incredulously as Clerides did the same before reaching into a second holster to retrieve another gun and then pulling a third gun that had been tucked into the back of his trousers.

Thinking Clerides had finally relinquished his weapons, Rauf looked on with surprise as Clerides, almost as an afterthought, raised his trouser leg to pull out a small gun concealed in a suspender. Having been relieved of their armoury, the two men finally began their talks.

Whilst the talks were in motion, Rauf became agitated as the attacks were still occurring and had extended beyond the borders of Nicosia. In Omorphita (Küçük Kaymaklı) houses were being subjected to savage arson attacks and evacuated on a daily basis. He confronted Clerides with the issue and stated the point of the talks was useless if

*Glafkos Clerides (born 1919 died 2013) was a prominent Greek Cypriot politician who later became the fourth President of the Republic of Cyprus for two terms from 1993 to 2003.

the attacks were still ongoing. Clerides responded with an apology and claimed the burning of the houses was the work of a 'lunatic on parole from an asylum'. He assured Rauf, although Makarios did not have the power to return the mentally-ill patient, he had ordered him to be sent back to the facility. Rauf had not been hoodwinked by the feeble falsehood but assumed the point had been made and the attacks would be halted.

Just two days later, however, four houses were set ablaze and Rauf telephoned Clerides asking if the unfortunate man with the mental illness was back on the streets. He was met with an emphatic 'no' from Clerides who persisted with the ridiculous subterfuge. "Well," responded Rauf, through gritted teeth, "there must be more of them out that need to be ordered back to the asylum!"

British Commonwealth Secretary, Duncan Sandys had also flown out to assist with the talks and witnessed the destruction of Turkish homes. He expressed his 'outrage' and 'anger' to the media in Cyprus and abroad but persevered with the discussions, which appeared to be floundering.

The suggestion was made for the conferences to continue in London with the Cypriot representatives. Makarios had already made statements to the effect the constitution was no longer valid and unworkable but still retaining his position as the legal governing body of Cyprus.

As a result of Makarios' position, Rauf rightly had concerns that the London conferences would be held under the banner of the government of Cyprus which — filled only with Greek Cypriots — was to the exclusion of Turkish Cypriots. With Dr. Küçük, and the ministers who had been forcefully withdrawn from governmental status, it was agreed the talks could only occur if it was in consideration of Greek and Turkish Cypriot communities attending

134

respectively. Sandys had agreed but Osman Örek, who was the then Minister of Defence, had a suspicious nature and insisted Sandys sign a document to confirm the conference would only include representatives of the two communities and interested parties involved as guarantors. The document was agreeably signed by Sandys and a satisfied Rauf and his colleagues, Örek and Halit Ali Riza, made their way to London.

On their arrival at Marlborough House to attend the conference, Rauf was furious to see each community accommodated but also had a table allocated for the Government of Cyprus. He approached the then Foreign Minister of Turkey, Feridun Cemal Erkin, and demanded the slight be rectified. To Rauf's dissatisfaction, Erkin suggested a compromise which included submitting a formal protest at the Government of Cyprus' attendance and a threat to leave if it took to the stand to speak.

A disgruntled Rauf left Erkin and decided to clear his head with a walk. As part of a VIP delegation, and the sensitive nature of Greek and Turkish clashes, he had been assigned protection. He asked his police protector for the nearest barber and was taken to a local 'Turkish' establishment. He settled himself in the barber's chair and struck up an amiable conversation of pleasantries with the barber in English. As the barber deftly moved the cut-throat razor back and forth across Rauf's exposed throat, the barber asked in Greek 'and how are the talks going Mr. Denktaş?' Rauf was left almost speechless and admitted later to feeling more than a little nervous by the unexpected encounter with what turned out to be a Greek Cypriot barber. "Very well," he responded, "I'm more than confident we can resolve the issues."

Luckily for Rauf the barber was not a fanatic but a genuinely interested party. However, leaving the barber's shop, Rauf was perturbed enough to ask the policeman 'what the hell were you thinking sending me to a Greek barber?' The policeman shrugged and offered his apologies saying he just thought the barber was Turkish and he couldn't tell the difference.

Rauf barely had time to consider the apparent indifference of the policeman as he had more pressing concerns — namely Erkin's approach to politics. On his return to the conference hall he insisted Erkin take up the matter of Sandys reneging on his documented promises that the 'Government of Cyprus' would not be in attendance. Erkin assured Rauf he would categorically state the Turkish Government's disapproval at a dinner party that night at which Sandys was a guest.

Rauf and his colleagues were staying at the same hotel as Erkin and waited in anticipation for his return. Whilst waiting, Rauf entertained his peers with his typical anecdotal humour describing in colourful detail how he had narrowly escaped the barber's knife. He peppered his conversation with impressions of the dull policeman that had delivered him to the barber before turning his attentions to more serious matters. The group agreed with Rauf's assessment that he had every confidence in Erkin and believed the Minister would return with satisfactory news. It was past midnight when they received word that Erkin had returned to the hotel and they rushed to his room to ask how Sandys had reacted at Turkey's displeasure and his intentions of how he would redress the situation.

Erkin didn't appear to mind the late intrusion but addressed Rauf and his excited peers as though he was speaking to a group of churlish children who had been excluded from a private party. He regaled them with the pomp and splendour of the ceremony that had accompanied the lavish dinner and Rauf listened with polite patience. Eventually Rauf interjected and queried how he had fared with Sandys' reactions to the concerns of the Turkish government.

Erkin proudly announced to his audience that Duncan Sandys had sat to the left of him and another minister had sat to the right of him. However, he had turned his back on Sandys and spent the whole night in conversation with the other man; he concluded his actions of ignoring Sandys for the duration of the dinner could only be construed as Sandys having understood his displeasure. Rauf was stunned by the so-called political tactic. When he recalled the incident later his voice barely concealed his sarcasm as he commented that Erkin had 'given us a real lesson on politics.'

Although Rauf and his peers did eventually succeed in halting any Greek Cypriot from speaking on behalf of the 'Government of Cyprus' no agreement was reached. The failure of the London conference took the Cyprus problem to the Security Council in February 1964. At the time the decision was made for the Security Council's involvement, Rauf had been in Ankara where he was reunited with his wife and children.

Aydın had flown to Ankara for an operation but had become accustomed to her husband's absences. She had only just left the hospital and was still in recovery when Rauf bade a hasty farewell to go to New York to attend the Security Council meetings.

The Security Council made the decision on 4th March 1964 to send a peacekeeping force to Cyprus. Despite his wife's ill-health at the time that had ended with her needing an operation, Rauf showed more emotion for the disagreeable actions of the UN. He was devastated as the United Nations Security Council had stamped the name of the 'Government of Cyprus' onto the agreement. In his memoirs he recorded that he 'cried at the fact...when there was not a single Turk in the so called "Government"'.

Rauf knew the agreement had basically endorsed Makarios' intended government and he would now act accordingly. He tried in vain to convince the Secretary General, U Thant, that Makarios would now use the legitimisation of his government to manipulate the UN peacekeeping force for his own gains. He believed Makarios would request the assistance of the peacekeeping force to aid the 'Cyprus Government' in 'quelling the Turkish uprising'. Whilst Thant had given Rauf an appointment, his neutral smile firmly fixed on his face at the meeting reminded Rauf of his impartial position.

It was a dejected Rauf that returned to Ankara to prepare his reports on the Security Council's decision and to consider how the new obstacle of Makarios' legitimised government should be dealt with. He didn't have long to consider the problem. Makarios had been busy removing his own obstacles and banned Rauf from returning to Cyprus. Rauf had been declared a criminal by Makarios and in consequence found himself unwillingly exiled to Turkey.

THE REPUBLIC OF CYPRUS IS BORN, AUGUST 16 1960
Seated from left to right, Archbishop Makarios as the first
President of the Cyprus Republic, Governor Sir Hugh
Foot and Vice-President Dr. Fazıl Küçük

Turkish Ambassador
to the Republic of
Cyprus,
Emin Dirvana

CHAPTER NINE
A Battle For Survival

By 1964, the Constitution, which had tendered a peaceful solution for a bi-communal Cyprus, had become openly ignored by Makarios and haughtily swept aside. The infamous *Akritas Plan**, written in 1963, and coinciding with Makarios' approach, had also outlined its objectives to remove any obstacles in the path of *enosis*. The bold declarations of the plan created a framework for the 'unalterable national objective' but were forced to recognise the political and legal implications of the Constitution. Seeking to remove the hindrances, an organised strategy, documented in stages, argued the urgent need to amend the Constitution and revealed unashamedly the reasons for doing so:

"...we must get free of all those provisions of the Constitution and of the agreements (Treaty of Guarantee, Treaty of Alliance) which prevent the free and unfettered expression and implementation of the wishes of our people and which create dangers of external intervention."

It is unlikely Makarios did not have knowledge of the plan (which was later attributed to be the work of the Greek Cypriot leadership with Yorgadjis as the main architect).

---

*Akritas was the code name for the plan that outlined its intentions to remove Turkish Cypriots and gain unification with Greece. It was written by the Greek Cypriot leadership with Yorgadjis named as 'Chief Akritas'.
See Appendix A for full version of the plan

He had already submitted his proposals* to amend the Constitution which then became the catalyst for widespread violence. He was aware that the Turkish Cypriot community would not consent to the amendments and would resort to loud protestations. Civil unrest would then follow allowing him to use the rejection as an opportunity to use force. The *Akritas Plan*, however, supplemented the proposals with its own militant tactics. Its objective was to remind Turkish Cypriots of their minority status and an inference rendering them as recalcitrant opposition to be brought under control was diligently recorded in the plan:

"...an immediate show of our strength may bring the Turks to their senses and confine their actions...effective use of force in dealing with the Turks will facilitate to a great extent our subsequent actions for further amendments."

The *Akritas Plan* had been a well-kept documented secret (until its publication in the Greek Cypriot newspaper, *Patris,* in 1966) but was distributed to high-ranking officials within EOKA groups advocating permissible attacks on Turkish Cypriots. EOKA members wasted no time in implementing the suggestions and a disruptive regime evolved designed to undermine and violently oppress Turkish Cypriots.

Acts of violence and intimidation flowed with alarming regularity and threatened the daily lives of Turkish Cypriots who were now openly targeted and placed under siege. Abductions were commonplace and hostages were 'held reportedly to be executed in case Turkey decided to intervene' as one observer wrote. Terrified Turkish Cypriots fled their homes and sought refuge in villages with a predominantly Turkish Cypriot population for safety, eventually finding

---

*In 1963, Makarios had put forward a set of 13 proposed constitutional amendments 'to resolve constitutional deadlocks'.
See Appendix B for full list of amendments.

themselves pushed into enclaves. The small, oversubscribed pockets of displaced Turkish Cypriot communities, having had their constitutional rights and their politicians removed, were left with no legal recourse and resorted to physically defending their confinement in an effort to preserve themselves. Resistance had now become their only option but they were ill-prepared. Their reduced status of residing in enclaves had occurred from frantic and frightened migrations over short periods of time leaving them with scarce resources and makeshift weapons that were of little consequence against a prepared Greek Cypriot force.

The desperate plight of Turkish Cypriots had their expelled leader Dr. Küçük sending frank messages to the international community appealing for support to aid them 'in their struggle against very heavy odds'.

DURING this time Rauf was in a wretched state and frustrated at being prevented from returning to Cyprus. He was a key speaker for Turkish Cypriots and a respected member of the leadership but was now being denied the opportunity to visit his people and organise practical help on their behalf. His banishment to Turkey had instead confined him to making trifling trips to the Foreign Office, where the Cyprus office was based, hoping to be of use. Days were spent busying himself with translating brochures and evaluating material sent to him by his assistant, Kutlu Adalı, who was still residing in Cyprus.

The reading material being sent by his assistant wasn't always palatable to Rauf and frequently left him feeling distressed. His exposure to an almost daily catalogue of compilations detailing Cyprus' shattered state had taken its toll; more disturbing was the endless reports he sifted through that demonstrated in detail the wanton destruction of property and villages.

Rauf recognised those that had managed to survive an onslaught would suffer in the long term as the implications of losing their homes would have devastating consequences; and the effect this could only have on all Cypriots. The most detailed and graphic reports regarding the social problem likely to affect Cypriots came from meticulous accounts submitted by the UNFICYP* They had been closely monitoring the events, recording in print, which Rauf had been privy to, before any agreements were signed in an attempt to curtail the mayhem affecting Cyprus.

One report composed by a UN worker known simply as Mr. A. Ortega was a comprehensive survey that had been gathered throughout the summer of 1964 illustrating the widespread destruction of villages and the number of houses lost. Ortega had been commissioned to examine each district and the damage incurred with a view to achieving an approximate estimate for 'reconstruction in Cyprus so that normal life can be resumed as soon as possible'.

To complement the report were photographs including aerial shots of stricken houses which exposed the extensive looting that had accompanied the deterioration of each village depicted. The statistics and photographic evidence that were pouring in from various quarters when they were released had devastated and saddened Rauf who recognised the Turkish domiciles.

To add to Rauf's woes was the ever-growing rift

---

*UNFICYP is the United Nations Peacekeeping Force in Cyprus. It was established under United Nations Security Council Resolution 186 in 1964. The purpose of UNFICYP is to maintain order between Turkish and Greek Cypriots following the inter-communal violence after 1964. The United Nations continues to present day in its aim to 'contribute to the maintenance and restoration of law and order and to facilitate a return to normal conditions.'

that was threatening to tear at the unity between the Communal Chambers' management (which was still taking responsibility for Turkish Cypriots) and the *Bayraktarlık* (central command in Cyprus). The situation had become turbulent and exacerbated by military influence. The commander of the Turkish land forces had fallen foul of Dr. Küçük causing confusion as well as rankling the leadership.

Adalı was keeping Rauf apprised of the situation which encouraged him to take up his pen and write volumes of letters in support of the leaders, reminding them they were all fighting the same cause. However, the contents of the letters were misconstrued and caused hostile reactions — opening a wound between Rauf and Dr. Küçük.

As well as the missives Rauf wrote lengthy articles for publications but they, too, didn't always encourage a favourable reaction. Many of his peers felt he was manipulating the situation from Ankara in favour of people who stood to benefit personally thus ensuring his own personal and political aims. Dr. Küçük, in particular, took issue with Rauf's influence from Ankara believing he was trying to usurp him as the Turkish Cypriots' elected leader. A flurry of desperate letters from Rauf to Dr. Küçük did not appear to settle the situation.

A report in the *Halkın Sesi* newspaper boasted Rauf was 'living it up' in Ankara in peace whilst his comrades were falling. Rauf had not taken kindly to the article and complained bitterly to an associate, General Turgut Sunalp, responsible for supervising military aid being sent to Cyprus, that he needed to return home.

Waves of young men were being called from overseas to fight. The returning volunteers would arrive in Turkey and then were secretly dispatched to Cyprus in a bid to support Turkish Cypriots. Rauf would meet the men, often students, with the Turkish Cypriot Ambassador, Mehmet Ertuğruloğlu, to prepare them and help raise their morale. Rauf decided that it would not be impossible to slip in with the troop of men bound for the next secret landing into Cyprus.

Unfortunately for Rauf, the General did not agree and dismissed Rauf's suggestion with a proffered attempt at congeniality, claiming the size of Rauf's 'head and nose were too conspicuous to camouflage.' Rauf countered he could be parachuted in, which prompted gales of laughter. A miffed Rauf recalled later to his wife that the General, between gasps of laughter, had told him 'the size of that bulk landing, you would break every bone in your body'.

General Sunalp did have some wise words for Rauf who was becoming increasingly upset with the disparaging remarks made about him. In serious tones, the General impressed upon Rauf that "for those leaders who choose to enter politics, they have to get used to being pelted with stones and have their noses rubbed in mud." He urged Rauf to 'ride above it' before reprimanding him that he needed to get on with the job and spend less time complaining about it. Rauf recalled later that they were words he would have chosen to give his younger self but at the time he had felt very differently.

He had every intention of supporting Turkish Cypriots the best way he could from afar but had no intention of giving up his desire to travel to Cyprus. He didn't have to wait long.

Rauf's chance to make the journey arrived in the form of Celal Mahmutoğlu who made a point of visiting Rauf to relay some dismal news. Mahmutoğlu, a Turkish Cypriot, was an active member of the resistance group (TMT) and frequently smuggled weapons to Erenköy by boat from Turkey. However, Mahmutoğlu had been disturbed by events occurring at Erenköy that was losing Turkish Cypriot occupied villages rapidly. Erenköy itself was in danger of completely diminishing as it was encompassed by the Greek Cypriot army and Greek National Guard; worse, was the internal problems of the unit of Turkish Cypriot men stationed in the area: whispered complaints made to Mahmutoğlu referred to the commanding officer stationed in Erenköy and a threat the men were intending to rebel if the commander was not removed.

Rauf informed the War Cabinet of the news, reiterating that the security of the villages and their inhabitants would be lost if something was not done to encourage the weakening unit not to fall. Rauf's friend and ally, Colonel Ali Riza Vuruşkan, made arrangements to go with the next troop of men and agreed to Rauf accompanying him — although he was not to inform the government until after his return.

On 1st August 1964, Rauf and Vuruşkan were mingling with a group of 60 pensive students aboard a vessel headed for Erenköy from Turkey. Erenköy had been severed from inland routes leaving the sea as its main access. The seas close to Erenköy were also exposed to dangers as it was constantly patrolled with reports of fishing vessels incessantly targeted and fired upon. Despite the possible hindrances, they were the ninth group out of eleven to arrive successfully at Erenköy.

The troop disembarked on the shore in the early hours and scrambled over rocky inclines to reach the makeshift camp serving as the headquarters. As Rauf came into view of the camps he was appalled at the sight he encountered: undernourished and poorly-armed dejected men milling around tents. He instantly approached as many men as he could offering assurances of Turkey's support and attempted to bolster their flagging morale.

As word filtered through of his arrival, several more weary

fighters made their way to the base to listen to him. Rauf saw as many men as he could in the vicinity and asked if there were any others within reach. He was informed there were a handful of men high up on the mountain range but it was a treacherous three-hour climb; he was discouraged from going as the peak was dangerously close to Greek occupation.

Güneş Menteş, a prominent lawyer in North Cyprus, was amongst the small groups of men situated in the higher altitudes at the time of Rauf's visit. He had arrived in the eighth group a month before after responding to the overseas pleas for university students to return to Cyprus to aid in the cause. The journey to the high peak was reluctantly climbed by the men who rarely volunteered to do so. As a newcomer, he had willingly gone to the top but became quickly acquainted with the harsh conditions and frightening aspects of being in such close proximity to Greek fire.

Rauf was also not deterred and made the arduous trek up the mountain range to meet the group of resistance fighters. Güneş remembered Rauf, despite his heavy size, looked fresh and jovial when he suddenly appeared in front of them.

According to Güneş, there had been visitors before to Erenköy with dignitaries gracing the troops with their presence but none had ever made it up to where the lone troops sat on the peaks. Rauf made an impression on Güneş and his fellow soldiers with his natural ease and humour that even managed to draw some laughter from the men. Güneş was also struck by Rauf's convictions and believes the men were all invigorated by his presence. He stayed with the men for more than an hour before making the journey back down leaving a distinct feeling of hope behind him.

Rauf's period of stay in Erenköy lasted for nine days

during which he witnessed for himself the terrifying aspects of war that showed no signs of curbing. In and around Erenköy heavy fighting was ravaging the land and disrupting the seas. The skies were also littered with menacing dangers as jets threatened the inhabitants below them with vicious assaults.

On 8th August, Turkish F-105 jets attacked Greek Cypriot positions around Erenköy in a bid to expel Greek forces who were keeping Erenköy under heavy fire. As the Turkish fighter jets were engaged in positions around Erenköy, two Greek F-84 planes emerged without warning over Erenköy firing indiscriminately succeeding in destroying an ammunition depot on the ranges. Rauf and the remaining villagers were vulnerable open targets with no refuge until moments later when they witnessed the welcoming sight of Turkish jets flying in. The Turkish jets engaged in an air battle and managed to track the Greek planes out of Cyprus space to the relief of Rauf and the terrorised Erenköy community.

Two days later, under the cover of nightfall, Rauf left the sorry sight of Erenköy and returned to Ankara. Within 24 hours, exhausted and agitated, he was standing in front of Turkey's Prime Minister, İsmet İnönü pleading the plight of the Turkish Cypriot fighters. İnönü listened patiently to Rauf explaining the severity of Erenköy's position and how soldiers were urgently needed to be sent to push back Greek Cypriot fighters who were closing in. He outlined the conditions of the men who were living on basic rations and it was imperative vitamins were also sent to supplement the men's poor diet. İnönü did not appear alarmed and retained a stoical composure throughout Rauf's report nodding calmly.

İnönü's reticent attitude had irked Rauf but,

unbeknownst to him, rapid developments had occurred during his absence. A day before, on 10th August, İnönü and Makarios had accepted the ceasefire resolution of the UN Security Council. With a temporary solution in place, İnönü informed Rauf with confidence it was not necessary to send anybody back and the men could 'now rest'.

Throughout Rauf's account of Erenköy, İnönü appeared more interested in the Greek jets that had attacked and disposed of the ammunition depot. Apparently he had consented to Athens for planes to fly over Nicosia for the 'purpose of boosting morale for Greek Cypriots'; however, two rogue planes from the squadron of seven had diverted and flown to Erenköy instead to wreak havoc there, causing him immense embarrassment. Any discomfort İnönü felt was not evident in the meeting he had with Rauf; although he was provoked enough to blast Rauf for leaving Turkey without governmental permission and consigned him once again to the Cyprus desk at the Foreign Office.

A pattern was beginning to emerge with Rauf who was consistently incurring the wrath of his superiors with his insubordinate behaviour. His fears for Cyprus' future and the fate of Turkish Cypriots were seemingly falling on deaf ears compelling him to take drastic measures regardless of the consequences to himself. Family members had privately expressed dismay at his actions but fared no better in their bid to restrain Rauf.

Increasingly worried about his safety, the family became a collective force concentrating their efforts on encouraging Rauf that he could still secure the interests of Cyprus from Turkey. Rauf gently brushed aside their approaches and intimated he would leave again — regardless of the concerns of his family or reproaches from his superiors.

Rauf's exploits had also reached the ears of his eldest

brother, Cahit. Initially, Cahit assumed the role of arbitrator seeking to find middle ground by encouraging Rauf to continue with his work in Turkey and of his obligations to remain with his wife and children. When he failed to elicit a promise from Rauf that he would not attempt to return to Cyprus again, he resorted to emotional blackmail; just as he had when Rauf left for the UK to study. He implored Rauf to stay in the protective confines of Turkey and threatened to disown him again should he leave.

Cahit was at a loss to understand Rauf's vehement passion for Cyprus. He himself had elected to stay in Turkey after completing his medical degree several years before and had a successful practice as a gynaecologist. He had married a Turkish citizen, which had not curtailed his lust for life, and he thoroughly enjoyed the cosmopolitan contrast of Turkey and Cyprus. His departure from Cyprus in the early thirties had only seen him return on one occasion — in 1954 whilst Rauf was working at the Attorney General's Office. However, Cahit's homecoming visit had left him feeling disenchanted with Cyprus and disconnected from his childhood environment; unlike Rauf who had remained devoted to the hopes of their father that his children would remain and contribute to the progression of Cyprus.

Cahit was forced to admit that Rauf could not be dissuaded and eventually accepted his youngest sibling's choices and his obstinate commitment to Cyprus. He had not taken on the authoritative mantle of father figure to Rauf after the death of Judge Raif and, apart from some half-hearted threats, was powerless to exert any pressure on Rauf to stay and make a life in Turkey as he had; he even understood Rauf's headstrong attitude and had a healthy respect for it. He too lived life to the full — albeit for his own pleasure.

Despite their different outlooks on life, Rauf and Cahit's

relationship remained intact based on mutual regard and were extremely devoted to one another. There was no acrimonious feeling between them and the difference of opinion over Cyprus did not evolve into a dispute. They continued to be supportive of one another and were in close contact — until Cahit's unexpected suicide a short time later.

Cahit appeared to have made the choice to take his own life in a determined and dramatic method but left no clue as to why. On a balmy evening in late summer, Cahit had returned home at his usual hour and sat down at the dining table patiently waiting for the customary *meze,* the apppetiser his wife would serve before a main course. As his wife fussed around him laying the dishes on the table Cahit reminded her to bring him the *rakı,* the aniseed-flavoured alcohol he always drank to complement his meal, sending his wife back to the kitchen. Before she could return, Cahit took his shotgun, placed the barrel in his mouth, and pulled the trigger.

Cahit's tragic suicide seemed inexplicable to all who knew him as there were no warning signs that he had been suffering from depression or any other concerns.   Yet Rauf, distraught at the news, was adamant that his brother would not calmly kill himself without any motive. In the absence of a suicide note, Rauf resorted to his lawyer background and the training it afforded him to painfully dissect Cahit's life striving to ascertain the reasons for such an unwarranted action.

Cahit was just sixty-three and had retired financially stable with no immediate discerning worries — leaving Rauf bewildered and none the wiser. He was never able to reconcile his brother's actions with his own memory of Cahit as a popular and jovial man who embraced life with gusto. He recalled his eldest brother was a man who lived for a distinctive purpose: "for him [Cahit], enjoying life was the purpose of living."

Rauf continued to tackle the unanswered questions hanging over his brother's death for several decades. He would sadly reflect on the events and could only arrive at the uncertain assumption that Cahit was no longer able to sustain his life — he had simply 'become disappointed and bored with it'. The unsatisfactory conclusion was of no consolation to Rauf who had obstinately clung to life even when he was responsible for placing himself in danger.

HIS work in the foreign office at the time of Cahit's death in 1964 up until 1967, had yielded no results for the Cyprus problem although he continued throughout in his capacity as a spokesman for Turkish Cypriots and met frequently with dignitaries assigned to broker a solution. Rauf worked fervently but gradually became disappointed and disheartened with the daily routine of meetings and working from behind a desk.

He worried incessantly about Cyprus and could not ignore the negative affect war was having on his community: he had witnessed for himself the physical effects that were slowly impoverishing his people. Refusing to succumb to the depressive confines of his desk, Rauf took a proactive stance and was determined to find a practical solution to solve the dilemma blighting Turkish Cypriots. Daily bulletins and unsettling letters from friends and family in Cyprus were sketching a bleak and dramatic picture. Economic sanctions and oppressive restrictions on Turkish Cypriots imposed by Makarios were becoming untenable for their well-being and preservation. Refuge camps were strewn across Cyprus and reports of villagers striving to survive, denied food and relief supplies, were filtering through to Rauf. He persevered with his quest to discuss a solution but was unable to ignore the realities of the situation. Diplomacy had averted a Turkish intervention but thousands of Turkish Cypriots were relegated to living under extreme circumstances that could not be ignored. Calls for his return to Cyprus were becoming more ardent and became an incentive to him to plan his next clandestine visit.

**Archbishop Makarios with Colonel Georgios Grivas
standing directly behind him**

Terrified Turkish Cypriot families forced to flee their
villages following the campaign to rid the island of ethnic
Turkish Cypriots in December 1963

Rauf visiting fighters in the enclave of Erenköy, 1964

CHAPTER TEN
High Seas Jinks

By 1967, the island's war-weary status remained unchanged with Turkish Cypriots forced into enclaves that amounted to just three per cent of the entire island. Damaging and harsh rhetoric being traded amongst community leaders added to the Turkish Cypriot woes. A besieged community with pitiful resources had the extra burden of being denied political strength as the leadership weakened and slowly disintegrated.

Rauf consistently sent messages of support appealing for unity and patience but was met with a stony wall of anger. Levelled accusations of his life-style in Turkey glared disapprovingly up at him from the pages of newspapers as well as personal missives from colleagues and opponents; all served to remind him of his absence from Cyprus and belittle his ongoing contributions made from outside of his homeland. The accusations were not solely limited to personal attacks — they were coupled with petulant demands that he should return before the community leadership collapsed irrevocably.

The troubled Larnaca communal leader, Dr. Müderisoğlu, went to Ankara with the purpose of meeting Rauf to discuss the community's anger and hoping to convince him to return to Cyprus. Rauf hardly needed convincing but lacked the means to travel. He was on a limited salary in Turkey that barely sustained his family. There were other complications but none more difficult than the fact he was still in exile. Since his last escapade to Cyprus he had been restricted in his movements and unable to travel undetected.

Dr. Müderisoğlu had an audacious plan ready to hand and insisting that secretly entering Cyprus was possible by boat via Larnaca. He assured Rauf that undercover operatives could be organised to collect him from the shore of Larnaca and then smuggle him incognito in the boot of a car to the city of Nicosia. Although the travel arrangements were less than glamorous, Dr. Müderisoğlu was confident the plan was foolproof. He had been encouraged by the support of sympathetic donors who had offered generous funds for the purpose of Rauf's return, determined to see him in Cyprus.

The journey was meticulously planned and arrangements made for Rauf, his under-secretary, Nejat Konuk, who had also been banished to Turkey, and a Sea Scout, İbrahim Erol, who was familiar with the sea journey and Larnaca.

A carefully-laid plan was to see the crew travel by fishing boat with a small speedboat in tow. They were to gain close access to Larnaca and then transfer to the speedboat which would be easier to navigate into a secluded bay. The speedboat also held another very important function which wasn't appealing but a necessary precaution: in the event of interception by Greek authorities, Rauf and his colleagues would be able to jump ship and use the speedboat to get themselves to safety.

Rauf knew from his family's response to his previous escapade he would need to create a ruse to allay their fears. He prepared an elaborate story for his wife, which only admitted to one fact — he would be returning to Cyprus. However, he assured her the visit was an official one approved by Makarios and embellished on the deception by purporting to have the luxury of travelling by helicopter from a military base to add weight to its authenticity. He then orchestrated with his friend, Vedat Çelik, assistant to the Turkish Cypriot Ambassador, a series of post-dated letters to be given to Aydın from him with fictitious tales of his daily routine in Cyprus and to allege they came via internal post from Cyprus to the Foreign Office in Turkey.

Aydın believed the ruse, convinced her husband was not at risk as his purpose in Cyprus was a 'necessary official duty'. His eldest son Raif, by now fourteen, had not been so easily swayed. He insisted he should travel with his father to Cyprus who naturally rejected the idea and instead gave him a binding duty by appointing him 'the man of the house'. With all the confidences he could muster, and knowing he was leaving a young family to fend for themselves, Rauf bid his family goodbye and would not be seen again for more than two weeks.

The small party of three were headed for Iskenderun and had been directed to make their way to a hotel close to the port. On their arrival they would be collected and taken to the harbour to board the fishing boat.

The journey to Iskenderun was a reasonably long one by car and the group had left late in the day. It was mutually decided that rather than drive through the night they would take a break half-way. Discovering a motel situated in an isolated area, the tired men agreed to stop and spend the night. The 'motel' turned out to be a very accommodating small brothel that lacked regular trade. Happily surprised to have a group of men spending the entire night, the trio were constantly disturbed with noisy tapping on the door to ask if they required 'service'.

In later years, Rauf would chuckle at the memory but remained adamant that he politely declined and even sternly reminded everyone that they needed all their strength for the impending journey to Cyprus.

In Iskenderun the jokey banter inspired by the experience of the 'motel' quickly faded when they were confronted with a rickety tug, and not the promised fishing boat that was expected to transport them to Cyprus. The tug was in an appalling state and minus the speedboat which was supposed to be trailing behind. The shifty crew manning the tug were apparently known for illegal activities on the seas and Rauf fumed at having been 'sold to smugglers'. Rauf and his companions, with grave reservations, boarded the tug and sat in silent protest whilst the boat chugged along at an agonisingly slow pace. It quickly became apparent the tug would not make the approximate 240-mile journey to Larnaca: it broke down twice and Rauf insisted the stricken tug turn around and head back to Iskenderun.

Undaunted by the ill-prepared journey and determined to continue his mission, Rauf summoned the incompetent contact and demanded he and his colleagues be furnished with the proper boats. Within 24 hours the fishing boat with its companion speedboat was bobbing gently in the port awaiting Rauf and his friends. With little trouble, a short time later, the boat and its cargo were sailing towards Cyprus and the group of men whiled the time away with nervous small talk.

The topic dominating their discussions was the possibility of being caught, with many scenarios produced of what might happen. For the good of their own welfare it was concluded Rauf's identity was best kept hidden if they were to stand a chance of surviving any possible ordeal.

The sailors of the vessel, who had not been given any information about their passengers, were clearly perturbed by the tone of Rauf and his companions' hushed conversation.

Unaware of Rauf's identity they wrongly assumed they were carrying drug smugglers and decided to take their own precautions. They dangled the men's luggage over the side, believing they were filled with narcotics, and intending to cut the ropes and safely dump the luggage with its 'illicit cargo' should they encounter a patrol boat.

With the crew satisfied the boat continued to sail smoothly with all on board hoping for solitude on the waters. However, by the second day the vessel's quiet journey came to an abrupt end. As dusk descended the unmistakable sound of a large powerful boat came spluttering towards them.

The illegitimate passengers followed the instructions they had been administered with and deftly lowered themselves into the speedboat. The drill had been for the men to wait in silence as the vessel sailed away to greet any obstacles before returning once the danger had passed. The reality had been distinctively different. Rauf had little hope of the boat returning for them as he had heard the distinctive sounds of ropes being furiously hacked at and knew instantly their luggage was lost to the seas.

The speedboat and its passengers had been abandoned and was a long way off shore. But, more worrying for the men, was the lack of promised supplies in the secondary boat. The agreements made had stipulated that essentials, such as water, basic rations and binoculars should be provided — none were in attendance.

By now the forlorn crew were in darkness and, as the boat did not possess a functional navigation system, they were unaware of their location and reliant on lights from the shore to guide them to land. They took the boat as far as they dared towards dry land hoping they had reached Larnaca. Without binoculars to survey the safety of the area, the Sea Scout İbrahim waded ashore to determine their whereabouts. He returned to the boat splashing wildly through the shallow waters in a panic to inform Rauf and Nejat that they had landed in an enemy military area and were nowhere near Larnaca.

They motored off in a southerly direction and eventually came upon another lit area of the coast. Unfortunately for the motley crew it was still dark and, as they were not familiar with the shore line, they blindly guided the boat in hoping to get close enough to send İbrahim on another reconnaissance mission. Their small vessel lurched from one large sea boulder to another before shuddering to a halt as it became wedged on a group of rocks. With the boat moored and in no condition to tackle the seas again, the group had little choice but to disembark and find shelter. They had spotted a small chapel which they realised stood as a community land mark for a Greek Cypriot village and took refuge in the nearby wooded area.

The group had not known it at the time but they were near Bafra and the wooded area of forest they had taken refuge in was patrolled by forest guards. They had barely time to consider their predicament before they were approached by a Greek Cypriot forest patrol guard.

He was young, excitable and armed with a pistol which he waved furiously in the faces of the exhausted trio. Rauf was the only one of the three who could speak Greek and he tried to placate the young guard by claiming they were lawyers from Larnaca on a fishing trip but had become stranded after their boat had hit rocks.

The guard did not appear to be impressed by their story and was resolutely suspicious of the three strangers who had strayed into his patrolled patch. Rauf recalled the solemn face of the young man that did little to mask his inexperience and desperation. "He kept yelling for his sergeant the whole time he began a search on İbrahim," Rauf explained, "but as he was busy with İbrahim he didn't see me sneak up behind him with my pistol!"

Rauf thrust his gun into the guard's back whilst growling at him that it was now he who was prisoner and to drop his weapon. However, to the surprise of all, the guard turned heel and ran off with his arms flailing in the air shrieking hysterically for his sergeant.

Rauf and his companions realised it wouldn't be long before the guard would eventually find his erstwhile sergeant. They left the wooded area and made their way back down to the coastline inching further along until eventually finding a cavernous area amongst the rocks that hinted at the possibility of sheltering them. Crouched amongst the rocks and hidden from view, the weary trio pondered their situation and options. Nejat appeared to concede defeat and had already resigned himself to the probability they were going to be caught, tortured and killed.

Nejat's morbid fear of being horrifically tortured compelled him to blurt out to Rauf his pessimistic plan designed to save them all. In anxious tones he suggested Rauf should shoot both himself and İbrahim; he then respectfully asked Rauf to turn the gun on himself afterwards which would leave no one alive to have to suffer the atrocities of torture. Nejat, having made the request, then shut his eyes tightly and braced himself to receive a bullet to his bravely protruding chest whilst an incredulous İbrahim looked on.

Rauf indulgently agreed with Nejat 'it had been a very good idea' up until the point where he had to shoot himself — he could 'gladly shoot' them both but decided he himself was rather partial to living. Rauf calmed Nejat by explaining they were all in this together and had no choice but to wait it out and accept the consequences of their fate. A clearly-relieved İbrahim, grateful for the reprieve, attempted to brighten their chances and told the others he would look for some water and try to find Turkish Cypriot assistance. He returned a short while later with water and enough sustenance in the shape of tomatoes given to him by a Greek Cypriot farmer. Whilst the ravenous group devoured the tomatoes, İbrahim explained they were again in a hostile Greek Cypriot area with little hope of finding Turkish Cypriot aid. His gloomy predictions were quickly realised. Despite the generosity of the Greek Cypriot farmer, it wasn't long before his patriotic senses had prompted him to sound the alarm and Rauf and his cohorts were discovered.

Rauf was the first to spot the army jeeps thundering towards them and knew their only chance of survival was to give themselves up. Emerging from the cave with their hands waving limply in the air, the three men were instantly surrounded by Greek soldiers demanding they hand over their guns. They did as they were told and Rauf repeated his story they were lawyers who had become stranded after a fishing trip but took the security of omitting his real name. The commanding officer appeared reasonably satisfied – although he had Rauf and his friends escorted to the nearest police station for questioning and verification of their identities.

They were taken to Agios Theodoris, a village situated in the Karpaz area. The commanding officer, not realising the value of his prisoners, left Rauf and his companions lounging outside in the mid-November sun flanked by a formidable escort as he went into the police station to ascertain their identities. Whilst Rauf had given a false name appearing to appease his captor it did not last long under scrutiny from the inquisitive crowd that was beginning to form around the guarded men. One eagle-eyed villager recognised Rauf and began an excited aria shrilly advertising Rauf's name and alerting the swelling audience to his real identity. His enthusiastic solo became an emphatic chorus as the surrounding ensemble joined voice and reached a crescendo with chants demanding Rauf's head be turned over to the village.

The commotion building up around him left Rauf with no alternative but to seek asylum from the commanding officer who had remained blissfully ignorant of his identity thanks to Rauf's persuasive story-telling. Fully aware of the risk he was placing himself and his companions under, Rauf knew it was still better to place himself in the custody of the commanding forces and take his chances with the Greek Cypriot authorities. The default option left him at the mercy of the baying crowd and a likely sentence of an unpleasant mob-lynching.

Increasingly worried about the crowd's bloodthirsty yells for his hide, Rauf began a desperate solo of his own shouting above the crowd to get the attention of the commanding officer. He begged a private audience with the officer and ventured to come clean about his identity. After admitting who he was, he then explained his need to conceal his identity was only to avoid scenes like the one occurring outside the police station. The commanding officer's reaction was of ego-wounding surprise to Rauf: he scanned the length of Rauf from head to toe, scratched his head in a quizzical fashion, before asking in muted disbelief 'are you *really* Denktaş?'

Apparently the officer, unable to accept the very dour appearance of Rauf, was plunged into confusion at being confronted with the short, squat and unassuming-looking man he had standing in front of him. "I suppose in his mind I was some sort of mystical giant," Rauf later recalled with a bemused smile.

It didn't take long for the officer to overcome his initial shock at Rauf's rather plain countenance before swiftly taking appropriate actions. Acting on received instructions from his superiors, Rauf and his companions were bundled blindfolded into a car and warned if they tried to escape they would be shot. There was little chance of resistance from Rauf and his comrades as once the commanding Greek officers were aware of their prisoners' identities a concerted effort was made to curtail their movement. Handcuffed and gagged, the group went on a seemingly endless drive, lasting several hours, designed to disorientate and delude them as to their final destination.

RAUF'S revealed identity had become of national interest as well as a conundrum for the Greek Cypriot authorities determined not to make a martyr out of Rauf. It had been hurriedly decided Rauf and his colleagues' exposure to the general public should be limited whilst Greek Cypriot superiors considered their fate. However, his arrival in Cyprus and subsequent arrest had already become noteworthy news and had alerted the community at home and abroad.

Rauf and his compatriots had been taken to Nicosia and secreted in the small holding cells of a secluded mental health institution. Imprisonment had not unnerved Rauf as he had heard on the radio in the police car of his capture and felt sure the Greek Cypriot government would be powerless to execute him lest they incur the wrath of Turkey. His detention was, however, creating ruffles and dividing opinions as Greek Cypriot superiors argued how best to handle their unexpected visitors.

Whilst the Cabinet was in session, in which Colonel

Grivas was in attendance, a soldier entered the hall and surreptitiously placed a piece of paper in front of Grivas for him to read; five minutes later, as he pondered the contents of his message, Makarios received his own piece of paper brought to him by a policeman. Grivas politely craned his neck in Makarios' direction and suggested without a trace of panic on his composed features they exchange pieces of paper. Makarios was far less controlled and blasted for all within earshot: "somebody is fooling us saying Denktaş has been caught!"

Several years later, Clerides admitted to Rauf that Makarios had hurriedly consulted with his peers over the question of what to do with him and was advised to have him shot: Rauf had entered the country illegally and had been branded a traitor of the Republic (the initial reasons for having him exiled). As he was deemed guilty of treason the authorities felt it was within their remit to have him executed. Fortunately for Rauf, Makarios' wily nature and concern for public backlash prevented him from sanctioning the execution. He also wanted to find out if Rauf had an ulterior motive for being in Cyprus and whether that motive had been approved by Turkey.

In a disused area of the mental hospital Rauf was subjected to questioning every twenty minutes in an effort to wear him down but was spared being physically assaulted (although he claimed his friends were not given the same respect). Rauf did, however, suffer the effects of sleep deprivation as the relentless questioning continued unabated. Eventually on the third day of his arrest Rauf's old courtroom adversary, Glafkos Clerides, appeared to demand answers from Rauf. He had the imposing presence of Yorgadjis with him who stood silently looming over Rauf as Clerides began his own line of questioning.

Clerides bombarded Rauf with demands to know what role Turkey was playing in Rauf's illicit excursion. He was not convinced by Rauf's truthful answers that Turkey were unaware of his departure and insisted on knowing his purpose for returning to Cyprus before finally asking in exasperation 'what the hell do you want Rauf?'

Rauf had adopted an apathetic approach during questioning but was beginning to wilt. He was exhausted from lack of sleep and having eaten little over the three-day period. Unable to contain himself he dispensed with the unemotional responses and blasted Clerides bitterly demanding to know what he would have done in the same position. "You closed the front door on me," he complained to an unmoved Clerides, "so I had no choice but to come in through the back window." Rauf then sat back with his arms folded staring defiantly at Clerides and his companion, Yorgadjis. Clerides, aware of Rauf's stubborn nature from their own courtroom duels, departed knowing he would not be able to procure anything further from Rauf.

A few hours after Clerides' visit, Rauf and his friends were transferred to the central prison in Nicosia and placed on death row. Rauf recognised the cells from his own visits to inmates during his lawyer days but wasn't fazed by the dramatic change of environment. He surmised later that he hadn't thought the move to death row was an intentional scare tactic but rather designed to segregate them from the general population of the prison. "If they had put us with the other prisoners we might have been in danger, I think it was for our own protection," he noted.

Rauf's charitable observations about the authorities' concern for him and his colleagues' welfare were possibly misguided. He was to remain a further ten days in detention but during his sojourn was released into the prison yard for the daily one-hour exercise along with the rest of the prisoners. Fortunately for the prison's newest inmate, the prison yard held little more than the threat of inquisitive young men intent on only leaning on Rauf for information and his thoughts on the Cyprus situation. Rauf happily obliged the prisoners and each day held a small seminar that would have the prisoners civilly debating and discussing the issues of Cyprus.

WHILST Rauf appeared to be relatively safe in Cyprus, back in Turkey concern for his well-being and whereabouts were raising questions and dominating the news. Rauf's deception to his wife had unravelled by the second letter he had organised to be sent. She had received his letter and satisfied herself that all was well from the humorous story Rauf had written describing his fictitious meeting with Makarios. She had then taken the children to the cinema only to return home and hear on the news of his capture in Cyprus.

Beside herself with worry, Aydın had gone to see every person of influence she could to determine Rauf's welfare. Although Makarios was benignly informing the international public that 'Denktaş is being treated as our guest' no other information was being imparted. Turkey along with Rauf's immediate family had not been given any evidence he was in good health leaving Aydın frightened and bewildered.

As Aydın raced back and forth to various government officials, it appeared she was not alone in her efforts. A huge pressure campaign had been mounted by politicians and supporters to secure Rauf's release. In a remarkable show of solidarity, that demonstrated Rauf's popularity, the Turkish public also took to the streets waving banners demanding

Rauf's release. The media ensured Rauf's face decorated the front pages of the newspapers as a persistent reminder to the public of his missing status as well as vilifying Greek Cypriots. Eventually the efforts from Rauf's supporters were rewarded when Makarios relented and gave permission for Rauf and his colleagues to be released from incarceration, thirteen days after their capture.

İbrahim was to be escorted to the border of the Turkish enclave in Larnaca where he resided. Rauf, however, learnt from his friend and lawyer, Ali Dana, he was being removed again from Cyprus and sent back to Turkey. Before Rauf would be able to board the flight to leave, a thinly-disguised attempt was made to have Rauf, and his fellow detainees, depart the island looking physically well and groomed. A barber was sent to each of the men's cells the day before their departure to shave and clean the dishevelled trio to have them appear presentable and fresh for media consumption — particularly in Turkey.

Assigned police officers, aware of the sensitive nature surrounding their prisoners, arrived the following day at the prison with two civilian cars to discreetly escort Rauf and his co prisoners to the airport. They were escorted to the airport with minimum fuss to board the plane that was to first take them to İstanbul.

It was evident as soon as Rauf entered the departure lounge, escorted by a formation of poorly-disguised policemen, that customs and airport security had not been informed about their illustrious traveller. The sight of him instantly aroused comments from shocked airport officials, as he overheard one astounded border control officer gasp in dismay: "that's Denktaş! He's escaping!" In his memoirs, Rauf recorded that he thoroughly enjoyed seeing the immigration officers 'looking at us with startled eyes'.

The police officers hustled Rauf through the throng of prying eyes to deposit him successfully on board the aeroplane. As the plane taxied down the runway they staunchly remained on the tarmac glaring up at the passengers with narrowed eyes. Rauf gaily waved goodbye to the sober-faced police officers observing with delight the sudden shift in their demeanour as they all broke into broad smiles waving enthusiastically back.

Not everyone on board was feeling as relieved and comfortable as Rauf. Once the aeroplane was safely in the air winging its way to Turkey, the skittish Nejat informed Rauf he would be disappearing once the plane landed. Although a Turkish Cypriot, Nejat also held Turkish citizenship and had left Turkey without a passport or permission and feared he would be in hot water with the Turkish authorities when he returned on home soil. Nejat fretted throughout the hour-long flight to Turkey provoking Rauf to consider the wrath he was likely to incur when he landed.

On arrival in İstanbul, Nejat was as good as his word and bolted from the airport taking advantage of the crowded reception of media and wellwishers to escape. "May Allah help you!" he yelled over his shoulder at Rauf who stood helplessly surrounded — unaware of the media storm he had created, as reporters surged upon him entreating him for his comments. An official retrieved Rauf from the clamorous swarm of microphones buzzing in front of him explaining the Minister of Foreign Affairs, İhsan Sabri Çağlayangil, was waiting on the telephone to talk to him.

Rauf had presumed he would be in for a roasting from the officious Minister and braced himself for the castigation to follow. As Rauf lifted the receiver to his ear he had a smattering of journalists around him and was acutely aware from Çağlayangil's cordial behaviour he was in the same position. Both men were extremely affable to each other with Çağlayangil in particular welcoming Rauf back into the secure folds and embrace of Turkey. After the brief telephone call Rauf was whisked off onto another flight bound for Ankara where he had been promised by Çağlayangil of a welcoming reception that also included his wife and children.

As the plane touched down in Ankara, Rauf was again exposed to the same enthusiastic horde of reporters and well-wishers who were thrilled with the images of Aydın and Rauf locked in a long-awaited embrace. Outside the airport Rauf was overwhelmed by the spirited crowd that had flocked to see him arrive and had begun to relax feeling that he would be quite safe from any form of retribution. The cortège of cars following him home to his house bolstered his confidence further as they expressed their heart-felt elation at his safe return with rowdy and boisterous horn blowing.

The excitement did produce one drawback as Rauf and Aydın's privacy was inhibited since they were now being swept along by the noisy chaperones to face more reporters camped on their doorstep. At the house Rauf was pelted with more questions about his exploits in Cyprus whilst Aydın remained politely tight-lipped.

Prior to Rauf landing in Turkey, Aydın had been sternly advised by İnönü she was 'the wife of a national hero' and should 'not express any weakness in front of the press' and she was expected to carry herself 'in a manner that is befitting of the Turkish people.' When it came to family matters, Aydın was a strong, outspoken individual who, like Rauf's own mother, was used to asserting herself. She was not willing to forgive her husband for putting himself at risk, and ultimately her too, by leaving her alone with four young children. When their front door was finally closed to the public, Aydın's first words to Rauf were a steely, "I hope you enjoyed your hellim *(traditional Cypriot cheese)* and olives..."

Although Rauf's family recovered quickly from the pain caused by the brief separation, it was obvious that the experience had left an indelible mark on the couple. Aydın never forgave Rauf for lying and refused to accept his description of the untruths as being mere 'white lies;' instead Rauf had succeeded in unsettling Aydın leaving her feeling apprehensive about the dangers Rauf faced as well as revealing to her a frightening ability to lie so convincingly to his family.

For Rauf, returning alive to his family did not compensate for his failure to reach his community. His unplanned incarceration had prevented him from completing his mission but had exposed him to the devastating reality that a Greek Cypriot regime was exercising its superiority and control over the island in complete comfort.

As Rauf and Aydın adjusted to the changes each had discovered, both took solace in the same hope that one day they might return to Cyprus.

**The speedboat with which Rauf attempted to reach Larnaca
now housed in a military museum in Lefkoşa**

Travel companion under-secretary, Nejat Konuk

173

CHAPTER ELEVEN

War Of Words

A S 1967 drew to a close, Turkish Cypriots already forced to govern themselves sought political remedies with a vehement determination. Rauf, along with his compatriots, felt there would be little hope of Makarios ever denouncing *enosis* or relinquishing his objective to undermine Turkish Cypriots' status on the island. However, despite Makarios' best efforts to reduce Turkish Cypriots' political rights, they had been resiliently managing themselves with a 'General Committee' since 1963. This was expanded on by 28th December 1967 when the Turkish Cypriot community, with the support of representatives from Turkey, established a separate administration from the government, the 'Provisional Turkish Cypriot Administration' (in Turkish *Geçici Kıbrıs Türk Yönetimi*).

The Administration was created during a precarious period for Turkish Cypriots when political relations between the two communities had been severed. The elected Turkish Cypriot ministers, including its vice-President, Dr. Küçük, had been given no choice but to withdraw from government in 1964 leaving them in a politically ambiguous situation and bitterly estranged from their Greek Cypriot co-partner.

Initially the Administration was a temporary measure designed to alleviate the problematic effects of not having a governmental base to refer to. Eventually the Administration's purpose was fuelled by its desire to gain autonomy and remain independent from what was now seen as Makarios' own government and regime that had expelled Turkish Cypriots.

A released statement advocating its intentions to stand independently declared: "Until the provisions of the Republic of Cyprus are implemented, all Turks living in the Turkish sector will remain committed to the provisions of the Turkish administration..." The message also made clear that Turkish Cypriots were no longer to consider themselves under a Greek Cypriot administration.

The naming of Dr. Fazıl Küçük as President and Rauf Denktaş as its Vice-President was fundamental in establishing a positive leadership role for the community to depend upon. As well as demonstrating that tensions had eased between the two men, it also affirmed Rauf's uncontested position as a senior leader in the newly-established provisional government exclusive to Turkish Cypriots.

During the formation of the Turkish Administration, Rauf was still in Turkey having been escorted back there for the second time a month earlier in November. Although his movements were restricted once again, his banishment did not prevent him from being involved with the social and political movements gripping Cyprus. The Presidential elections were due in a few short months and Rauf had noted a change in Makarios who was now hinting at the possibility of inter-communal talks — albeit on his terms.

Prior to 1967 (and after the withdrawal of Turkish Cypriots from government in 1964), Makarios had always refused to meet with the Turkish Cypriot community leaders referring to them disdainfully as 'rebels' with no political authority. His belittling attitude of a community's elected leadership had become his typical approach which emphasised his intent to remove the validity of the Turkish

Cypriot leadership. He would only consider discussions or make concessions based on their willingness to accept 'minority rights' and climbing down from their insistence on being viewed as equal partners.

It appeared several factors, including being on the brink of war with Turkey and the withdrawal of Greek military forces at the end of 1967, prompted Makarios to issue a statement in January 1968 suggesting 'a realistic reappraisal of the handling of the Cyprus problem' was necessary. The statement did little to disguise the fact Makarios was attempting to distance himself from his earlier convictions of *enosis* and deliver a sugar-coated bitter pill to Greek Cypriots: he alluded to Cyprus having to accept the limitations 'of what was feasible, which did not always coincide with what was desirable'.

His statement was made during his Presidential campaign a month before the elections (held on 25th February 1968) to the 'people of Cyprus'. It was a blatant attempt to influence the balloting by suggesting his heartfelt goals were to achieve 'sovereign independence' and cast vague doubts on the possibility of *enosis*. Makarios had gone to arbitrary lengths to cast his net to ensnare all sectors of society in order to gain the optimum amount of votes. He most likely needn't have worried as his popularity amongst eligible voters was fairly secure; he was overwhelmingly successful in being reinstalled as President — as one caustic journalist pointed out later, 'he gets votes thanks to his relationship with heaven.'

Despite having a faithful voting flock Makarios conceded that the people of Cyprus were divided and far from living in amicable peace under his direction. He knew there were still the discontented Turkish Cypriots he needed to tame. Reflecting the gulf between the communities, Turkish

Cypriots flouted their displeasure by ignoring government protocols and insisting on holding their own elections which unanimously voted Dr. Küçük as the Vice-President.

Shortly after his re-election in March 1968, Makarios, under pressure from the UN, tentatively agreed to 'exploratory talks' to be held between the two communities. Rauf, who was still recognised as the President of the Turkish Cypriot Communal Chambers, had his passport returned and permission to enter Cyprus to begin talks with Glafkos Clerides, the President of the House of Representatives*.

Although it had been Dr. Küçük who had insisted on Rauf's presence at the negotiating table with Clerides, concerns were being bandied around in the parliamentary circles of Turkey doubting the Doctor's sincerity. Rauf and Dr. Küçük's differences during Rauf's exile in Turkey had become well known with Çağlayangil also having received letters from the Doctor regarding his thoughts on Rauf.

Çağlayangil, who had become close to Rauf after his return from imprisonment in Cyprus, was concerned at the type of reception Rauf would receive on returning home. He feared Rauf's chances of success at the negotiating table would be damaged if the public and media were distracted by any negative images of him and Dr. Küçük; and he was not convinced the Doctor would not look for opportunities to undermine and berate Rauf publicly in an effort to keep him from usurping him as the recognised Turkish Cypriot leader; it did not bode well, in Çağlayangil's opinion, if the two leaders were to be seen squabbling at such a critical juncture for the Turkish Cypriot community.

*The House of Representatives is the parliament of Cyprus. Before 1964, Turkish Cypriots occupied 30% of the seats but the entire Greek Cypriot remainder had voted in 1965 to abolish the Greek Cypriot Communal Chambers with all responsibilities of the Chambers to be transferred to them.

Rauf assured Çağlayangil he and Dr. Küçük would work successfully together without incident — even predicting the publicity-conscious Doctor would be at the head of the crowd to welcome him on his return. Whilst Rauf managed to settle any doubt for Çağlayangil he did point out to the minister he remained unhappy with the slights. Rauf had no intentions of confronting Dr. Küçük but informed Çağlayangil he would use the next elections as a forum to challenge the Doctor's former statements about him. Rauf was adamant he could use the elections as leverage to extract a retraction from Dr. Küçük or, at the very least, force him to explain the negative statements he had made to the public about him.

To the relief of Turkey, the two men recognised far more was at stake than defending bruised egos ensuring Rauf's forecast for a calm partnership with Dr. Küçük would be proven true. The two leaders embraced warmly on Rauf's return in March 1968 and strode through Cyprus in a public show of unity to rapturous applause from jubilant Turkish Cypriots lining the streets. Neither man discussed or confronted the other on the issues that had led to their rift preferring instead to set aside their differences for the time being and concentrate on the talks.

The eagerly-anticipated talks threatened not to get off to a good start as the two community representatives could not agree on the venue to begin them. Rauf's stubbornness surfaced when he refused to start talks in Cyprus' capital, Nicosia, as Makarios had proclaimed they would. Various offices belonging to neutral third parties were offered but Rauf was immovable on the subject. He deplored the idea of beginning in Cyprus under the auspices of EOKA and Greek arms who he stated were still dominating the island and persecuting his people. Rauf also had his own agenda with a not so subtle message to Makarios. He reasoned the power

178

denied Turkish Cypriots needed to be addressed and it was not for Makarios to dictate the terms or make declarations without consultations involving the Turkish Cypriots. "I [was] trying to teach Makarios that we have to agree and then declare something. He is not the master of us and he should understand this," Rauf explained.

After a laborious two months of wrangling over a venue, the community leaders jointly agreed the initial talks would be held in Beirut. The exploratory talks had both leaders gingerly dipping their toes in uncertain waters to ascertain if there was any hope of dialogue; if they both agreed there was a possibility of constructive communication then the talks would be referred back to Cyprus for the leaders to start bartering for their respective communities.

Although Clerides and Rauf had shared many courtroom dramas, and as such were no strangers to confrontation, they had always maintained a civil relationship and mutual respect for each other. The opening sessions, paving the way for the talks, saw both men eying each other warily across the negotiating table as they attempted to establish a basis from which the talks could continue from.

By day, the representatives would spend several hours sat on opposing sides thrashing out the details; in the evenings the interlocutors, who were residing in the same hotel, would enjoy sociable dinners together in the hotel's dining room leaving any unresolved issues behind in the board room for the following day. The companionable get together of the pair at dinner, however, would always end with polite declinations from Clerides to venture out of the hotel to explore the borders beyond the dining room with Rauf.

One evening as the men were at their usual dining table, a waiter approached to inform Rauf he had a telephone call.

The call was from an Armenian who Rauf had known in his school days and had got wind of his arrival in Beirut. The old class mate had a thriving business as a 'contractor of cabaret artistes' near the hotel and invited Rauf to join him in his office for drinks. Rauf suggested to Clerides they both went over but was given a polite refusal by Clerides saying he was 'far too tired'. Clerides then appeared to feign a yawn as if to punctuate the point, which didn't go unnoticed by Rauf who shrugged his indifference at Clerides and left the hotel.

The short walk led him directly into the garishly-decorated foyer of his friend's establishment where he was confronted with 'beautifully dressed girls' rallying to greet him. Not for the first time, Rauf found himself in a brothel as his friend admitted to being an agent — of prostitutes. Rauf turned on his heel and made a dramatic sharp exit fully aware of how his visit to a friend at his questionable offices could be perceived and exploited in the press. At breakfast the following morning Rauf responded to Clerides' wry probing about his evening with a feigned yawn of his own and dismissive shrug claiming he had changed his mind and had coffee at a late-night cafe instead.

The atmosphere in Beirut had been congenial enough to persuade both leaders they were ready to commit to dialogue. The first round began on 24th June in Nicosia for a month before both retired to their respective corners to seek advice from Turkey and Greece. When the two leaders resumed a month later, it was clear the negotiations would require a great deal of patience as the talks had generated challenges for both communities. It was also apparent to the international community of spectators that both leaders were in for the long-haul and prepared verbally to fight tooth and nail to preserve their rights.

Early in the inter-communal talks Rauf appeared to be the more liberal of the two, winning him admiration from some quarters and rebuke from others. Whilst he consistently made demands of self-government for Turkish Cypriots, Rauf was prepared to relent on many issues — which didn't go unnoticed by the British observers. The British High Commissioner, Sir Norman Costar, reported to the then British Foreign Secretary, Michael Stewart, that Rauf had 'made far-reaching and realistic concessions' unlike Clerides who 'had proved almost totally inflexible on all political issues.'

Rauf had wanted the preservation of the Turkish villages that had haphazardly grouped together, as a result of the inter-communal violence, to become permanent. He focused on the villages gaining local autonomy by submitting to Clerides the possibility of having the island organised by 'geographical federation.' A difficult first task was to try and legitimise the banded Turkish Cypriot villages by delineating their existence on the map. He used as his principle basis an article from the Constitution that allows for a community made up of solely Turkish or Greek Cypriots to install members from their own community in the local government, administration and police force. Clerides was obstinately adverse to the idea and rejected any scheme that would lead to Turkish Cypriots gaining any form of independence.

Although Rauf refused to withdraw the proposal from the negotiating table he was prepared to loosen many of the Turkish Cypriot percentage rights which earned him the ire of his peers. The TMT, still with a heavy presence in the villages, was particularly upset with Rauf's concession-making and would often berate him both publicly and privately for doing so.

In later years Rauf was philosophical about what he could and could not have achieved during the inter-communal talks. Contrasting his own experiences of the talks with that of his successor, Mehmet Ali Talat*, in contemporary times, he pointed to the extreme circumstances he was forced to negotiate under. He recalled in his observations of the period how the ever-present threat of violence retained a menacing grip on the talks. Every potential agreement was subject to disruption as objecting Greek Cypriot groups would frequently resort to terrorist tactics in a bid to undermine any agreement offering a favourable amendment for Turkish Cypriots. Rauf argued Talat had no such worries to contend with as the Turkish army resides in Cyprus offering security. "...Turkish army is here, we are a state," Rauf pointed out, "[and] we rightfully go and say [to Talat] 'why the hell did you give this up?' But then, during [the] 1968-74 talks, we had absolutely nothing if they attacked."

The talks managed to continue unabated with Rauf choosing to ignore the heckling he received both from his peers and the threatening opposition. He contended later his stalwart approach had only ever been influenced by the abject conditions Turkish Cypriots were living under and the community's confidence in him. Since the early 1960s, Makarios had systematically reduced living standards with his imposed trade restrictions. By 1967, he had also made virtual prisoners of the villagers by barricading the roads to prohibit movement of travel. However, at the time of the talks, in a goodwill gesture, Makarios had removed the blockades allowing villages to trade — even if it was only

*Mehmet Ali Talat (born 6 July 1952) was the leader of the left-wing Republican Turkish Party (*Cumhuriyetçi Türk Partisi*). He became prime minister in 2004, and subsequently won the Presidential election held on 17 April 2005. Talat was inaugurated on 25 April 2005, succeeding retiring President Rauf Denktaş

amongst themselves. Taking advantage of the relaxed laws, Rauf safely toured the villages giving him the opportunity to survey the general welfare and morale of his people.

The tour was very revealing as Rauf's emerging popularity was apparent in every excited face that rushed to greet him. Rauf's support from the community undoubtedly gained some merit from his newly-found status as a national hero. (His exploits, a few months previously, as a gun-toting rebel then becoming a detainee in (and surviving) Makarios' Greek Cypriot-run prison had both enthralled and emboldened the community.) Less enamoured with him and not possessed with the same positive enthusiasm, as he discovered in the early months of the talks, were the leadership and its associates representing the community. Rauf had been impressed by the strength of the villagers' resistance and believed the overwhelming opinions of the villagers coincided with his own: continued resistance until a satisfactory settlement could be achieved. However, he felt the community's leadership was in direct conflict with the general view held by the population; instead they were rashly prepared to settle for any agreement.

According to Rauf, he was prepared to make a 'few concessions', although this did include giving up many Turkish Cypriot privileges in central government providing they were able to have local autonomy enabling them to organise their own villages under a geographical arrangement. Rauf was certain these rights were not only achievable but could also work. Whilst he put all his energies into these aims he began to realise that Dr. Küçük and his colleagues had other ideas. They were in disagreement with him and instead encouraged him 'to find any agreement' that would 'save them' from annihilation. Disappointed, Rauf surmised Dr. Küçük and his colleagues had lost hope that a Turkish intervention would occur leaving them with no alternative but to desperately accept a solution on virtually any terms.

In December 1969, with the talks still active, Rauf also appeared to contradict himself and began back-tracking from his earlier admissions. However, it was the fault of the leadership that had flexed its complaining muscles strongly enough to exercise their right of veto. Dr. Küçük had reeled Rauf in preventing him from implementing and sanctioning the concessions he was prepared to make. Rauf was forced to deviate from his original terms leaving him to face furious Greek Cypriots who accused him of executing a 'U-turn' after appearing to make an acceptable offer which was then callously withdrawn.

The discontentment felt by both sides did not prevent the talks from shambling on although they showed no tangible signs of reaching a solution. Rauf was an experienced interlocutor, as was his counterpart, Clerides, but both men were at the mercy of their superiors. A memorandum to the British Foreign and Commonwealth Office in 1970 also discussed the problematic talks labelling the weaknesses of the Turkish and Greek Governments but reserved their apprehension for the 'obstinate and ingenious Archbishop' as being the major obstacle.

Rauf's biggest stumbling block would indeed prove to be Makarios who had no intention of ever giving up his deep-seated values or his powerful position as the president in which to administer them. Even after the events of 1974, which led to a Turkish intervention*, Makarios (safely secure in London) gave an interview to Italian journalist, Oriana Fallici, emphatically reiterating his superiority.

---

* A military operation was launched on 20th July 1974 by Turkey in response to the 1974 Greece organised *coup d'état* in Cyprus. In Turkey it is known as the 'Cyprus Peace Operation' (in Turkish: *Kıbrıs Harekatı*).

The interview was also used to reduce Clerides publicly to the role of messenger making clear he still dominated the talks: "Oh, naturally, it's understood that Clerides won't make any decisions without my consent. It's understood that when I speak of going back to Cyprus, I mean to go back as president. I'm the president, I'll go back as president. I'll never agree to go otherwise. And the question of whether I'll remain president for a long time or not concerns me alone."

Whilst Makarios' arrogance was a well-known personality trait, it was his blatant attempts to impede the talks that had become embarrassingly obvious to all — as well as a hindrance to the communities' respective representatives. He was notorious for using stalling tactics to delay proceedings hoping it would increase his bartering chances to acquire any agreements which would encourage a path for *enosis*. But Rauf's stubbornness was equally legendary and had not gone unnoticed by the international bystanders who painstakingly followed the talks in progress for the purpose of reporting.

Communications between weary diplomats, concerned with the lack of progress, were running back and forth between offices and included their own personal observations. Their frustrations with the two communities were evident and spilled out onto the reports as they cited the differences between Turkish and Greek Cypriots. The two communities had virtually become a source of ridicule as the diplomats traded anecdotes with Rauf marginally earning himself slight favour as the representative of the more compliant side.

The British Ambassador to Ankara, Sir Roderick Sarell, felt it prudent to warn an inexperienced representative from the Foreign and Commonwealth Office of the mottled history that entangled the Cypriots. His entertaining but abbreviated version of Cypriot history was marked with some scornful observations on some Cypriot diplomatic idiosyncrasies:

185

"It is the belief in this Embassy, and of our US and Canadian colleagues, that the Greeks and Greek Cypriots tend to be more devious than the Turks (we are not sure about some of the Turkish Cypriots). On the other hand, the Turks may be more stubborn — as indeed the side with the relatively consistent, straightforward and 'unimaginable' policy, is liable to be: the Greek counsellor here [in Ankara] recently confessed to Edmonds that, in Athens you could easily get ten different versions of a story in one day, whereas in Ankara it would take ten days to get a single version".

The written communications between the diplomats exposed a profound misunderstanding of the two Cypriot cultures but did reveal the exasperated sentiments felt. By 1973 the talks were no further on serving only to earn more misgivings from the international community. The problem seemed to lie with both leaders' insistence of clinging to their respective agendas, causing grave doubts of ever achieving a mutually satisfactory outcome.

Clerides, under instruction from Makarios, had kept up his refusal of allowing any suggestion of a geographical federation being considered. Makarios was more than aware Rauf's agenda was tinged with the ideology that promoted *Taksim* and feared the consequences of accepting geographical federation would lead to partition of the island. Rauf, by equal measure, refused to deviate from his own course at the negotiating table. He ploughed on relentlessly seeking necessary amendments and rights that would enable self-autonomy.

As all the key players involved battled for political advantages, Rauf had become embroiled with another pressing issue which had petitioned his ambitious inclinations. He had been hauling his deep-seated frustrations for Dr. Küçük wordlessly from one political stage to another since his return to Cyprus. However, with the elections approaching, Rauf had decided to settle his grudges very publicly by challenging Dr. Küçük for his seat as the Vice-President of the Republic. Having made the decision before he left Turkey, Rauf waged a campaign that saw both leaders pitted against each other for a restless public to choose between.

It was shortly before the elections in 1973, that a stunned Dr. Küçük learned Rauf planned to stand against him. Dr. Küçük had apparently underestimated the extent of Rauf's discontent and ambitious nature and the serious threat that the combined characteristics posed to his leadership. Rauf's popularity also proposed a risk to Dr. Küçük who was slowly being undermined by Rauf's very public deeds.

Rauf's profile had been raised considerably — derived in part from his escapades on the seas when he attempted to return to Cyprus covertly. The renowned adventure had catapulted Rauf into folklore status and characterised him as 'a man of action' by his impressed peers. It had also endeared him to a new and excitable generation looking for an actionable hero and forceful defender. (Ironically, this status had also impressed a teenage Mehmet Ali Talat who confessed in an interview that his own youth was influenced by Rauf's exploits; although his adult political years were in opposition to Rauf).

Whilst Dr. Küçük was revered for his role as the acclaimed leader, Rauf was the charismatic guardian struggling dutifully to obtain equality for Turkish Cypriots during the inter-communal talks. He had become well-known for his defiance and rebellious nature that appeared to fly in the face of Greek Cypriot edicts; and his involvement with the highly-publicised talks ensured he was a newsworthy item, keeping him buoyant in the eye of the Turkish Cypriot public who were demanding change from their cramped existence.

Dr. Küçük had not taken Rauf's challenge lightly and took the precaution of going to Turkey to seek advice and elicit support. Unfortunately for the concerned leader, Rauf had not only won the favour of the community but had spent his years of exile in Turkey courting influential supporters.

Although there is no substantiated documented proof of how Dr. Küçük was received by Turkey, Rauf's assertion was that Dr. Küçük was smartly dismissed by Turkey. They thanked him for his services but told the disappointed doctor he was no longer needed and had suggested 'it would better if you leave it to Denktaş". Thus armed with political assets denied to Dr. Küçük, Rauf had little trouble overthrowing his opponent who had declined from entering his own candidature on his return from Turkey.

Rauf's subsequent election as Vice-President was a keenly-felt blow to Dr. Küçük who felt betrayed by him. Dr. Küçük had been an integral part of defining Turkish Cypriots' political society and unhappy he had been relegated to the background by the young man he had groomed to become an essential member of the political leadership. After the elections, the men retained openly-strained relations up until a few months before Dr. Küçük's death in 1983. The two leaders made tentative peace over their joint interest for the newly-formed independent state for Turkish Cypriots although their relationship had been irrevocably soured by Rauf's actions.

As a retired elder statesman in 2010, Rauf may have been pondering his own fortunate position to have spent over three decades as a leader virtually unchallenged when he expressed remorse for how Dr. Küçük was eased from the leadership. In the relaxed atmosphere of his own home he spoke freely of how he felt a sense of responsibility for the 'broken heart' he had inflicted on Dr. Küçük. "I should not have done it. I should not have opposed him," he ruefully admitted in an interview. "He was our leader and but for his leadership and his efforts in making Cyprus a case for Turkey we would not have been here."

It was an honest admission of how important Dr. Küçük's contributions were in laying the foundations of Turkish Cypriot society as it is recognised today; but Rauf still rejected the notion that his motives were based purely on ambition. Despite his ruthless approach that won him the elections in 1973 from Dr. Küçük, Rauf maintained his only goal was to end the dispute between Turkish and Greek Cypriots; for Rauf this meant division of the island which would allow Turkish Cypriots to be free from the 'minority' status and enable self-autonomy.

He was aware the talks were unlikely to bring about a satisfactory conclusion and decided any hope of independence could only come from Turkey.

Clerides and Rauf facing journalists after talks in Beirut, 1968.   *Below* Dr. Küçük and Rauf

CHAPTER TWELVE

The Enemy Without

The talks in 1973 between Clerides and Rauf, as the newly-appointed Vice-President, were still unable to end the cloud of uncertainty that all Cypriots resided under. Makarios had seemingly adopted a new approach that suggested an interest in removing *enosis* from Cyprus' future, showing instead a determination to concentrate on achieving an independent Cyprus. The apparent change in attitude from the acknowledged President of the Republic should have brought a collective sigh of relief from the Turkish Cypriot community but instead confusion and fear reigned in its place.

Enosis had been an issue trailing faithfully behind Makarios for many years. Despite waxing lyrical on the subject with passionate speeches declaring his commitment to *enosis*, he had chosen to prolong its stifled existence. Makarios' stance was that *enosis* was best left to time with the hopes Turkish Cypriot resistance would dwindle.

It did not stop Makarios from frequently indulging in lengthy political discourse seen arguing for its immediate realisation and turning a blind priestly-eye to terrorist actions committed in the name of *enosis*. However, it was under his controlling guidance that *enosis* was simply left to remain a controversial subject — talked about and fought over but never brought into fruition.

Makarios' complicated but lengthy flirtation with

enosis had often seen him veering between his Hellenistic patriotism and his own personal ambitions. He had refused to 'close the door' on *enosis* in negotiations, but had been reluctant to usher it in as he knew too well the threat it posed on his grip on Cyprus: if *enosis* came into being, the supposition for Makarios was his political departure and the expectation of dutifully handing over the reins to Greece.

Unsurprisingly in later years he was seen to express a preference for an independent Cyprus with himself firmly in control. A candid interview with the celebrated journalist Oriana Fallaci in November 1974 revealed just how keenly Makarios objected to being undermined whilst at the same time artfully painting a representation of himself as being in opposition to *enosis*. In a reference to the frustrations he had caused Greece, he stubbornly declared:

"I was too big an obstacle to *enosis*, and they were too anxious to have *enosis*...Anyway, they expected me to take orders from Athens, they wanted me to obey like a puppet, that's absolutely impossible with my temperament. I obey only myself."

Makarios' failure to comply with any one's wishes other than his own naturally became something of a millstone for '*enosis*.' However, his reluctance to make a formal declaration in favour of *enosis* and consign it to a position of *non grata* in Cyprus' history provoked the ire of Athens.

A *coup d'état* staged in Greece on April 21st 1967 by the Military Junta had caused drastic changes to the face of Greece that had also been adversely affecting the island ever since. On seizing power, the Junta, under the leadership of Col. Georgios Papadopoulos, had been aggressively promoting their stratagem on *enosis* creating conflict within Makarios' now predominately Greek Cypriot government and politically-displaced Turkish Cypriots. Undeterred by the intricate policies that underscored Cypriot politics, the Junta, eager for results, forged ahead in its determination to declare Cyprus' union with Greece.

The only real obstacle preventing the Junta from realising their goal was Makarios. His inconsistent policies threw doubt on his allegiance to *enosis* and Greece was becoming increasingly impatient. It was after several years of reasoning, the Junta had finally concluded *enosis* was destined to remain just a simple threat under his supervision. With its own army presence on the island, and strategically-placed officers in the National Guard, Greece was poised to remedy the situation by snatching power from Makarios and imposing *enosis* with or without his consent.

Snapping at Makarios' heels, and sharing Greece's views, as well as revelling in their support, was Cyprus-born Georgios Grivas — a prominent figure in the Greek army and the man responsible for the EOKA campaigns in Cyprus. Despite the threats he was surrounded by, Makarios continued to defy the Junta even though he suspected they were plotting to overthrow him. Assassination attempts on Makarios' life had managed to be averted but clarified to the priest his fears that Greece was seeking his removal in order to secure an instant declaration of *enosis*.

As Makarios tangled with Greece and tried to preserve his defiant hold over Cyprus, questions were being raised by the Turkish Cypriot community as to their own fate. The instability of Makarios' government and the external factions that threatened to topple him disturbed Rauf in particular. Regardless of who swiped power, Turkish Cypriots, in a Cyprus united with Greece, would be at the mercy of Greece with even less opportunity to safeguard their own identities and rights as they became submerged within Hellenistic rule. The circumstances were further exacerbated for Turkish Cypriots who were still living in enclaves under strained conditions. Segregated villages lived under a fragile cease-fire that had been instigated by the UN but remained at risk as the subject of *enosis* continued to rage fiercely showing no signs of dissipating.

For hard-pressed Turkish Cypriots it meant daily lives were disrupted by sporadic outbursts of violence and also thwarted by illegal economic sanctions in an effort to oppress them. A swift conclusion to the talks had begun to dominate the existence of Turkish Cypriots' who were naturally restless for a solution.

Originally, in 1968, the talks had inspired hope in Turkish Cypriots but that hope had steadily faded. Over the years leading up to the Turkish intervention, the inter-communal talks had begun to falter with signs of dialogue breaking down between the leaders. The respective community leaders would often find themselves at an impasse over fundamental principles prompting speculation and anxiety from the international and local communities for their success. One persistent bone of contention was the reluctance of Clerides and his government to dismiss *enosis* completely; Clerides was also insistent the Zurich agreements* would never be returned to which was in direct conflict to Rauf's policies that were based on them.

On 14th March 1971, Rauf was furious after a familiar speech delivered by Makarios to bolster his popularity at an EOKA memorial service in Karpaz announced 'Cyprus has been Greek since the dawn of history and shall remain Greek.' He ended the speech with a glorious burst of rhetoric publicly trumpeting Cyprus' intended future: "We

---

*The London-Zurich agreements, of 1959, had formed the basis for the 1960 Constitution. It set out the abiding principles and was the agreed foundation for the final settlement of the 'Cyprus Problem'.

have taken it [Cyprus] over as a wholly Greek island and we shall preserve it as an undivided Greek island until we hand it over to Mother Greece."

The entire speech was duly reported in Greek media although his last comments were omitted as they were seen as too provocative. However, the speech, including the climatic finish, was tape recorded and Makarios' statements during the politically sensitive era of the inter-communal talks had reached the ears of Rauf.

At the time of Makarios' speech, the talks were still continuing with one slight alteration. Rauf and Clerides had removed the oppressive atmosphere of a boardroom and would meet at an appointed time in informal surroundings at each other's house. Both interlocutors enjoyed the familiar surroundings and were always encouraged by it to debate and converse in a congenial manner. After listening to the inflammatory speech, Rauf dispensed with politeness and angrily questioned Clerides about Greek Cypriot intentions and commitment to procuring a peaceful solution. He let his disappointment thunder through the halls of Clerides' well-ordered house as he queried the worth of continuing the talks. After venting his frustration he quietly added the end of the talks was not his decision but a full report to Ankara would be sent along with his recommendations regarding 'the usefulness of the talks.'

Despite the affable climate created by their mutual home environments it still wasn't unusual for the leaders to suspend the talks temporarily due to detrimental statements made by public figures that they believed were damaging and hindering progress. Clerides had also stormed out of a meeting in early 1974 after comments made by Turkey's Prime Minister, Bulent Ecevit (he had made a statement effectively suggesting Cyprus would be better off with a federal system). Constant halting of the dialogue, however, cast doubts on the likelihood a solution could be found as well as creating damaging effects on the relations between the communities. The deadlocks between the two caretakers of the communities ensured long periods of uncertainty for all concerned Cypriots whilst they waited for the talks to resume.

Rauf sought to diminish the idea of *enosis* and its pernicious intent on the talks once and for all. He demanded Clerides release a statement declaring *enosis* was no longer a considered option for Cyprus. In return Rauf offered to make a statement which would dispel any fears *Taksim* was the desired objective of the Turkish Cypriot community.

Clerides refused citing he was not in a position to do so; Rauf then appealed to the sympathetic constitutional advisor from Athens, who had been assigned to Clerides, to make a statement. The advisor made a simple counter-argument claiming his capacity as constitutional advisor prevented him from making any public announcements.

Rauf recalled Clerides raising his shoulders and hands in a sympathetic gesture but would only venture a half-hearted commitment to say 'if Athens says *enosis* is out, all I will be saying is that Athens has said *enosis* is out.'

Rauf had despairingly waved an olive branch at Clerides' camp, knowing he was burying his own nationalistic hopes, and had still been ignored. He was deflated by the momentary realisation of knowing anything he offered was never going to dispel the threat of *enosis*. Makarios' occasional simpering on the subject calling instead for an independent Cyprus was only ever designed to appease the community and fulfil his own ambitions; it was not enough to convince Rauf that Cyprus would not be offered up to Greece at the first opportunity.

Rauf's fears for the Turkish Cypriot community had

grown considerably and he was consumed with pessimism for the future. It was his firm belief they faced an inevitable future under *enosis:* destined to be subjugated to a lesser role within the population and eventually cleansed from Cyprus; and it was only marked by time, in his view, that Turkish Cypriots would succumb to their prescribed fate.

He mounted a frantic mission to make Turkey aware of the increasingly unstable situation triggered by the growing tensions between the Junta and Makarios. Rauf had kept a wary eye on events noticing how the Junta had stepped up its efforts to procure *enosis* and Makarios, fearing his expulsion from Cyprus, dug his heels in deeper to prevent its formation — all of which exposed Turkish Cypriots to further risk.

Makarios' grievances with the Junta became a very public affair dividing Greek Cypriot loyalties. Many Greek Cypriots were loyal to Makarios and did not wish to have *enosis* foisted on them by a military regime. In contrast, Greek Cypriots led by Grivas had formed paramilitary groups to remove Makarios to make way for the Junta and allow *enosis*. Makarios had already accelerated the situation with his challenge on the National Guard. He had reduced military service, which pared down the size of the army and the Junta's stronghold in Cyprus, and attempted to expel officers from the island. He further pushed at the Junta by writing a letter to General Phaedon Gizikis (the figurehead President of Greece), openly published in the media and holding the regime responsible for the terrorist campaigns tearing at the Cypriot community.

Rauf began a ruthless campaign of his own to encourage Turkey to prepare for the worst. He admitted to obsessively bombarding all the related offices with daily bulletins — sometimes several in one day — informing Turkey of the slightest movement or rumour he had heard relating to the dilemma building between Makarios and the Junta. Reports to Turkey became a relentless duty of Rauf's as he dashed off reams of paper minutely detailing the political developments of the situation; the communications were always accompanied with forecasts predicting catastrophic results that ended reiterating the urgent need for Turkey's aid.

Çağlayangil, in his capacity as the Foreign Minister of Affairs as well as Rauf's long-time friend and supporter, had already responded to Greece and the coup in 1967 as rumours of an intended coup against Makarios swiftly followed. Without any subtlety, Çağlayangil had warned Greece in a public statement of the consequences should they take action in Cyprus:

"Everyone, and especially our neighbour Greece and the Greek Cypriot administration, knows very well that Turkey will never accept a solution based on *enosis*. If they intend to obtain this result by force, or by way of a *fait accompli*, and are ready to assume the responsibility for the consequences, then we will all see how the Cyprus problem will be solved."

Seven years after Çağlayangil's stark warning, Rauf was pursuing Turkey, hoping she would invoke her rights as one of the guarantor parties and intervene on Turkish Cypriots' behalf.

By January 1974, Bülent Ecevit* had assumed the role of Prime Minister for Turkey and since that time Rauf had ensured the newly-appointed premier was apprised of all the developments in Cyprus. Rauf and Makarios

*Bülent Ecevit (born 1925 died 2006) first entered parliament in 1957. He was the leader of the Republican People's Party (Turkish: *Cumhuriyetci Halk Partisi*) and later the Democratic Left Party (Turkish: *Demokratik Sol Parti)*. He served as Prime Minister of Turkey on five occasions.

had an opinion in common: both believed the Junta were conspiring against Makarios to replace him with a willing marionette eager to have his strings pulled to dance to the tune of *enosis*. More frank reports from Rauf expressing his opinions and sent to Ecevit were followed up with a visit to Ankara to receive the premier's thoughts in person.

In the ministerial office, Turkey's congenial prime minister stared thoughtfully at Rauf considering the reports very carefully. He nodded his head sagely and made reassuring noises of approval at each sentence Rauf leant across the desk to direct him to. Rauf was in an agitated state, worrying he would not be able to impress upon Ecevit the urgency of Turkey's aid. He pressed Ecevit further by asking the premier to comment on his paragraph in the report that discussed the assassination attempts on Makarios. Rauf had offered his own conjecture by outlining the probability of the Junta's intentions to make another attempt on Makarios' life in order to replace him. The ensuing mayhem that would swiftly follow for Turkish Cypriots would assure their removal from Cyprus as *enosis'* roots would be planted. Ecevit smiled benignly at Rauf and told him he had agreed with everything written and Turkey was more than ready to intervene.

Rauf returned to Cyprus reasonably satisfied that Turkey would respond in any eventuality and made statements to the press and waiting Turkish Cypriots. However, Rauf was plagued with personal doubts that Turkey would arrive too late. He agonised over Cyprus' fate and whether Turkey would actually have the legal right to intervene if *enosis* was given the chance to be established first; the fear of which drove him into a fitful sleep on most nights.

On one such night, Rauf had a prophetic dream about Turkey's founder, Atatürk, which left a lasting impression on him. Rauf had retired to bed at a late hour after spending a typical evening working into the small hours. As his wife slept peacefully, Rauf clambered wearily into bed beside her and fell into a restless sleep that was disrupted by flitting dreams.

He claimed not to have been asleep very long when he experienced an unusual phenomenon: a dream-like state of semi-consciousness during which he was confronted with the image of Atatürk walking towards him. A mixture of elation and terror ran through Rauf as the spectre looked directly at him with a calm demeanour. Drawing strength from the kindly-looking form, Rauf begged the General for help as the 'Turkish Cypriots could not withstand any more suffering.'

In response to Rauf's pleading the entity imparted an ambiguous message: 'conjecture is important, Denktaş watch out for the conjecture.' Rauf awoke a short while later drenched in sweat with the haunting image of Atatürk still smiling at him.

The vision had a considerable affect on Rauf who was unable to accept it held little importance as being anything more than a vivid dream; or the product of an over-worked imagination due to his lack of sleep in the recent months making him vulnerable and distorting his senses. Risking his professional reputation, Rauf disclosed the contents of his dream to Çağlayangil the following morning at a meeting. He explained to the bemused minister the importance of the 'conjecture' as 'told' to him by Atatürk. The symbolic meaning was obvious to Rauf: Turkish Cypriots would be saved. Çağlayangil appeared confused and questioned what and to whom did the 'conjecture' refer to.

Refusing to be distracted by 'the minor' details, Rauf became very animated on the subject claiming the message was a clear reference to Turkey's plans of coming to the island. Çağlayangil gently encouraged Rauf back into his seat and insisted he had a cup of strong Turkish coffee to calm his nerves. "He thought I had gone," snorted Rauf with laughter, coupled with finger-twirling motions at his temple.

Several decades later, Rauf managed to recall the dream with such clarity suggesting it may have been embellished on over time. However, known as a significant story-teller, Rauf enjoyed recounting the story for the amusement of his audience when discussing the events of 1974. "I had spoken to Atatürk that night," he continued to insist shortly before his death, "it was more than a dream...I mean he was very much alive..."

Whilst Rauf had been impressed by his nightly vision the significance of the dream lay more in its timing rather than its prophetic properties. Rauf had felt strongly the Junta had set their sights and a date for Makarios' disposal. The ominous coup appeared imminent and Turkey's timing was unknown but vital if it was to prevent *enosis* being declared amidst the carnage. Within days of his dream the coup against Makarios became a reality.

On 15th July 1974, Makarios, *en route* to the Presidential Palace from his summer retreat in Troodos, was contemplating his day ahead. Unbeknownst to him, the Junta (now under the instruction of the more sinister, Brigadier Dimitrios Ioannides) had sanctioned his demise, known as *Operation President* to take place that day.

Intriguingly, the attempt on his life was not made on the comparatively quiet roads travelled by Makarios with his light complement of guards; Makarios was able to wend his way onward to the Palace oblivious to any dangers. Once at the Palace a haphazard plan appears to have been hastily thrown together in an effort to maximise the drama leading to the event of forcibly removing Makarios. With every intention of seeking out Makarios for death or capture, heavily-armed gunmen led a vigorous assault on the Presidential Palace.

The Palace was stormed with enough gunfire to raze the building to the ground but the would-be assassins were foiled in their attempts to remove Makarios. Amidst the blazing gun-battle Makarios had managed to slip unharmed out of a back door. Flanked only by two aides Makarios avoided further detection by stripping himself of his cassock and into civilian clothes and eventually made his way to Paphos. On his arrival there, Makarios contacted the British who spirited him away by helicopter to the safety of the British bases before flying him on to London via Malta.

Four days after the event an appalled Makarios stood in front of the United Nations Security Council. Despite not wishing 'to occupy the time of the Security Council' with his 'own personal adventures,' he managed to give a graphic account of the attack that took place: he had apparently been entertaining school-children in the reception room when the first shots were heard.

Whilst the Presidential Palace was 'shaking from mortar shells' he escaped but the fate of the children was left unknown as they fade from his narrative allowing his address to then concentrate on the 'providential miracle' of his safe exit from danger. Finally, aggrieved that the Junta had 'extended its dictatorship to Cyprus,' Makarios firmly deplored their actions and labelled EOKA B, amongst other things, 'terrorists.'

Back home on Cyprus soil, the general public were in turmoil. The death of Grivas in January 1974 had allowed the ascension of the notorious, self-confessed 'Turk hater,' Nikos Sampson*. A more acceptable face for Greece with his fanaticism and devotion to *enosis*, Sampson was installed as President of Cyprus by the Greek regime. Knowing how unsettling this would be for his community Rauf wasted no time trying to reassure Turkish Cypriots and made appeals for them to remain united. He made public statements suggesting the issues that had arisen from the coup were an internal matter involving the Greeks; nothing would change for Turkish Cypriots and their ongoing struggle to obtain their rights under the auspices of the 1960 constitution; although privately he maintained the hope that Turkey would intervene before *enosis* was proclaimed with the risk of leaving it too late for his people.

The moment the coup had been initiated Rauf had been engaged in hectic discussions with Ecevit at how best to intervene. Rauf maintained it was his suggestion to have the two remaining guarantor parties (Turkey and Britain) involved in a bloodless intervention through the British bases — a token intervention that would see Turkey land at a British base to launch their operation. Turkey and Britain would then take action from there should Sampson's administration refuse to step down.

Ecevit flew to London on the 17th July apparently taking with him the proposal suggested by Rauf and made the appeal to the then Foreign Secretary, James Callaghan, and Prime Minister, Harold Wilson.

The idea was rejected with Wilson later stating

*Nikos Sampson (born 1935 died 2001) became President of the Republic of Cyprus after the *coup d'état* by Greece in July 1974. Sampson was a journalist and fiercely loyal member of EOKA. He was widely believed to be the 'chief executioner' for the group and suspected of being involved directly in the murders of several policemen and civilians. He was later imprisoned in Britain after a death sentence was commuted but returned to Cyprus after the formation of the Republic emphatically, "He asked us to allow him to use the Sovereign Base at Akrotiri for the purpose. He received a courteous, but declaratory 'no'."

Rauf was exasperated by the responses and felt time was slipping away if the Turkish Cypriot community were to survive. It was critical that Turkish Cypriots were defended and Rauf spent each day at his office working on the conundrum of how an intervention could be executed.

He was plagued by journalists who camped outside his offices and hounded him for answers whenever he came into view assuming he had information. They were relentless with questions that centered on Turkey and whether she had any intention of landing. Rauf did his best to avoid the reporters and remained tight-lipped giving non-committal responses to the probing questions whenever he was unable to elude them.

By the third day, Rauf, tired and stressed allowed his usually cool-headedness to slip. He told the waiting journalists that if Turkey didn't arrive 'within a few days then this is the end.' The hacks rushed to Kyrenia and waited by the harbour suspecting, wrongly, that Rauf knew the Turks were on their way and causing mild panic in their wake.

By 19th July, Rauf did receive very specific news from Turkey: they accepted the conjecture Rauf had outlined in his reports and were making preparations. Just as Atatürk had promised: 'conjecture is important.'

Burnt-out presidential palace in Nicosia following tank artillery during the *coup d état* of 15th July 1974. *Above* Nicos Sampson as *de facto* President of the Republic of Cyprus, 1974.

Rauf and Turkish premier Bülent Ecevit

PART 3

*Invasion, And
Counter-Invasion*

CHAPTER THIRTEEN
The Sky's The Limit

THE 15th of July in 1974 saw the Greek-inspired coup invade Cyprus, rendering Makarios' newly-inspired visions for an independent Cyprus useless and Rauf's hopes of equal rights for Turkish Cypriots fade even further into the distance. Any interests and concerns from the general population, as well as those from political and government representatives, were ignored as the newly-installed President, Nikos Sampson, set about ruthlessly implementing the foundations that would act as a springboard for securing *enosis*.

Sampson went on to solidify his despotic image, instigating a merciless fratricidal campaign involving the persecution of Makarios supporters to accompany his crusade against Turkish Cypriots. His actions against Cypriots were designed to sweep aside any opposition to Greece and her intentions but placed Cyprus once again in jeopardy.

Violent clashes between Makarios supporters and the opposing pro-Junta forces broke out over the island as news of the coup spread. Meanwhile, Rauf's anxiety increased as he worried about the inevitable consequences likely to affect Turkish Cypriots caught again in the cross-fire. Rauf, who had always pursued Turkey relentlessly to fulfil her obligations to protect his community, was by now utterly desperate. In an interview with author Brendan O'Malley in 1985, he made no secret of the dependency Turkish Cypriots had on Turkey; it was imperative Turkey intervened and on the morning of the coup he recalled his immediate thoughts and how he was spurred into action:

"In the morning I was in my office as usual at 7.30 and at 8.30 shots started to be fired from the Greek quarter and particles of bombs started falling on my roof. Then we heard that there was a coup and Makarios was dead. We contacted the Turkish government immediately [saying] that this was a takeover by Greece and all our safety, the lives of our people, were endangered and Turkey should honour her treaty obligations. Our concern was to bring Turkey to our aid, otherwise we were finished."

Rauf continued to pound on Turkey's door for an active response, but Ecevit hadn't been idle in his attempts to restore order. On the 18th July, Ecevit demanded from Greece the resignation of Sampson and the instant withdrawal of the 650 Greek officers present in the National Guard.

Greece rejected Ecevit's demands with a confidence bordering on arrogant defiance by proposing only to rotate the officers. All other requests were met with a bold refusal and an indication there would be no deviation from the course taken involving Cyprus' newly-installed administration. Greece's response was baffling considering the threat they faced from Turkey's army. One eminent observer, Prof. Dr. Salahi R Sonyel, claimed however that Greece's reaction was hardly surprising as they were apparently convinced that 'US pressure, as before, would dissuade the Turks from resorting to force.'

As concerns continued to mount over Greece's authoritarian administration, Ecevit was being urged to 'restore the equilibrium' that was now lacking on the island. Ecevit made his decision on 19th July to intervene based on the terms set out in the Treaty of Guarantee and then sent word secretly to Rauf via the Turkish ambassador, Asaf İnhan. İnhan went to see Rauf in person at his office but was disappointed not to find Rauf in residence and left a coded message asking Rauf to contact him immediately. Rauf's nerves were already at straining point by the time he received the ambassador's message but knew the veiled message could only mean Turkey had made a decision to come to the aid of Turkish Cypriots.

An impromptu meeting was held at the ambassador's private residence with the commander of the TMT also in attendance. Rauf was ushered into the house and told in solemn tones his 'prayers had been answered' which caused him to utter a very audible sigh of relief. Turkey would be landing the following day at 5am, explained the ambassador, but absolute discretion was vital if the landing operation was to be successful.

The ambassador warned Rauf he was not to utter a word to anybody until one hour before the intended strike. Although Rauf had been desperate for Turkey to arrive on Cyprus' shores, his relief was overshadowed as he agonised over how he could best prepare his community beforehand. To add to the dilemma, he was expected to organise statements in Turkish, Greek and English and arrange for their distribution at a precise time — again with just one hour to spare. "Well, that was a nonsense," Rauf recalled with a shake of his head. "How could I get ready? Have the things translated and not tell anybody..."

The impossible task had Rauf racking his brains on how to overcome the impracticalities. It didn't take him long to find the best approach. He made an executive decision to ignore the edicts and rounded up a few of his closest colleagues to elicit their help. After informing them of what would be taking place the following day, Rauf insisted all would be staying with him at his home that night to help prepare the statements for the community. There were some mild protests as some of the men wanted to telephone their wives to explain their absence. Rauf adamantly refused their requests and asserted in previous times he had refrained from telling his wife anything. However, on this occasion, Rauf's wife was safely out of the country with her children in Turkey which drew a few disgruntled comments from his friends.

Nevertheless, the close-knit group of men remained with Rauf and to ease tensions Rauf fed his companions a good meal and kept their wine glasses full to help them sleep later. During dinner the conversation was interrupted by an Austrian colonel and his assistant dropping by to visit Rauf. Lieut. Colonel Franz Rieger was commanding the Austrian UN contingent and had been assigned to Rauf by UNFICYP after the coup.

The unstable atmosphere prevalent in Cyprus ensured the two men spent a lot of time together over a short period which had encouraged them to strike up an informal relationship. They often shared their opinions and thoughts on Cyprus in a candid manner over a brandy. Rauf had always felt relaxed in the colonel's company but, despite their amicable relationship, was unable to tell him of Turkey's plans for the following day; and all of the men gathered in Rauf's living room were under pressure to finish their task but could do little else other than sit and smile awkwardly at the officer who had joined them in a nightcap.

The uncomfortable atmosphere, and his unwanted place in it, saw the disquieted colonel and his assistant drain their drinks silently and quickly before bidding Rauf and his companions an uneasy good night. A collective sigh of relief went around the room as Rauf and his colleagues finished their assignment of creating public statements, which included a dramatic pre-recording by Rauf to be aired at 5am informing Cyprus that Turkey had landed on the shores. After all the statements had been finalised, the group retired for a night of nervous sleep. Rauf was agitated and unable to sleep. He spent the night pacing the house with worried footsteps whilst frequently checking his public address along with the rest of the statements.

At just before 4am, he woke his aged father-in-law Münür, who had been living with Rauf and his family, to move to the basement in an effort to keep him safe. The old man listened patiently to Rauf's explanation for disturbing his sleep before he gently patted Rauf's arm and begged to be left to sleep in his own bed. He had decided if he was 'to be killed by a Turkish bomb, let it be so.' Rauf didn't have any time to waste and decided the best course of action was to respect his elderly relative's wishes and left him to the comforts of his bed.

By 4.15 am, Rauf was in front of the Austrian colonel's house fulfilling another obligation — to apologise for his behaviour the night before and inform Lieut.Colonel Rieger of the impending intervention which he wanted the colonel to witness personally. Rauf banged on the colonel's door with gusto alerting all the sleeping occupants inside. A dazed and undressed Rieger stood in front of Rauf to receive the news of Turkey's imminent arrival with blinking dismay.

He quickly gathered his thoughts and told Rauf he would have to telephone HQ to which Rauf calmly stated would not be possible. Rauf had taken the precaution of cutting his telephone line and those in the surrounding area. The colonel rushed upstairs to dress and came stumbling back down with one leg inside a pair of trousers whilst the other tried to negotiate the steps. Rauf recalled the incident as one of the few light-hearted moments during a precarious time although he conceded he 'had no idea how the man didn't fall and break his neck.'

Upright and dressed Lieut. Colonel Rieger followed Rauf to the makeshift headquarters of Rauf's group, which had been set up in the basement of the Cooperative bank in Nicosia, to wait for the long-anticipated strike to begin. At exactly 5 am, they listened to Rauf's pre-recorded address splutter into life after a protracted silence over the airwaves on *Bayrak* — the Turkish Cypriot radio station.

The dramatic monologue was laden with herculean language and aimed at all Cypriots with Rauf announcing the intentions of Turkey were 'to eliminate the pro-Junta elements' that had usurped the rights of the Greek Cypriot community as well as the Turkish. He ended with a heartfelt pledge that reassured the Greek community Turkish Cypriots 'wished to live on friendly terms as co-founders of independence.'

When Rauf's voice had stopped transmitting an eerie silence descended over the villages of Cyprus as many Cypriots were just beginning to shrug themselves awake to the news. They didn't have long to digest the impact. Rauf's speech had declared the strike would be imminent and warned people to stay in their homes and not risk being in the open air and exposed to armed assaults.

A series of busy movements replaced the quietude with most people foregoing their daily routines and rushing to find safety. Cypriots from all corners of the island grabbed provisions and began migrating to their nearest form of shelter to wait out the storm of bullets that were expected to rain down. The hour that followed after the announcement was uncharacteristically quiet — without any of the noises normally associated with air strikes. Rauf waited in nervous anticipation for the shrill sounds of war jets to cut through the air indicating Turkey had arrived.

Defying his own orders, Rauf ventured outside dragging a small group with him to scan the skyline for signs of action but was met with resolute stillness. Adding to his confusion of Turkey's elusive absence were news bulletins being broadcast on Greek Cypriot channels claiming the Turkish fleet had arrived but had been pushed indignantly back into the sea and overhead fighters chased off.

The propaganda achieved its desired effect on at least one Turkish Cypriot: "You can't imagine what a state I was in," Rauf recalled when recounting the moment. "I said, my God if they have done what they said...if this is true then I have really messed up telling everyone."

At 6 o'clock, Rauf heard the distinctive sounds of bombardment commence from the Kyrenia side and caught the breathtaking sight of planes streaming over Boğaz. The first Turkish soldiers to land had actually been at Five-Mile beach west of Kyrenia but had rapidly spread themselves over the North of Cyprus much to Rauf and his friends' relief.

The small party of men erupted with euphoria at the sights and sounds of Turkey's charge with some even kissing the asphalt gratefully as Rauf looked on. Although Rauf found himself caught up emotionally by his friends and fellow Turkish Cypriots' reactions, it was the UNFICYP's Austrian colonel's reaction that intrigued him the most. He grabbed Rauf's hand and held it tightly between his two palms and quietly offered his congratulations before turning on his heel to contact his superiors.

The mystery of Turkey's tardiness was never solved although Rauf had his own opinion that the hour difference between Cyprus and Turkey at the time may have been an issue. Regardless of what had influenced Turkey's lateness it was within hours of the landing that Turkey's representative, Asaf İnhan, suggested to Rauf a visit to the Turkish contingent was necessary. As well as being an expected duty, İnhan was of the view that Rauf should also show an interest in the welfare of the landing Turkish soldiers.

It wasn't difficult to persuade Rauf as morale-boosting had become a trademark characteristic of his. He took the duty very seriously whilst showing a genuine concern for the people he encountered. As a result of his personable behaviour Rauf had been made a firm favourite amongst the Turkish people alongside his own Turkish Cypriot community. Often when Rauf visited Turkey he would find himself herded into a humble village home who would insist on treating him like a long-lost relative.

There was no doubt, even amongst his opponents, that Rauf possessed the communicative skills many of his peers lacked but the difference for Rauf was that he actually enjoyed talking and listening to the different people he met. He readily agreed to meet the soldiers and brushed aside the warnings that he was told he might encounter along the route.

Rauf joined İnhan and they made their way to a camp just outside Ortaköy and met with one of the first wave of Turkish soldiers. As the two dignitaries wandered around the hastily-organised camp, that Rauf described as looking like 'something out of a war film,' neither could imagine just how close they came to losing their lives.

They picked their way through the busy scene to a tent housing the commanding officers who were hunched over maps planning routes and attacks. Seeing Rauf and his diplomatic colleague, the commanding officers snapped to attention and gave the pair a courteous greeting. After exchanging information and assessing the volatile situation, Rauf and İnhan were escorted out of the tent by all the officers. Minutes later a mortar shell hit the tent and flattened it but thankfully did not explode on impact.

RAUF'S close brush with death was not to be his last that day. By the afternoon, the situation had become more turbulent with bombs and mortar shells flying in all directions. Undeterred by the chaotic disturbances, Rauf, having learnt that the Commander of the forces, Nureddin Ersin, had arrived in Boğaz, decided to drive up to make his acquaintance. Accompanying him was Osman Örek who still held the position of Minister of Defence under the Republic of Cyprus government. Rauf had gone back into Nicosia to collect Örek and the two men with the ambassador in tow left to meet the Commander.

The official car allocated to government officials was still in their service and pressed into use for the journey which took them along the mountainous road near Gönyeli. As the trio and their chauffeur sailed through with the Turkish flags flapping proudly on the car, none of the occupants were aware they were passing through a war zone. The area gave the impression of being deserted but the sounds of gunfire belied the fact that there were several people in the vicinity.

A little further into the journey the first reminder of armed conflict became apparent as a house they were passing was hit by a bomb and just a few seconds later an electric pole crashed on their left side just a few terrifying feet away from the car. The car with its distinctive flying banners had advertised its passengers and attracted attention. Rauf's intuition told him they had become the prime target and he screamed at the driver to turn the car around and head back. Guided by his own instincts, the driver refused and pressed his foot down sending the conspicuous car hurtling forward to pummel its way through the war zone.

Despite a bullet hitting the car, the driver earned the gratitude of Rauf who was quick to acknowledge that his actions had saved the lives of all the occupants in the car: "he was right [to carry on driving through] – one bullet hit us one side but it did not pierce the car," Rauf wrote later of the incident. The trajectory of the bullet demonstrated if the driver had stopped and executed a u-turn the bullet would most likely have cut through the windscreen and reached one of the passengers.

Having escaped the scene intact, the men managed to continue the journey with no further problems. They arrived in Boğaz and found Commander Ersin, surrounded by his officers, poring over maps. The Commander had evidently been expecting Rauf for he had a list to hand of supplies he hoped Rauf could provide. The brief meeting ended with Rauf clutching his list of instructions but determined first to meet with some of the soldiers who had been steadily arriving despite the adverse conditions.

RAUF had once again found himself in the midst of a war zone as he attempted to make contact with the soldiers. Smoke was billowing in neighbouring fields and pockets of fire sporadically breaking out — although it did not hamper the ranks of soldiers spilling into the area that had been commandeered by the Turkish army: there had been ceaseless activity as helicopters landed briefly to release scurrying soldiers from their bowels before taking off again.

Rauf's attention, however, had been distracted by the parachutists who were falling from the sky and landing adroitly in the field. It was a source of wonder for him at how the parachutists coped as they plummeted to earth. From their aerial viewpoint they witnessed first-hand the disconcerting images of devastation hundreds of feet below them. He marvelled at their bravery and their insistence to battle on despite the sights awaiting them.

On landing, Rauf noticed that after all the parachutists had organised themselves they would then make their way to a solemn young man standing in the field with a clipboard. Rauf followed the parachutists' trail and, with the intention of striking up a conversation, sought out the young officer to whom they had been reporting.

Once he had the attention of the officer he expressed his admiration for the young men and questioned the officer, who didn't appear to be beyond his early twenties, about his own experience when he too had parachuted onto the island. Without thinking, Rauf asked impertinent questions which had the potential to embarrass the young officer:

"I asked a question which should not be asked of a soldier," Rauf recalled ruefully. "I said when you jumped into this hell — burning fields, fire from all directions — were you not afraid?"

Rauf knew it wasn't an appropriate line of inquiry as it called the soldier's bravery and integrity into question. However, the soldier's response came as a surprise to Rauf with the parachutist appearing unperturbed and ready to give a forthright answer; furthermore, the soldier had an unnerving story to tell which he was eager to impart. He swore to Rauf he was a university graduate of sound mind but he had witnessed something he could not adequately explain.

The parachutist claimed as he had jumped from the aeroplane, he had initially been overwhelmed by the burning fields below him but then an unexplainable event occurred: an apparition unfolded before his eyes showing 'tens of thousands' of armour-clad horse, their riders thundering across the skies with swords drawn. Reliving the experience for Rauf, he adamantly claimed that what he had witnessed was the 'martyrs of 1571'* who had descended with him and his fellow comrades. Any fear he had experienced due to the sights below him had instantly vanished at the sight of the sword-brandishing riders.

The story left an impression on Rauf as well as providing him in later years with an introduction when he was attending Islamic conferences. The references made to the martyrs by the parachutist were alluding to verses in the Koran that state martyrs did not die; in fact, martyrs would reappear in a righteous war and manifest themselves as part of the home front to strengthen the numbers and resolve of the men at war.

Rauf would relate the parachutist's story with theatrical flair to his Arabic audiences during the time he was trying to court Islamic countries and gain their recognition for the then newly-formed TRNC. As the narrative reached its conclusion with the colourful visions of white horses and their saintly riders, he relished in the reactions of the Muslim audience. To his delight the devout Muslims would begin yelling with great vigour "Allahu Akbar!" (God is great) several times which

---

*In 1571 the Ottomans invaded Cyprus in order to free the Orthodox Greeks from Catholic repression. There were 80,000 martyrs during the siege under the command of Lala Mustafa Pasha.

would last for the best part of ten minutes. Rauf's objective at the conferences was to gain support for his country, and he believed the passionate reactions signalled a hopeful future.

Unfortunately, after the fervour had died down, Rauf would be disappointed to receive just a firm handshake with good wishes for the TRNC's future. Despite the setback, Rauf confessed later the sight of 'Arabs throwing their arms in the air' and chanting so ardently was very appealing and never failed to bring a smile to his lips.

HOWEVER, during 1974, Rauf rarely had occasion to smile as he watched Cyprus struggle with the bludgeoning burden that war had inflicted on her shores and inhabitants. Locked in political conflict for much of the time in 1974, it was Rauf's eldest son, Raif, who was instrumental in revealing the painful realities to him affecting Cyprus. Rauf's family had returned in late July to be with him but Raif had never left Cyprus. He had elected to stay behind with his father becoming caught up in the war.

Raif was just 23-years-old and at university but like most of the young men of his age he had been dividing his time between school and taking up arms in Nicosia to fight. His defensive position along the perimeters known as the Green Line* was a notoriously difficult border to protect. The young men were mostly made up of inexperienced young Turkish Cypriot students hurriedly drafted to fight. Those of them stationed at the frontline found themselves constantly engaged in battle and under fire causing them to be mentally and physically exhausted as a result.

*The Green Line is a United Nations Buffer Zone: a demilitarised zone patrolled by the UN that was established following the events of 1974. The neutral Green Line separates the South and North of Cyprus and remains in existence to date.

Whilst Raif had insisted on being a part of the war effort and placed himself at the forefront, Rauf admitted his son leaned on him to arrange for more troops to be sent to the Green Line. Greek radio stations had periodically broadcast potentially damaging propaganda falsely claiming to be the victors in the war which had worried Rauf's son.

An anxious Raif had sat with his companions clustered around a tiny transistor radio that defiantly blared out the success of the Greek contingency and their strength at pushing back the Turkish army. Raif saw the men around him losing heart and begged his father to send extra troops in the shape of the Turkish army to bring solace to their flagging spirits.

The Turkish army were heavily engaged in battle and had yet to cross Boğaz — a fact Rauf tried to explain to his son. Raif countered his father's argument by insisting the frontline depended on seeing a show of Turkish soldiers. Against his better judgement, Rauf contacted Commander Nureddin Ersin of the forces. Ersin listened to Rauf's request over a crackled line but only managed to muster up a small unit of soldiers which he dispatched with some misgivings to Raif's position on the Green Line. A tired and worn group of eight Turkish soldiers presented themselves at the front, driving up the length of the line to reassure the men that Turkey was behind them. The demonstration of defeated-looking soldiers parading proudly had a positive effect on Raif and his grateful friends.

Raif had often come under criticism for exploiting his relationship with his father (particularly in later years) which prompted angry denials from Rauf. Even during the conflict, Rauf found himself under fire for allowing valued Turkish soldiers at his son's request to present themselves at the Green Line. Incensed at the suggestion his son had asked for special treatment, Rauf pointed out Raif was trying to support his comrades and cement a crumbling frontline when he was asked to intervene.

At the same time his son was stationed on the frontline, Rauf's own position at the forefront of politics made him a target. He waged his own daily battles politically that exposed him to danger but he admitted it was far more difficult to ignore his own feelings as a parent with a child exposed daily to gunfire. Alarming statistics were revealing the gravity of the situation as the mounting toll of Cypriots becoming fatal casualties continued to rise steadily. Rauf was routinely informed of losses to life and plagued with fears that his own son would one day appear as a name amongst the dead.

Just one day after arranging for soldiers to be sent to the Green Line in support of Raif and his colleagues, Rauf had been told a consequential amount of soldiers had been killed. The lifeless bodies of almost one hundred men — all soldiers of Turkish and Turkish Cypriot descent, were lying in a small Nicosia hospital corridor waiting to be identified. An order from the commander of the area had stated that the men could not be buried without being formally identified, much to the overcowded hospital's despair. Rauf had decided before he contacted the commander to discuss how to resolve the situation: he should go to the hospital to talk with the hospital staff.

More used to morale-boosting visits with a rousing welcome, it took considerable effort on Rauf's part to steel himself against the harrowing sight of the soldiers' blood-soaked bodies and expressionless faces.

An orderly from the hospital had led Rauf through the rows of corpses piled atop of one another in the limited corridor space and then stood silently by his side as they came to a halt. Rauf was in a dazed stupor when he suddenly became aware of a lit cigarette that had been placed between his lips. Rauf had quit smoking two months beforehand and angrily ousted the offending cigarette. "They won't come alive if I smoke or not," he snapped at the orderly.

Rauf left the brutal scene grateful that his son's face was not amongst the dead. Despite the overwhelming sense of relief he felt, Rauf was keenly aware there were parents who would probably never know if their son was one of the motionless bodies lying on the floor in front of him. He made a heartfelt phone call to the commander pleading with him to reconsider his decision. The mostly young men lying cold on the floor of the hospital needed a dignified burial regardless of whether or not they could be identified.

The commander relented and those who could not be identified were laid to rest in a simple ceremony attended by only a handful of official mourners. The last resting place of the ill-fated and nameless soldiers, Rauf claimed, was behind Dr. Küçük's printing press in the middle of Nicosia.

Top left above Rauf's son, Raif Denktaş, standing on a stool with gun aimed, at a border post prior to the arrival of the Turkish Troops in July 1974

Turkish troops landing in Cyprus for peacekeeping operations on 20th July 1974

**Turkish paratroopers landing on Messoria Plains,
Lefkoşa**

CHAPTER FOURTEEN
Wistful Thinking

DURING the short eight days of Sampson's Presidency, Rauf had persisted with his statements, supported by Ecevit, that Turkey's involvement was purely a peace operation to prevent the Junta-inspired coup from taking absolute control in Cyprus. With Turkey's aims being systematically broadcast, and to Rauf's satisfaction, it was a resolute Turkish army that marched steadfastly resulting in rapid advances in the north of Cyprus posing a problem for Sampson.

Sampson appeared to have been caught off guard by Turkey's arrival and was only roused into action just one day before Turkey's landing operation on 20th July. Prior to Turkey's appearance on Cyprus' shores, Sampson had been kept busy with rebellious supporters loyal to Makarios' regime which left him little time to assess the threat imposed by Turkey.

He had embarked on an anti-Makarios drive, rounding up the loyalists and then imprisoning them; all other important combat resources were used to defend areas against attacks from Makarios supporters that were still at large.

According to an interview given by Clerides to journalist and author, Brendan O'Malley, several years later, news of Turkey's combative action was met with disbelief by Sampson. He claimed the Junta had been duped by the CIA into thinking they would be protected against an invasion by Turkey. Sampson, backed by the Junta, was 'panic-stricken' and uncoordinated but he made a clumsy effort to remedy the issue. Realising that Makarios' supporters and his own had a common enemy, he released the several thousand men he had interned and gave them weapons hoping to stave off the advancing Turkish army.

Meanwhile, as territories were slavishly fought over, Sampson attempted to legitimise his position as the leader of Cyprus. With remarkable speed and confidence, he had organised his cabinet to represent the new government and in a show of self-assuredness sent an emissary to the Green Line to inform Rauf that he was still recognised as the Vice President of Cyprus. However, Rauf had curt words to offer the nervous envoy who had the unfortunate job of delivering the message: "it's not a question of whether he recognises me," snorted Rauf, "the question is whether I recognise him!"

Rauf had been both shocked and disgusted by Sampson's installation as President of the Republic likening his appointment to another notorious figure in history. In an undisguised display of contempt, he bitterly spat that Sampson was 'as unacceptable as Adolf Hitler would be as President of Israel.' He went on to underscore his convictions of a non-recognition policy for Sampson's government with a frank explanation — and one that would continue to prevail for subsequent Greek Cypriot Presidents until the end of his life. For Rauf, the Republic of Cyprus, and its government, meant a wholly Greek Cypriot regime which no longer represented even a marginal element for Turkish Cypriots.

With Sampson firmly rejected by Rauf, the internal political machinations of Cyprus were churning erratically and heading in a worrying direction during 1974. However, it was behind the scenes that an even more ominous threat loomed. Relations between Turkey and Greece were damaged enough to suggest both countries were on a collision course for battle. Despite the American Secretary of State, Henry Kissinger, urging both countries not to go to war, Kissinger was worried. He offered up slim chances that war could be averted and was quoted in the *New York Times* as warning 'there is nothing to bet money on' after attending a meeting that he had hoped would reduce the threat.

The job of preventing war between Athens and Ankara fell on American official, Joseph Sisco — Kissinger's representative. Sisco's endeavours saw him spending much of the time scuttling back and forth between the two giants. Aware of the affect Sampson was having on events, Sisco beseeched Athens to remove Sampson and replace him with Clerides. Ignoring the request, Athens responded with its own demands on Turkey effectively asking her to restrict her actions of invasion.

Turkey had no intentions of leaving Cyprus and co-ordinated her movements with the Turkish Cypriot resistance fighters to reinforce her presence on the island. By 23rd of July, a general ceasefire was called and Sampson eventually removed from office along with the collapse of the Greek Junta. He was quickly supplanted by Clerides (who took on the role of caretaker until Makarios' return) which left him feeling bitter about his uncompleted objective for Cyprus. It was apparent that Sampson had not been willing to quit his post as the disgruntled would-be leader only offered his resignation amidst protests he was 'about to proclaim *enosis* when I quit.'

Although Sampson's hasty departure was met with nods of approval, this left Cyprus once again exposed to dealing with the aftermath of an unresolved tussle between the two communities. Accompanying Clerides to the official chair were the remnants of Sampson's Greek Cypriot government. The undesirable arrangement meant Clerides and Rauf had their work cut out for them and having to come to a practical arrangement. Rauf and Clerides also needed to prevent further calamities by seeking solutions that would appease those watching from Ankara and Athens. Resistance on both sides was wearing the patience of the international community; and the conferences being held in Geneva for all parties concerned were not yielding any satisfactory results.

Despite their respective stances on government issues, there was the expectation for Rauf and Clerides to do what they could to resolve the threat and find a peaceful solution for Cyprus; in doing so it would alleviate the tensions between Greece and Turkey.

The standoff between the Aegean power houses had been a powerful factor for the talks but had also spilled over onto the meeting between Rauf and Clerides creating an unusual atmosphere. As the men strode toward one another for an uncertain meeting, their faces were etched with strain. Neither man in all their years of negotiating had ever embraced before, as is the normal customary greeting of Cypriots, preferring instead to rely on a handshake and a flippant joke to reacquaint themselves.

This first meeting between the men, since the events of Turkey's landing, saw both men dispense with their usual politeness and hug each other warmly before kissing each other briefly on the cheeks. Clerides then opened negotiations with a practical statement reminding Rauf that they both had to work hard towards 'saving the situation'. Rauf readily agreed and yet another round of talks began.

The primary concern, at least for Rauf, was the plight of the Turkish Cypriots stranded in the South after the events had caused a division of the island. Several thousand Cypriots were residing unwillingly in areas on both the north and south of the divide. Clerides, however, was adamantly working on a different agenda: he had received a warning from Makarios (still residing outside Cyprus) that the subject of acquired territory by Turkey needed to be addressed with his vain hope that Turkey would diminish her hold.

Rauf and Clerides, each certain of their objective, embarked on a series of humanitarian-based talks in an attempt to settle the Cypriots who had been swept up in the conflict and separated from their respective communities. The talks, held in Vienna, were lengthy discourses that raised and disappointed the expectations of both men in equal turns.

Rauf argued emphatically for an exchange of population which Clerides, under pressure from his superior, Makarios, was reluctant to agree to. Clerides held fast to Makarios' principles to regain an integrated Cypriot community that would allow a Greek Cypriot administration and bias. In spite of their fierce opposition and differences of opinion in the early meetings, Rauf managed to raise the point of population exchange eloquently enough to place Clerides in a difficult position with Makarios.

Clerides walked away from one particular conference and straight into a rebuke from the Archbishop for caving in to Rauf's demands and not making more headway over territory. At the Archbishop's insistence, Clerides was expected to take a more proactive stance in the next meeting.

In the second round of the talks, Clerides was on his feet speaking passionately at great length in defiant refusal of allowing an exodus of Cypriots and determined to draw Rauf in over the question of territorial concern. As Clerides warmed to his subject, Rauf remained unusually silent without offering up any of his usual interjections. Instead, with his head bowed, Rauf wrote vigorously in his notebook only glancing up to offer a bland expression of indifference on his face to Clerides when a pause had occurred during the talking.

With his pen racing noisily across the page punctuated with the occasional theatrical sigh, Rauf's behaviour began to irk Clerides. 'For Heaven's sake Denktaş what are you writing?' he asked in exasperation.

Rauf deliberately took his time to finish writing his last sentence before looking up. "Oh, my dear Clerides," he offered with a smile. "Are you not aware you can be hanged for what you're saying? I'm making sure I get every single word you say down on paper — I intend to gather all the evidence I can!"

Rauf's wit had Clerides perplexed and he gently lowered himself back into his seat, speechless. However, Rauf noticed with a wry smile, at the next meeting, Clerides poised his pen at a rakish angle before brandishing it at Rauf with dramatic flourish. After making the gesture, Clerides then began writing with furious intent whilst keeping a bemused expression on his face.

The scribbling in notebooks may have initially served to antagonise Clerides and later provide some light relief but Rauf was serious about securing the right for Turkish Cypriots to relocate to the north.

The difficulty in achieving such an agreement lay with Makarios, who feared a population exchange would lead to a permanent division. Although he was happy at the estrangement of the two communities, Makarios was adamant that Turkish Cypriots should not occupy any part of Cyprus under their own separate administration.

Clerides had his hands firmly tied by Makarios which Rauf had to find a way to loosen. He knew Clerides could be a reasonable man from his years of interaction and would make decisions based on a sensible advantage. Rauf's own advantage was his stubbornness and having the support of his community which he fully intended to exploit.

Rauf combined the two favourable assets he possessed to overcome Clerides' intransigence by imposing a simple threat knowing that Makarios would be warned to take it seriously: if an agreement could not be reached in Vienna, he stated his intentions to call upon all Turkish Cypriot citizens (who wanted to leave the South), on a certain day at a particular hour to walk to the north; should there be any opposition, Rauf sternly advised, the Turkish army would be in swift attendance to ensure their safe passage.

Clerides was left in no doubt from Rauf's fixed look that the threat was not an idle one. The Turkish army had already proved to be a formidable and, so far, unstoppable force. Resistance to Rauf's proposition for allowing the exodus would only ignite further violence and produce more blood-stained scenes that Greek Cypriot administrators needed to avoid. After frantic conversations with Makarios, Clerides assented to the proposals which Rauf later described as a 'hard fought round'.

The dispute had ended in Rauf's favour but he was not content to accept an agreement that would be open to interpretation, and worse, could be stretched enough to lead to more dialogue — he wanted immediate action without any hindrance. Rauf knew this might only be achieved if proceedings received the international community's blessing.

His close friend and ally Vedat Çelik had been in attendance at the meetings and was impressed at how Rauf artfully managed to make the population exchange agreement a binding one with an international stamp of approval. According to Vedat, Rauf began putting forward a series of sly suggestions referring to the limited resources of the Turkish Cypriots. He pointed out with a beguiling smile to Clerides that his community did not possess large modes of transport in which to carry their belongings for the migration to the north; nor did they have any hope of organising a large scale operation to ferry busloads of villagers out. After each example demonstrating Turkish Cypriots' lack, Rauf was quick to assuage the problems by suggesting the UN should organise the process 'as a neutral party'.

Clerides accepted each of Rauf's suggestions as reasonable which naturally had included the UN's assistance. With the UN firmly locked in and committed to supplying transport and aid, documentation would be generated after each meeting requiring a signature from the UN and Clerides. The whole process was to be entirely managed by the UN which Vedat concluded had only been due to 'Rauf's gentle encouragement.'

As the action had been witnessed and executed by the UN it meant that the agreement (known as the Vienna lll Communiqué) was watertight and not able to be reneged on. It was a small victory for Rauf but for one grateful Turkish Cypriot, the Third Vienna Agreement, signed on 2nd August 1975, meant his entire village was able to relocate to the north. Kenan Atakol, wrote about his experiences in his book *Turkish and Greek Cypriots, Is Their Separation Permanent,* maintaining the villagers of Yayla 'were all jubilant and happy' at having made it safely to the north. He highlighted how crossing the border was a treacherous journey with many Turkish Cypriots losing their lives trying to get across the borders but the assistance of the UN had been able to guarantee their protection, as Rauf had known it would.

Little has been recognised regarding the obstacles Rauf faced to secure the agreement and its success of resettling Cypriots. In fact, the Vienna lll Agreement is often maligned by the Greek Cypriot administration that chose to view the independent migration of Cypriots as compulsory. In later years, Aytuğ Plümer (later to become the under-secretary for the Foreign Minister under Talat's administration) felt forced to defend Rauf's success in the Vienna talks and wrote to the General Assembly Security Council in December 1997. He reminded the Council of how 'displaced persons [were] settled' as a result of the agreements and not as the Greek Cypriots claimed by a forced expulsion.

Apart from the settlement of Cypriots in 'their own respective territory' Plümer also pointed out another important aspect of the Vienna agreements: he went on to suggest, with Cypriots safely segregated, the agreement had paved 'the way for a bi-zonal settlement of the Cyprus question.' And it was the very question of Cyprus' 'bi-zonal' status in 1975 that had raised the heckles of Makarios.

The Vienna talks had been surprisingly swift (they had begun with the first round of talks on 28th April 1975 and concluded by 2nd August of the same year) and Rauf felt strongly about the accomplishments that were achieved by himself and Clerides. He was optimistic about the ground covered and believed positive steps in the right direction had been taken. Makarios, however, did not share the same enthusiasm. He had returned in December, 1974, regained control of the Presidency and immediately set about putting his house in order. Shortly after the Vienna agreements Makarios expressed his displeasure with Clerides' performance and removed him from the negotiating table with Rauf. His source of ire had been the population exchange and the long term effect this proposed.

It wasn't until nearly two years after the Vienna III Agreement had been signed that Makarios agreed to make the diplomatic effort and meet with Rauf beginning the inter-communal talks again. Rauf had taken the initiative and invited Makarios to a summit meeting on 27th January, 1977, which coincided with Rauf's 53rd birthday. The talks were to be held in a less than glamorous environment — Nicosia airport, but were at least on home soil in Cyprus allowing both parties to feel comfortable.

Under the auspices of the UN with the UN special representative Javier Peréz de Cuéllar attending, Makarios and Rauf entered the conference room and began to eye each other warily. The protracted silence was broken by Makarios who was the first to offer a winsome smile mentioning he knew that it was Rauf's birthday. With his fixed smile still in place, Makarios politely asked Rauf how old he was. Rauf mustered a smile of his own and replied he was 23-years-old. A quizzical look from Makarios, prompted Rauf to elaborate further that he didn't 'count the last 30 years of living under your policy of *enosis* as having lived.'

Makarios appeared unruffled by Rauf's slight although an icy atmosphere threatened to settle on the conference. Peréz de Cuéllar attempted to ease tensions with a short introduction encouraging the two sides to continue in a conciliatory manner. Makarios was the first to take the floor and declared his intentions to 'accept a federal solution to our problem' for the sake of safeguarding an independent Cyprus. However, before Makarios would proceed with the talks he first wanted to ascertain if the Turkish Cypriot side were genuinely interested in working together with the Greek Cypriot administration for the benefit of a federal solution. It was also to be an opportunity for Makarios to take a swipe at Rauf for claiming to be President of an unrecognised Turkish Cypriot administration.

A letter sent to Makarios from Rauf a few weeks earlier had provoked outrage. The offending missive had been signed off with Rauf declaring himself the 'President of the Turkish Federated State'. Makarios bristled at Rauf's intentions to be seen as a President and launched into a long tirade aimed at reminding Rauf of his lower status. He stated in punctuated tones at the meeting that he most certainly did not recognise Rauf with such a title; Rauf was instead to be recognised by him in the lesser form of 'leader of the Turkish Cypriot community'.

Rauf was not about to be outdone by Makarios' haughty attitude and indicated he was equally affronted and determined to hold onto his self imposed title. Staring defiantly at Makarios across the table, he shot back a scathing response: "neither do I recognise you as President of the Republic of Cyprus," he spat. It was Makarios, however, who ended with the last word on the subject. "I know it," he drawled disdainfully. "Others, however, throughout the world, do recognise me."

Both leaders eventually settled for stifled politeness in a bid to continue the meeting constructively. Makarios, in a largely repetitive speech, challenged Rauf on his views and sincerity to work towards achieving federation. Rauf was forced to state 'at least three times that the Turkish side aims are for the creation of a federal state and not a confederation.'

Although Rauf was on record for agreeing to federation, Vedat Çelik, who had also been present at the conference, candidly admitted that Rauf had only ever felt the opposite. Despite his denials to Makarios, Rauf believed that confederation was the only viable solution for Turkish Cypriots. He had privately admitted to being bitterly disappointed that the population exchange in 1975 had not altered Cyprus' path. In his opinion, Turkey had missed an opportunity in its failure to establish independence and legitimise Turkish Cypriots now living separately after the Vienna agreements. "They wanted to leave it to the international community," Rauf had later rationalised — although he did accept the timing for Turkey couldn't have been worse as she was battling her own internal problems.

Despite Turkey's reluctance to intervene and create a separate Turkish Cypriot state, Rauf was not deterred and on the advice of Turkey pushed for federation as being the most likely springboard to securing independence at a later time. Makarios had also agreed to move forward and consider the best approach to implementing federation. However, in keeping with Makarios' usual pedantic behaviour, he wanted preliminary discussions to identify specific ground rules. The lengthy discussions with Rauf, Makarios hoped, would first lead to an undertaking that 'basic principles' would be agreed upon.

Makarios had already consented, albeit with a guarded view, to the population exchange. This in turn had led to an official recognition of the demographic changes that couldn't be denied later by Makarios. His acceptance of the segregated status of Greek and Turkish Cypriots gave hope to Rauf (as well as the many Turkish Cypriots now living in safety) that the division would be permanent. By March 1977, Makarios had appeared to have mellowed considerably further and offered a statement suggesting contrition: "I regret many things and most of all *enosis* on my part," he was cited in print as saying to a Danish correspondent.

Unfortunately, it was Makarios' death a few months later, in August 1977, that ended any thoughts of how he proposed to make amends or, more importantly, produce an executable plan with Rauf for federation; his death did, however, produce endless speculation. In a wistful conversation with Vedat, several decades later, Rauf spoke at great length on what might have been — had Makarios lived. The two seasoned politicians stretched the realms of possibilities using suppositional methods to ponder how far Makarios might have gone. "Who knew what 'federation' meant to him?" Vedat claimed Rauf had asked himself. "It's possible that had he lived the Cyprus question may have been solved."

According to Vedat, Rauf had indulged himself with an entertaining theory that Makarios may well have been genuine with his consideration for federation. It was an unusual departure from Rauf's confirmed opinion that Makarios would always cling to *enosis* and its ideological path of unification with Greece. Rauf had apparently reasoned that Makarios had agreed in principle to a federation solution for Cyprus and could only have continued to see it through to fruition. Despite never making his opinions public on the subject, Rauf's view was hotly contested by Makarios' successor, Archbishop Chrysostomos II.

During a ceremony in January 2013, to mark Makarios' contributions as the first President of the Republic of Cyprus, Archbishop Chrysostomos II stated Makarios would have withdrawn 'his support for a federation in Cyprus if he were alive today.' Dashing Rauf's proposed theory that Makarios had accepted the notion of federation, Chrysostomos went on to imply that Makarios had been coerced into accepting a federative solution: "Makarios accepted a federation with much heartache...simply because he had to make that concession to solve the national issue..."

Rauf's own contemplations on the subject usually began and ended with frustration. The 'Cyprus problem', as it had become known as, had raged on over the decades after Makarios' death causing endless disappointments for Rauf. An unsettled Cyprus hung precariously in the balance as the talks continued after 1977 yielding no satisfactory solution. The uncertainty was to leave Rauf surmising the talks with Makarios had only ended as a result of his death; with Makarios' successors, however, the talks would consistently end in failure as the two sides perpetually disagreed.

Despite Makarios' contradictions (which were frequently accompanied with a temperamental outburst) Rauf had still managed to forge a working relationship with him that suggested a solution might have been achieved. Unfortunately the relationship would not be mirrored in Makarios' successor, Spyros Kyprianou.

After meeting with Kyprianou, Rauf felt the chances of reaching an agreement were less favourable than with his long-time adversary, Makarios. Of all the representatives for the Greek Cypriot government, Rauf found Kyprianou the most difficult to deal with. He knew without a shadow of a doubt that Kyprianou was not a man he could negotiate his way round the Cyprus table with; for his own part, Kyprianou immediately set about undoing any progress that had been made under his late leader, Makarios.

Left to right, **Archbishop Makarios, UN Secretary-General Dr. Kurt Waldheim and Rauf, February 1977.**

Left to right, **Makarios' successor Spyros Kyprianou, UN Secretary-General Dr. Kurt Waldheim and Rauf during the conclusion of the 10-Point Agreements, May 1979**

Rauf with his close friend and ally Vedat Çelik.

CHAPTER FIFTEEN
The Archbishop's Heel

IN the post-era of Makarios, a long and arduous decade with Kyprianou beckoned for Rauf. Kyprianou was a seasoned and staunch hardliner who had been an active campaigner for *enosis*. His approach to the Cyprus issue not only conflicted with Rauf's own but also contradicted Makarios' final acceptance of a solution based on federation. He disputed that Makarios had agreed to the existence of two political bodies based on territory and viewed the notion of bi-zonality with deep suspicion. Kyprianou's deep-seated resistance would complicate matters later for the inter-communal talks as it became the push Rauf needed to make a controversial decision. This would lead to an arrangement which would prove both challenging and changing for the political environment in which future Turkish Cypriots would negotiate.

Kyprianou shared some similarities with Rauf as a determined character and veteran on the issues pertaining to Cyprus. Whilst studying business and then law in London, as a young man who had barely turned twenty, Kyprianou had been appointed by Makarios as a personal aide. Within only two years of the appointment, Kyprianou's status was upgraded and he was given the responsibility of promoting Makarios' objectives which included diligently 'informing the British public opinion on the Cyprus issue.' He eventually fell foul of the British authorities for 'developing sympathy' for the independence of Cyprus and was forced to quit Britain in 1956. Expulsion from Britain did not appear to dampen Kyprianou's ambitions or loyalty to Makarios whom he had known since childhood. Just one year later, still under the Archbishop's sponsorship, he reappeared in New York to again press the Greek Cypriot cause.

These experiences gave Kyprianou an early education in Greek-influenced ideologies that would later shape his own political agenda to see Cyprus become Greek; it also gave him a valuable introduction to the influential players, with allegiances to Makarios, whose edicts he would claim to follow religiously; and later, as the legally-accepted President of Cyprus, Kyprianou worked tirelessly to convince the international community to accept a solution based on a Greek Cypriot-occupied administration.

Kyprianou obstinately rejected any notion of a partition of Cyprus but didn't appear to be keen on any concepts that allowed for Turkish Cypriots to be an influential partnership in administration either. On the advice of Turkey, and under Rauf's leadership, the Turkish Cypriot community had already declared The Turkish Federated State of Cyprus* in 1975 and had continually asked each successive Greek Cypriot leadership to also form a federated state from which The Federal Republic of Cyprus could be then established.

It came as no surprise to Rauf that Kyprianou and his government rigorously fought against recognising any aspect of a Turkish Cypriot administration. Echoing the sentiments of his predecessor, Kyprianou considered Turkish Cypriots

"The Turkish Federated State of Cyprus (in Turkish: *Kıbrıs Türk Federe Devleti*) was declared on 13th February 1975 with Rauf Denktaş as its President until 15 October 1983. Amongst the international community it was recognised by Turkey only.

a troublesome handicap and snatched every opportunity to downplay their legitimacy and eliminate their influence over the future of Cyprus.

Rauf's iconic status as the leader of the Turkish Cypriot community would also be used against him to sabotage any chance of reconciliation between the two sides. From his advantageous position as a recognised President, Kyprianou would frequently sneer at Rauf's position as the President of an unrecognised state and refused to acknowledge him as such — allowing him to use it as a pretext for declining to meet with Rauf either publicly or privately.

Kyprianou's slight to Rauf was making a less than subtle point but he was also able to have his actions indirectly supported by the international community. In New York, where both Rauf and Kyprianou addressed the UN Assembly's Political Committee, Kyprianou was given an even wider audience when he went on to address the General Assembly — the all-important debating forum — but a privilege denied Rauf as he was not representing a recognised government. Rauf instead seethed by the sidelines as Kyprianou took centre-stage and made every effort to gain the attention and sympathy from the UN for the 'plight' of Greek Cypriots.

Despite being cold shouldered by prestigious elements of the Security Council Rauf attempted to reach out to Kyprianou on a private level. He sent a polite invitation to Kyprianou suggesting dinner but was curtly declined. Several more attempts by Rauf were all met with the same negative response. Each rejection was grounded with a condition that claimed that to meet Rauf, in any capacity, would be accepting of his status as leader and endorsing the *status quo* which Rauf had apparently created.

Rauf was left frustrated without any recourse as all appeals to win over Kyprianou had failed.

The intentional snub to Rauf was eventually waived for the resumption of talks that began on 15th June 1979. Although Kyprianou had signed an agreement to resume the talks, he entered the discussions with misgivings and gave the impression of an unwilling participant. During their meetings, Rauf would often be aggravated by Kyprianou's reticent behaviour, which, unlike his previous liaisons with Clerides, created a stifling atmosphere. Clerides had been an entertaining negotiator and both he and Rauf had injected some life into the meetings with their banter.

Rauf had not been able to 'warm' to Kyprianou and complained within the privacy of his inner circle that he had been a difficult man and certainly somebody he 'could not share a coffee with.' According to Rauf, Kyprianou was devoid of a sense of humour — at least with him, and frequently remained tight-lipped in an all too obvious attempt to avoid even polite conversation. In characteristic style, Rauf would seek to ease the tense atmosphere and loosen Kyprianou's terse attitude with humour.

Rauf's entertaining anecdotes would elicit guffaws of laughter from most in the conference room but his jovial efforts were met with a deafening wall of silence from Kyprianou who refused to be drawn in. Throughout their meetings, Kyprianou instead maintained a stiff countenance shifting only to offer a disapproving glare.

Despite Rauf's failure to prise a smile from Kyprianou's expressionless face, it had no real bearing on the outcome of the meetings. Of more concern to Rauf was Kyprianou's 'obsession' with resurrecting Makarios' Hellenistic legacy to make Cyprus wholly Greek. It would have a notable affect on the meetings and made working toward a solution impossible. Furthermore, Kyprianou's inability to introduce any flexibility into Makarios' policies turned him into a petty adversary with poor negotiating skills causing more frustration for Rauf.

Kyprianou exhibited an exasperating tendency to disrupt the inter-communal talks with his indecisiveness which Rauf deposited the blame for on Greece. An obvious pattern was emerging Rauf noted after each meeting. With the support of the UN's Secretary General's Representative, Peréz de Cuéllar, the representatives were able to break through some of their opposing points and subsequently arrive at viable solutions which Kyprianou appeared to initially agree on. Unfortunately for the talks, the meetings would then be followed with a jaunt by Kyprianou to Greece.

Heavily influenced by Greece, Kyprianou would back-pedal on the settlements reached and return with a fresh set of demands. As well as spending fruitless hours in meetings, Kyprianou saw to it that the two sides were never able to move beyond verbal discussions and allow agreements to be formalised with his signature.

In an address to Strasbourg on 23rd April 2002, Rauf ventured his opinions very publicly on Kyprianou's attitude towards the talks. Although Kyprianou had died just weeks before on 12th March 2002, an unrepentant Rauf stated the difficulty lay with Kyprianou's loyalty to 'sustain and to protect the will and testament of Makarios.' Rauf also hinted at Kyprianou's arrogance in the same speech referring to how 'proud' Kyprianou was for not agreeing to any solution that involved a partnership of the two communities.

The 'pride' that Rauf alluded to reared its ungainly head constantly in the shape of Greece. Kyprianou was openly known to have little regard for Turkish Cypriot welfare and harboured a deep-seated prejudice towards them and, coupled with Greece's influence, it greatly impinged on his ability to accept a concept which offered balance for both communities.

Kyprianou had viewed the difficult years prior to 1974 as a 'golden age' that had enabled a Greek Cypriot influenced administration to keep a controlling hand over their Turkish Cypriot neighbours. Greece undoubtedly reminded Kyprianou of the benefits gained from having a superior and fortified position for a Greek Cypriot administration, and to lose it would spell disaster for Greece's long-term plans for Cyprus.

However, Kyprianou's loyalty to Greece would backfire on him. His dogged determination toward expelling any Turkish Cypriot influence earned him the unflattering reputation of being intransigent even amongst his own peers. Dignitaries and Ministers alike grew increasingly tired of Kyprianou's stubborn behaviour and vented their frustrations publicly. Kyprianou's Foreign Minister, Nicos Rolandis, openly criticised him — even going as far as to refer to Kyprianou as the 'enemy of Cyprus.'

Whilst Kyprianou continued to disrupt the talks, and provoke both communities, privately Rauf was delighted as it gave him some respite from the international demands seeking a solution. Several years after their contact Rauf quipped during an interview that Kyprioanou 'made my job easier.'

Rauf was shrewd enough to realise the media backlash meant much of the international pressure being exerted was then mainly borne by Kyprianou. Playing to the advantage, Rauf instead spent his time monitoring Kyprianou angering his own compatriots as well as unsettling an anxious international community. By 1983, however, Rauf was no longer willing to just sit back. He watched with dismay as a smug Kyprianou returned from one of his excursions to

Greece boldly exhibiting a victorious sign made famous by Churchill. It was Kyprianou's response to rejecting yet another agreement brokered by the now UN Secretary General, Peréz de Cuéllar. The defiant gesture left Rauf feeling he had no more options open to him.

Earlier in the year, Kyprianou had again suspended talks and was refusing to continue dialogue with Rauf. Resorting to his age-old ploy, Kyprianou cited his reasons as not wishing to be seen encouraging the notion that Rauf was an equal head-of-state. It was a destructive action that left the talks *in situ* and sparked anger and despair in the communities on both sides.

The criticism levelled at Rauf's political rank was swiftly met. Rauf, backed by Turkish Cypriot leaders, would reason that Kyprianou's refusal to negotiate with 'a person of inferior status' could only be answered by raising his status.

Rauf was already the widely-accepted choice as leader amongst his own community but he needed the acceptance of the international community. His own community had become adept at providing for itself (albeit with Turkey's aid) but it too needed to shed its stateless system and acquire stability. Both issues could only be resolved by declaring independence for Turkish Cypriots and Rauf decided the time had come to send the message that Turkish Cypriots would no longer play the inferior cousin to their Greek Cypriot counterparts.

It was a monumental undertaking and Turkey's continued military and economical support remained essential. Rauf reasoned the Greek Cypriots had the political advantage which had completely isolated the north side and decided to plough on regardless.

Discussions began in earnest during the summer of 1983, with Rauf and his like-minded allies, and centred around the prospect of creating an official state. They argued that the foundations of a government were already in place — it was simply lacking an official status. The 'imbalance did not allow a settlement' Rauf went on to protest to Turkey. Fortunately, Turkey had also become exasperated with the ongoing talks and accepted Rauf's frustrations as being legitimate; it was no longer acceptable to remain known in simple terms as 'the community' whilst Kyprianou and his administration were deemed the 'Government of Cyprus.'

Rauf didn't anticipate any resistance to the proposal from the Turkish Cypriot Parliament to declare independence, and knew that public opinion would be with him, but chose to be discreet and not make direct announcements — contradicting his usual habit of venturing into public with passion-filled speeches to elicit support.

Even with family and friends, Rauf remained oddly coy on the subject and took pains to steer conversations away from the topic when questioned. One close friend had spoken to him just days before the issue went to vote in the Parliament of the Turkish Federated State of Cyprus and spoke of his surprise at Rauf offering no hint of the exciting announcement to come. Rauf did break his silence, however, to visit an old friend who had initiated him into the annals of the Cyprus problem and had also played a vital role in trying to solve it — Dr. Küçük.

The two men had at one point in their own shared history become estranged as they wrangled very publicly over their differences. Their infamous war of words, waged in Küçük's own newspaper, had divided loyalties amongst the Turkish Cypriots as well as placing a strain on their personal relationship. Although clearly affected, relations had not been completely severed between the two. Rauf's ambitious nature had prevented him from alienating Dr. Küçük who still held an iconic place in the heart of the Turkish Cypriot community. Rauf paid a visit to Dr. Küçük (now suffering from cancer caused by years of endless chain-smoking) in an ill-disguised attempt to gain his support before he headed to Turkey. Rauf knew of Küçük's failing health but had hoped the news of the long-awaited birth of the TRNC* would act both as a peace-offering and soothing balm.

To Rauf's consternation, his intended grand gesture was met with only a lukewarm reception and instead received a barrage of worried questions from the ailing Küçük. Dr Küçük was a pragmatic man and did not immediately embrace the suggestion for an independent state. He had mixed feelings which mainly stemmed from his concerns about possible repercussions that could be expected from the Greek Cypriot side.

He offered Rauf a slew of examples as to how the Greek Cypriots could terminate shared services including the provision of power and LPG cooking gas which was still being supplied to the north by the Greek Cypriot south. He advised Rauf to consider waiting until the Turkish Cypriot side had time to be fully self-sufficient and prolonging the declaration for six months or even a year until the issues could be resolved.

Küçük had known that Rauf was headstrong and unlikely to heed his advice but he was a tired man who had conceded the reins to Rauf years previously. The outcome was inevitable for North Cyprus and any misgivings Küçük felt were not evident on the day of the declaration.

---

*Turkish Republic of Northern Cyprus (in Turkish: *Kuzey Kıbrıs Turk Cumhuriyeti*) is a self-declared state rejected by the UN and the Republic of Cyprus and only recognised by Turkey. The TRNC proclaimed its independence from the Republic of Cyprus on 15th November 1983 with Rauf as its first President and Nejat Konuk as its first Prime Minister.

As crowds of excited Turkish Cypriots surged into the divided capital of Nicosia*, they were greeted with a trio of proud men which included Küçük and Osman Örek, waving enthusiastically from a balcony overlooking Atatürk Square.

Several years after Küçük's death, Rauf would airbrush away any suggestion of doubt in conversations by claiming Dr. Küçük had been 'excited' about the impending declaration and had no concerns. 'He had been moved to tears,' insisted Rauf whose memories of the doctor's reaction had also seen him offering at once his support and allegiance. More importantly, Rauf was satisfied that the pair had 'made up' and had put their warring past behind them.

The journey for Rauf to the eventual destination of the Presidential balcony had not entirely depended upon a nod of approval from Dr. Küçük. Over time Rauf had built a political fraternity of his own which ensured he was not without his resources or influential friends — particularly those in Turkey. He had successfully managed his campaign to bring about independence and adroitly sidestepped any opposition to his targets but this, in part, had largely been due to being on the receiving end of prestigious aid and encouragement from a handful of loyal but influential supporters.

One such friend who had keenly supported Rauf was another senior member of the politically powerful — Süleyman Demirel. He had been a close friend of Rauf's since the mid-1960s and, by the time of the impending declaration, had already served six terms as Prime Minister

---

*Nicosia (in Turkish: Lefkoşa) is the largest city and the capital of the island of Cyprus. It functions as an important economical and governmental base for Turkish and Greek Cypriots.

of Turkey. Although the military coup in 1980 saw Demirel faced with a ten-year ban from an active role in politics, he was able to shrug it off as a mere inconvenience and remained largely unaffected. Throughout his political exile he continued to meet with Rauf frequently and threw his full support behind the proposal.

Rauf was adamant that partition was the only viable solution and believed it was achievable with Turkey's assistance. Demirel bolstered Rauf's confidence by reassuring him that Turkey would not leave Turkish Cypriots to fend for themselves. The Greek Cypriots' only real power was in their ability to isolate Turkish Cypriots by their being recognised as the 'sovereign' government of Cyprus. However, they could not expect to have their 'powers' restored on the whole island as Turkey was too strong and had a firm foothold on the island. Turkey would continue to support North Cyprus economically as well as militarily, Demirel concluded.

Still wielding a huge amount of influence, despite the political ban, Demirel became a compelling force who exerted all his efforts to help Rauf achieve 'self determination for his people.' He still had the ear of the Turkish government and was consulted on a regular basis by officials.

The Foreign Minister of Turkey at the time, Melih Esenbul, who had served as Ambassador in Washington during Demirel's term as Premier, also appeared unperturbed by the ban. In an unconventional move, Esenbul approached Demirel for his approval regarding the declaration of the TRNC. Demirel naturally gave a resounding 'yes'. The bold approach was later followed up with a delegation from Cyprus seeking Demirel's opinions.

Rauf and Demirel had been in complete agreement over the issue of declaring independence for the Turkish Cypriots.

Apart from the necessity of raising the Turkish Cypriot profile in politics, they believed it to be part of a natural process: the formation of an independent state would also be preserving the Turkish identity and re-establishing roots previously laid down by Turkey.

The men had bonded years previously over their shared interest and admiration for the Ottoman Empire which saw their mutual ancestors first conquer and then rule Cyprus for 300 years before leasing it to Britain in 1878. Given Cyprus' history, they both believed that Turkish Cypriots had a natural place on the island. Demirel, in particular, took pride in the Ottomans' achievements and was unmoved by any arguments suggesting Turkish Cypriots did not have any rights of stay on the island.

Unfortunately for both Rauf and Demirel, the UN did not share the same sentiments. On 18th November 1983, three days after the pomp and ceremony that accompanied the public declaration of the TRNC, the United Nations Security Council formally disapproved and made their own declaration: they adopted resolution 541 stating categorically "Northern Cyprus' decision to declare independence legally invalid." As well as urging other members of the UN club not to recognise the TRNC, the UN insisted the only valid authority should remain the Greek Cypriot government recognsed as the Republic of Cyprus.

The resolution was a huge disappointment to Rauf but it changed very little for him. Fighting against larger establishments for 'self determination' had become a way of life for Rauf and he certainly had no intention of retracting the rights of Turkish Cypriots now that he had announced their independence. It was soon after the resolution had been adopted that Rauf began a series of high-profile visits to the UN offices in New York hoping to highlight his case.

Although Rauf never made it to the floors of the General Assembly, he did find himself better received by certain sections operating within the UN offices. Rauf's presence in the UN offices was not unusual as he was accepted as the community leader of the Turkish Cypriots and received politely. However, his self-imposed title as a President (of an unrecognised country) was not tolerated and therefore not deserving of a security detail normally befitting an important position. Despite Britain having consistently communicated with Rauf over the years she never offered protection; America, on the other hand, appeared to have a different approach.

The USA installed a group of large men, complete with buzz-cuts and square jaws that towered over the much shorter Rauf, to accompany him at all times. Entering a lift with the intimidating group of men swarming around him hadn't ruffled Rauf at all but his close friend and aide, Çavlan Süerdem, was clearly intrigued by the silent rocks surrounding them.

He watched with fascination as one mound of a man raised his wrist to his mouth and delivered in a monotone voice that 'potato head' was safely in the elevator and heading towards his destination. As the lift doors sprang open and the group walked down the corridor, another impassive voice mumbled into his sleeve that 'potato head' was now on his way to the conference room.

"Mr. President, do you realise these men have code-named you Potato Head?" a captivated Süerdem revealed to Rauf in hushed tone.

"Is that so?" Rauf responded in a theatrical whisper, "I wouldn't worry too much about it as I'm quite sure potatoes are very well respected here."

Aytuğ Plümer, as a TRNC representative working closely

with Rauf, had also noted that the attention paid to Rauf's security was always a dramatic affair in New York. Plümer recalled being issued with bruising instructions on how 'your President' will be protected in the event of an attack.

Using Plümer as a model, the burly security agent demonstrated how he would need to 'grab the President by the scruff of the neck, lift him off his feet and throw him to the floor.' The action was intended to place Rauf low down to avoid any missiles that may be levelled at him. As an added precaution, the exceptionally large security handler would then land on top of Rauf to cover him from any further onslaughts. Rauf watched the demonstration with a concentrated expression throughout before asking Plümer in Turkish — 'will my security guy be trying to kill me or save me?' Plümer replied he hoped it was the latter but wished Rauf all the luck nevertheless.

Fortunately Rauf continued his visits over the years to the UN offices without incident but he made no headway in persuading the international community to accept his statehood of the TRNC; nor was he able to win approval from his counterpart, Kyprianou who would still dig in his heels at every opportunity with his refusal to meet Rauf.

Much to Rauf's annoyance, Kyprianou also continued to turn down the efforts of Peréz de Cuéllar, who produced the Draft Framework Agreement in 1984 from which the two communities were expected to negotiate. In January 1985, another modified version by the Secretary-General after a 'long and arduous shuttle diplomacy between the two Peoples,' had again not been inked with Kyprianou's signature despite indicators suggesting otherwise. The Secretary-General, under considerable pressure to reconcile the two leaders, went back to the drawing board intending to produce yet another version.

It was four months later in April that Peréz de Cuéllar's reworked draft appeared which he described as a 'consolidation' of the earlier 1984 agreement. Whilst the earlier agreement had been a comprehensive text that had satisfied both communities, the new document bore all the hallmarks of Greek Cypriot influence.

It transpired later, the new document had been negotiated with the Greek Cypriot side and had excluded Turkish Cypriot input. The document was already in possession of the Greek Cypriot side but Rauf's own first glimpse of the newly 'improved' document came from his morning perusal of the Greek Cypriot dailies. The Greek Cypriot press had managed to publish the draft before he received it from the UN leaving no doubt in Rauf's mind of the slight intended. Despite being outraged, he waited until he received confirmation of the document from the UN hours later; only then, in a calculated manner designed to embarrass the Secretary-General, did Rauf write a lengthy letter to de Cuéllar, listing his reasons for rejecting the draft before expressing his surprise at how the document had come to the public's attention before his own.

Peréz de Cuéllar's response was swift. In a bid to salvage relations he organised a round of talks between himself and each respective community for November and December later in the year and again in February and March of the following year. However, before the talks with de Cuéllar, got under way, Rauf had been busy heading up a new Constituent Assembly which had busied itself with the drafting of a new Constitution.

On its completion Rauf was delighted when the new Constitution received an overwhelming acceptance from the public after it was put to referendum on 5th May 1985.

The success of the vote by the people paved the way for

Presidential elections with Parliament setting a date for the following month. Rauf was quietly confident he would have the backing of the voters and was pleased when six out of the eight political parties also endorsed his independent candidature as President.

Although there had been no doubt in Raufs mind, on 9th June, 1985, he won a landslide victory and became the First President of the Turkish Republic of Northern Cyprus. Rauf had just barely six months to settle into the role before once again he had to confront a personal challenge that shook him to his very core.

Declaration of the Turkish Republic of Northern Cyprus, 15th November 1983. *From left to right*, **Osman Örek, Dr. Fazıl Küçük and Rauf**

Veteran Turkish Premier Süleyman Demirel greets Rauf
after the Declaration of Independence, 15th November 1983

Süleyman Demirel sharing his memories of Rauf during
an interview on 21st December 2012 at his home in
Ankara

CHAPTER SIXTEEN

An Accidental Death?

On December 23rd 1985, Rauf was spending a rare quiet evening at home when he received an alarming phone call to tell him that his eldest son, Raif, had been seriously injured in an accident. Raif taught at a university in Famagusta and was travelling back from the university campus when he inexplicably ploughed into the back of a Turkish military lorry.

The stretch of road Raif had been driving on was not well lit with street lighting at a minimum. Adding to the poor lighting conditions was the time of evening Raif had been behind the wheel: he had been working late and dusk had started to descend by the time he left for home.

However, the driving conditions would not be enough to satisfy Rauf as a possible cause for the accident. His reactions later on the accident were deeply resentful, blaming third parties, and controversial by suggesting the accident had too many rogue factors — the stationary vehicle's role in the accident would come under particular scrutiny from Rauf because of its military status.

On the night of the accident Rauf would be given little time to question the cause of the accident. He had been herded into a waiting car that careered through the streets in a dramatic effort to get him, and his wife, to his son's bedside. The wailing siren that announced their arrival at the State hospital in Lefkoşa served only to confirm the situation was critical. Despite reassurances that everything possible was being done to ensure Raif received the best medical care, his chances of survival were waning. The flurry of activity and parade of grim-faced doctors that swarmed around the intensive-care unit were enough to convince Rauf there was little time to waste.

He spent the night pacing floors and placing phone calls to various medical facilities in a bid to obtain the best advice and support for his son's care. By the following morning, Rauf's worst fears had been confirmed. Raif had suffered terrible injuries, including brain damage, leaving his future and quality of life hanging in the balance.

Rauf was faced with making a decision for his son and opted to use his influence to get a second opinion from Turkey. Believing that Lefkoşa did not have the facilities to cope with the level of specialist care needed to support his son, Rauf contacted the military with a request that their service could be utilised to provide medical assistance. Although Rauf would later play down the suggestion it was his position as a public figure that afforded his son preferential treatment, he admitted it appeared to be a substantial factor that enabled him to call on Turkey and allow special priority to be given to Raif.

The response was immediate. A military air ambulance was swiftly dispatched to take Raif to the renowned Gülhane military hospital in Ankara, Turkey where a team of specialists was assembled and ready to treat him.

Rauf and Aydın had escorted their son on his journey spending the arduous hour fretting about the outcome. Aydın had been inconsolable throughout the flight with her distress clearly visible and captured by waiting photographers despite the over-sized sunglasses worn to disguise her grief. On arrival at the hospital, the desperate parents were ushered through a private staff entrance to the corridor leading them to their son. Raif had just returned from the operating theatre after emergency surgery but his condition remained unchanged. After finally being permitted to see his son, Rauf was unable to prevent the gasp of shock he emitted when he saw the extent of Raif's injuries. Raif was lying motionless in a coma and Rauf and his wife were greeted with a gruesome image of their son who showed visible facial injuries of trauma sustained from having been thrown in a violent impact; worse was the sight of tubes protruding from his body and connected to complicated machinery obstinately keeping him alive.

The dreadful injuries and physically shocking sight of their son had a sobering effect on the parents. Forced to push aside their shock, Rauf and his wife set about keeping a determined bedside vigil as they waited for Raif to open his eyes. He never did. He died from his injuries with his mother holding his hand as Rauf silently looked on.

Raif was just 35-years-old and had been Rauf and Aydın's first-born child. Both parents had forged a close relationship with their eldest child and, Aydın, in particular, had been in close contact with him — with mother and son meeting on a regular basis up until his premature death. Their grief at losing a third child had also been compounded by the knowledge that Raif's own children — all under the age of ten, were now without a father of their own. The extended family grouped together in an effort to shield Raif's young family but each member of the Denktaş clan struggled on a deeply personal level.

The tragedy for Rauf would become a deeply painful episode that he would never come to terms with and capable of invoking a plethora of emotions from him. Over the years, like an errant pendulum, Rauf would swing hopelessly between tears and anger at the mention of Raif's name. It was particularly noticeable during interviews and when Rauf appeared at his most vulnerable. He would frequently infer that external forces had been responsible for his son's death and rage with anger at an anonymous establishment which he held accountable; often the interviews would be concluded with a visibly upset Rauf.

Rauf's mixed emotions spilled over very publicly with his revelations regarding Raif's demise but did not appear to affect his influence over the voting public. They maintained a strong confidence in his leadership and his nationalistic policies. This may in part have been due to family values being an integral part of Turkish Cypriot culture with the community expressing an understanding of the devastating loss Rauf had experienced. His public displays were met with mixed reactions but still deemed heartfelt and accepted as a result of unexpectedly losing his eldest child.

Despite the wealth of support Rauf received it didn't erase the overwhelming grief he felt. He was already dealing with the unnatural process of a parent losing a child, but had been profoundly affected by another loss: the loss of a friend. The father and son had not only been bound by the familial ties connecting them but also by their shared values and interests; and over the years, as Raif matured, these shared interests had become an integral part of their relationship.

Work had always ensured Rauf had been absent for much of his children's formative years but he had adopted a creative method to maintain a link to his children: he wrote letters to his children to remind them of him and used the medium to broach a variety of subjects.

The letters would become a useful tool and an opportunity

to mete out valuable advice based on his own experience. Raif had been much older than his younger siblings and became the first recipient of the letters that were littered with poetic references and worldly advice. It appeared Rauf had been intent on grooming his son for a productive future which included a leadership role. A heartfelt letter he once wrote to Raif was crammed with wise words but also gave clear instructions on how leaders were expected to behave. The letter was followed up with many more of Rauf's musings that he frequently penned whenever he was absent or unable to speak to his son.

Rauf's diligence and fluent penmanship had a great deal of influence over Raif whose life was remarkably similar to his father's: he too entered into teaching and politics after completing university. Raif's home life also reflected his upbringing as he mirrored his parents' relationship with a stable marriage and children. Raif's childhood friend, Mehmet Küçük, had grown up alongside the Denktaş family and also noted the similarities — although he believed the relationship between the two men was not quite the comfortable portrait that Rauf painted.

The Küçük family had been closely linked to the Denktaş clan over the decades as a result of the close working relationship between Dr. Fazıl Küçük and Rauf and their joint political contributions. The two families had at one time lived next door to each other with the Denktaş family renting a property owned by Dr. Küçük. Living in such close proximity meant the families were often together and socialising; the informal atmosphere between the families encouraging the children to slip uninhibited back and forth between the two homes.

Mehmet Küçük was about the same age as Raif and remembered with a degree of fondness the childhood they shared. Contradicting Rauf's assertions that he never had time to spend with his family, Mehmet claimed that Rauf was a brilliant father who could always be found at home and frequently showered his children with toys. "He [Rauf] would go to a toy shop called Mavros in Ledra Street where he bought toys for his children. He was like Father Christmas to us," Mehmet recalled.

Rauf's gifts to his children were expensive but always shared with the neighbouring children. Mehmet recalled how, much to the delight of all the children, Rauf had purchased an 8mm cine film projector. Rauf, who had always been passionate about westerns, complemented the purchase with a 'Cowboy and Indian' film each day for the children to watch. The projector was only able to depict films in silent mode but it did not deter the children who were entranced by the action flickering silently on screen.

Although Rauf had been generous with his children, it had not been so much for the pleasure he derived from the look on their faces. Mehmet insisted Rauf's tendency to indulge his children had stemmed from his 'flamboyant' nature and the need for ostentatious displays; and all too often looking for approval.

Rauf freely admitted his grand gestures to his family were an act of over-compensating for his absenteeism from home but Mehmet offered his own perspective — a different side of Rauf that was rarely discussed but was well known: his egotistical nature.

Rauf's 'flamboyancy' would frequently surface as he craved attention and deliberately tried to impress those around him — regardless of whether that was a member of his family or the public. With a shake of his head, Mehmet offered that typically Rauf resorted to behaviour that would earn the public's attention rather than their respect; unlike his own father, Dr. Küçük, who had a distinctly different method that was designed to support the community rather than excite a fanfare from them.

Mehmet felt the differences between the two men could be easily defined by their alliances during the troubled years of Cyprus: Rauf had been a well-known associate of the armed TMT which was later criticised for being responsible for killing Turkish and Greek Cypriots alike. Dr. Küçük, on the other hand, had founded *Volkan** which had claimed to be a passive resistance that even the Greek Cypriots had respected. For Mehmet, it was proof enough of Rauf's gung-ho attitude versus the calmer attributes of Dr. Küçük that could be clearly seen by the different resistance movements each man had aligned himself with.

Whilst bitter clashes between Dr. Küçük and Rauf were frequent and often made public, Mehmet claimed that Rauf was also experiencing problems with his son at home. Raif had inherited his father's brash nature and dominating personality, according to Mehmet, which caused friction. Arguments were not an uncommon occurrence inside the Denktaş home and was apparently enough to drive Raif to seek solace in Dr. Küçük's 'calm' demeanour.

Mehmet's assertion that the spats between father and son would prompt Raif to confide in Dr. Küçük 'more than his own father,' did not impact on Raif's anger when he felt his father had been insulted. In a weekly newspaper he established, Raif rushed to his father's defence aimed at Dr. Küçük's criticism towards Rauf (regarding his administration after the events of 1974) with the cutting headline: "Dr. Fazıl, are you now working for the Greek Cypriots?"

---

*Volkan (in English: Volcano) was an early Turkish Cypriot movement created in the early 1950s in response to the emergence of EOKA. It was an armed resistance organisation that preceded TMT but eventually replaced by TMT.

The defensive action implied Raif had a great deal of respect for his father which was reciprocated. Father and son had developed a mutual respect and friendship stemming from them finding common ground that both men were able to relate to. As well as being a journalist and teacher, Raif had pursued a career in politics and was passionate about Cyprus. He had strong opinions and, not unlike Rauf, was not afraid to voice them even when they didn't coincide with his father's. His objections would often upset the political apple cart that would anger his Rauf's supporters.

Raif had been a staunch member of his father's political party until his attempts to break away and start his own party. Shortly before his death Raif had founded the Turkish Cypriot Social Democratic Party. He failed to win a seat in the parliamentary elections but still managed to rile the elders of Rauf's political allies and enemies alike. It was seen as a betrayal by some of Rauf's peers and an impulsive move by others who queried his motives.

Raif also had to contend with accusations of nepotism as about the same time of his failed attempts to win seats in parliament, his father had appointed him Special Political Advisor to the President. There were many who viewed Raif as being too young and inexperienced for the role leading to calls of preferential treatment. The charge was constantly being answered by Rauf who argued his son was more than qualified having cut his teeth growing up in a political atmosphere and was European-educated (Raif had been an Oxford University graduate).

Throughout the years, Raif never lost the support of his father. Rumours began circulating after Raif's death claiming Rauf had been extremely upset by some of his son's views and actions. Refuting the rumours in interviews years later, Rauf insisted he had always been proud of Raif but their familial relationship meant he could not be seen to support him publicly. However, Raif was a controversial figure who often forced Rauf to walk a thin line between his duty as a President and his emotions as a father.

As the son of the TRNC President, Raif found himself constantly under scrutiny and on more than one occasion at the mercy of publications looking to defame his family name. One such headline to cause worry appeared in the popular Turkish newspaper, *Hürriyet*. It openly claimed Raif had been harbouring a public enemy suspected of murder and terrorism, Hüseyin Kocabaş, who was wanted for questioning over the murder of the then Public Prosecutor, Doğan Öz.

Rauf was in New York at the time with Kyprianou when he was called by his son in an agitated state. Raif, who always sought his father's counsel, would also seek out Rauf when he needed reassurance. He had been distressed by the news item and horrified by the apparent association made about himself and a terrible crime. Also at stake was the damage to his image and the portrayal of a shady criminal being painted of him. He dreaded his children being made aware of the accusation and how he would explain it.

Raif had been raised in a high-profile family and had worked hard to raise his own independent profile — publicly as a political party member and as a university lecturer — and feared his life would be left in tatters by the false allegations.

Rauf advised his son that a public figure could always expect to be hauled across the pages of the media but this situation, and its libellous nature, warranted taking the case to court. Raif duly followed his father's instruction and started an action to sue the publication which later resulted in a judgement in Raif's favour and the sum of 50,000 TL being paid by way of an apology. Rauf, however, remained concerned. Although he didn't express his thoughts to Raif, he feared that the action, whilst bringing a triumphant outcome, would still not be enough to repair the damage to his son's reputation.

BEFORE his return home, Rauf had a pre-arranged meeting with Bülent Ecevit in Ankara to discuss the events that took place in New York. Although the former premier was banned from active politics (like Demirel, he had become a political casualty of the 1980 military coup in Turkey), his influence and experience were still recognised. Rauf also held a great deal of respect for Ecevit who had been responsible for Turkey alighting on Cyprus' shores in 1974 during the conflict. Although the meeting with Ecevit was intended to discuss issues relevant to the talks on Cyprus in New York it became dominated by Rauf's personal issues.

Rauf made no apology for using the time to express his outrage and upset at the defamatory storm that had been whipped up over his son. It was the surname of Denktaş that had fired the imagination of the media, Rauf protested to Ecevit, and Raif was 'paying the price'.

Ecevit didn't have any children of his own but managed to sympathise with Rauf's fatherly concerns. He assured Rauf that the Turkish intelligence officers present in Cyprus would certainly know if a wanted fugitive was hiding in Raif's home and would have apprehended him immediately; Ecevit regarded this as proof enough of Raif's innocence.

Rauf argued that it wasn't the falseness of the report — he was satisfied his son would be found innocent — but rather the damage to Raif's name that was the concern.

The pragmatic stance by Ecevit hadn't appeased Rauf but he admitted later that his intention had been to get the former premier's attention: he had succeeded in lodging his complaint with one of the highest authorities of the time and he had extracted a sympathetic attitude towards Raif.

Despite being exonerated from any wrong-doing and incurring compensation, it seemed *Hürriyet* had not finished with Raif. A few months prior to his death another scandalous story appeared alleging that Raif had been part of a drugs ring operating in Cyprus. The story had formed its roots from the statement of a suspect being held in custody for drug-running who claimed Raif had been an accomplice.

The accusation was lacking in evidence and based on one suspect's testimony but it gathered momentum and piqued the public's interest. Raif again turned to his father who repeated his advice of battling the publication through the courts. Rauf's keen sense of the law and legal skills had no doubt influenced the counsel that he gave to his son; Raif, however, was not as confident a second time round. He had once more been thrust into the limelight of negative attention and was deeply troubled by the affect it would have on his children. He became withdrawn, clearly tormented by the new set of allegations. Rauf tried to console his son and offered his own experiences. "I've been called everything under the sun," he volunteered, "has any of it stuck?"

Raif bore many of his father's traits but did not appear to have inherited his father's thick skin and could not be convinced, instead sinking further into depression. He had written to the *Hürriyet* for the second time protesting his innocence but the newspaper declined to publish his comments reducing his morale even further. It was whilst Raif was faced with the challenge of proving his innocence that he was killed in a traffic accident. Rauf, consumed with grief, immediately set about finding a scapegoat to take responsibility. Threatened with the possibility of being ruined by the allegations, Rauf rushed to his son's defence claiming he had been under immense 'psychological pressure' and in a 'confused state of mind'—all factors which had contributed to Raif's cause of death. In darker times Rauf would hint that the strain Raif was under had been caused by certain parties, making them the perpetrators of his son's death— holding the MİT*, in particular, responsible.

During an interview with a reporter from *Vatan Gündem* Rauf hinted at the coincidence of Raif driving into the back of a Turkish military vehicle. As the journalist probed further, Rauf's trace suspicions gave way to vehement passion of condemnation adamantly stating his 'son died because of MİT'. To justify the claim he reminded his audience of the politically difficult time: he had been 'engaged in an argument' with Turkey over the signing of a draft framework agreement presented by the UN for a bi-zonal, bi-communal** federal Republic.

The parties concerned with the agreement had apparently not been directly involved in the drafting although they had been briefed on its contents. Under pressure from Turkey, Rauf eventually agreed to sign the document on the basis that the details would be worked out in separated talks. Kyprianou refused to sign and the 1985 summit collapsed.

* The National Intelligence Organisation (in Turkish: *Milli İstihbarat Teşkilatı*) was established in 1965 (to replace the National Security Service) and is the governmental intelligence organisation of Turkey.

**. There are conflicting views on the definition of bizonality and bicommunality between Turkish and Greek Cypriots. In the recent Joint Declaration, the terms are rephrased as the Turkish Constituent State and the Greek Constituent State. However, for the Turkish side this means two zones whereby the majority of populations will be Turkish and Greek respectively; whereas the Greek side considers this a temporay arrangement for a maximum of seven to ten years.

Although the failure of the talks had been disappointing, particularly for Turkey who had stressed the need for a solution, the tension arising from Turkey's insistence on Rauf's acquiescence to sign had created discord and disrupted political unity. All of which came at a personal cost for Rauf who insisted he was being 'leant on quite hard' as well as enduring malicious character assassinations in the press. The smear campaigns that accompanied the pressure were not just restricted to him. According to Rauf his son's own public spats with *Hürriyet* were a direct result of the 'muddying campaigns' too. The outcome saw Raif's journey to and fro from the university conducted under stress 'and that is when he had the accident' Rauf flatly pointed out.

Raif was given a military honour service at his funeral which left Rauf feeling profoundly dissatisfied. "What's the use?" he would utter later when referring to the service. Rauf had instead begun to feel his political life had encroached on his personal life with dramatic consequences too hard to ignore. He began to question the sources of information that had led to the offending article and once again used his influence to extract information.

He wrote to several government departments in Ankara with no attempt at careful wording. Demonstrating his outrage, Rauf let slip his anger whilst demanding answers. "I had been defending a common national problem with sacrifice," he curtly informed his reader before adding "it is unfortunate that my son hit a military lorry and died in consequence." Rauf then made clear the point that his son died with a 'constant worry' looming precariously over his head. For the family to be able to move on it was imperative for them to have answers and know that Raif was innocent of the accusations he added.

Luckily for Rauf one of the recipients of his letter was a Commander who had been a part of military operations in 1974. His work had been in the intelligence department and he was able to send Rauf two CDs of the interrogation involving the suspect who had alleged Raif was involved in the drugs ring.

Rauf listened to endless conversations as an anonymous voice repeatedly referred to a man known as 'Raif Kamyoncu'. 'Kamyoncu' was not a surname but actually a reference to the man's occupation as a lorry driver (a characteristic of Turkish Cypriot culture often saw people identified by their occupations or associations). The CD, which ran for several hours, remained consistent in its accusation of 'Raif the lorry driver' being the main culprit in the drug smuggling. The second CD eventually threw more light on the matter when towards the end of the interview the suspect was asked about the identity of the 'Raif' he repeatedly names. The interviewer questioned if the man 'Raif' being referred to is the son of Denktaş and receives a simple but damning 'yes.'

The taped conversation had been leaked to the *Hürriyet* by an unscrupulous source with Rauf offering the possibility MİT was the culprit. Regardless of who was actually responsible for the leak, *Hürriyet* made quick work of releasing the information in its pages. However, contradictory reports began flying alongside the story garnering attention. Shortly after the publication appeared the suspect involved also gave an account, on his release from custody, claiming his statement had been extracted by force and had been untrue.

Rauf was never able to determine the truth or prove his son's innocence but his legal experience had directed him to refuse the interview would ever be enough to convict his son. At every opportunity Rauf would raise issue with the 'flimsy evidence' and would come out in defence of Raif — although he admitted much later in his life that it did him no good. 'Raif is gone,' he eventually conceded and there was nothing he could do to change it.

The only remedy for Rauf remained, as always, to deal with Cyprus and the challenges for the community. A huge shift in power and attitude was beginning to take shape in Turkish Cypriots led by a younger generation. The changes occurring would eventually force Rauf to reconsider his own position in the community.

Raif Denktaş

CHAPTER SEVENTEEN
A Bitter Pill

THE tradition of spending time at the negotiating table with a Greek Cypriot President had always been a key part of Rauf's life. It was meeting the demands of the Turkish Cypriot community eager for a settlement that had become a daily concern and a matter of contention Rauf needed to resolve. However, Rauf's efforts to bring an end to the problems blocking Turkish Cypriots' progression and recognition were continually thwarted proving tiresome for his own community. The constant setbacks suggested Rauf's retirement loomed as a wave of younger, disgruntled Turkish Cypriots expressed dissatisfaction with the elder statesman and his policies.

By 1988, his meetings with Kyprianou had proved ineffectual at securing a solution. Both leaders had persistently objected to the tabled suggestions despite a lot of pressure being strenuously applied on both leaders. The negotiations had reached critical levels with heavyweights like the US and UK wading in and reminding the community leaders this might be their 'best and last chance' at achieving a solution. Although some Islamic countries such as Pakistan, Bangladesh* and Indonesia were threatening to recognise

*Pakistan and Bangladesh had initially declared their recognition of Northern Cyprus as a sovereign state shortly after its declaration of independence, but withdrew their recognition after the UN deemed the Turkish Republic of North Cyprus declaration illegal (noted in UN Security Council resolutions 550 and 541).

the TRNC if the negotiations failed, Rauf knew it would not be enough to push Kyprianou. He had already resigned himself to the fact a solution based on negotiations with Kyprianou were highly unlikely. Their joint efforts were only successful in as much they managed to achieve the 'Ten-Point Agreement'.

The agreement secured by Rauf and Kyprianou amounted to a confirmation of the 'Four Guidelines' originally produced from the meetings held by Rauf and Makarios in 1977. Its purpose was to highlight the foundations and direct the leaders in their negotiations. It was successful in that it became the blueprint for present-day meetings between the North and South leaders. Apart from its hope to act as a springboard for the leaders to work from, it also remains the last significant document that Rauf and his counterparts appeared to publicly agree upon. Although he would later find greater flexibility from Kyprianou's successor, Georgios Vasos Vassiliou, Rauf didn't feel encouraged.

Vassiliou appeared to be a broad-minded individual with a progressive attitude. He had succeeded Kyprianou after the elections in February 1988 based on his energetic campaign to solve the 'Cyprus problem'. A successful businessman, Vassiliou had been a determined candidate when he stood as an independent for the Presidency despite not having a political party base which could be used to wield influence (although he did receive support from the communist party AKEL). Vassiliou's subsequent election appeared to be a reaction to Kyprianou's policies on the Cyprus settlement issue and his positive statements to drive Cyprus forward and bring about change.

Vassiliou proved to be an effectual guardian for Greek Cypriots and was responsible for a number of reforms that delivered important revisions. Under his direction, the Greek Cypriots enjoyed a period of economical growth and had oppressive restrictions lifted. He settled an uncomfortable existence for Greek Cypriots by protecting their civil liberties and removing the regime that policed them for their political convictions. (Vassiliou had introduced the reforms that assured Greek Cypriots' political beliefs were no longer held on file by the police).

However, Rauf's first experience of Vassiliou threatened to topple an already fragile relationship between the Turkish and Greek Cypriot communities. On hearing Vassiliou had been elected, Rauf immediately went on the charm offensive sending his congratulations along with an offer to meet with the Greek Cypriot President at a neutral location.

Vassiliou rejected the suggestion of having 'a cup of coffee with Denktaş' claiming it would be 'absurd' and tantamount to renouncing the 'very existence of the Republic of Cyprus'. Vassiliou, no doubt warming to his rigid theme, had no intention of leaving the insult there. He added that if Rauf wanted to meet with him then he was welcome to make an appointment with his secretary 'like any Cypriot citizen'.

Vassiliou's arrogance did little to ruffle Rauf as he had become quite immune to the rejection stance he encountered from the Greek Cypriot leadership. He was accustomed to having his leadership role undermined and pin-pointed as a reason not to meet and knew the statements aired by the Greek Cypriot administration was never likely to change. He also resisted exploiting his counterpart's rudeness and refrained from appearing publicly indignant.

Rauf often chose to respond in a private forum with a congenial remark wrapped neatly around his caustic sentiments. With his tongue firmly lodged in his cheek, Rauf later referenced the insult by suggesting Vassiliou 'was a man I could share a cup of coffee with' unlike Kyprianou, who he 'couldn't even raise on the telephone.'

Despite appearing to be an able and productive leader for the Greek Cypriots, Rauf's experiences with Vassiliou were not as satisfactory. During his time with Vassiliou, Rauf complained of being pulled backward and forwards through long, often whimsical notions, presented to him by the Greek Cypriot administration.

Before the talks collapsed in early 1990, Vassiliou had offered favourable concessions to Rauf and his team. The concessions did pique Rauf's interest particularly as they included alternative options regarding territorial issues that offered a smaller but virtually exclusive Turkish Cypriot zone, a 'willingness to phase in' the all important 'three freedoms', and even the possibility of a 'rotating Presidency' amongst other suggestions.

Not entirely convinced, Rauf reacted with caution. He had not been moved by the sincerity of the proposals and expressed his concerns citing he had 'legal reservations' regarding their validity. It hadn't escaped a wary Rauf's attention that many of the proposals had been made in private by Vassiliou or a member of his team. The informality meant most of what had been presented to Rauf was not considered binding as it did not appear in official written form and therefore not sanctioned as legal documents. Rauf's objections had apparently been noted as they coincided with the Greek Cypriot side withdrawing many of their newly-formed ideas and intentions.

Rauf wasn't too disappointed over the change of heart by the Greek Cypriot side and had decided to push for changes of his own. Almost a decade earlier, Rauf had added his signature to the United Nations Security Council resolutions in acceptance of respecting the sovereignty of

Cyprus (according to the UN, the sovereignty is a shared feature enjoyed by both communities) and also indicated the same at the 1977 and 1979 Summits. Rauf now wanted to implement his own concept of a 'separate sovereignty for each community' but first had to convince the UN that his government should be treated as an equal.*

Another round of meetings began in late February 1990 between Rauf and Vassiliou in New York with Peréz de Cuéllar. Rauf wanted to impress upon the UN representative that he was only interested in direct talks with Vassiliou but that the talks 'should be firmly anchored in reality' if they were to be able to progress. Introducing a list of 'talking points' Rauf launched into an eloquent lecture beginning with a statement to promote his intentions of being there as only to represent his people and having 'no claims to represent anyone else'. It was a statement that Rauf clarified by pointing out that the Greek Cypriot leadership should also only be responsible for its own people and could not present itself as an authoritative figure over the Turkish Cypriot Community.

Vassiliou was a competent businessman and knew when Rauf was pitching an idea that had every intention to sell the validity of equality and undermine the advantage held by Greek Cypriot superiority. As soon as Rauf had finished his presentation Vassiliou rose to his feet and declared he had 'not come to New York to be criticised by the Turkish Cypriot leader' but to discuss the Secretary-General's proposals. An embarrassing exchange quickly followed with Vassiliou being sharply reminded by the Secretary-General that he had not presented any formal proposals to be used

* The United Nations accepts that the Republic of Cyprus has *de jure* sovereignty over the island and its surrounding waters despite the fact the island is partitioned with the *de facto* Turkish Republic of Northern Cyprus in existence.

as a basis for all talks. Not to be outdone, Vassiliou then argued that Rauf had been trying to introduce new subjects which were not 'within the parameters previously agreed to for future negotiations.'

Having made his point, Rauf appeared to make some headway as terminology did change in the UN. On 12th March, 1990, the UN Security Resolution 649 wording reflected some of Rauf's attitudes as it stated 'the two communities were to be treated on equal footing'. Partially mirroring some of Rauf's opinions, the resolution removed the asymmetrical references 'the Government of Cyprus' and 'the Turkish Cypriot community' and instead juxtaposed the 'two communities' by referring to their respective leaders in the text. Rauf recognised the changes as a positive step in the right direction but refused to accept it as any sort of victory; it was, in his view, simply edited wording.

Despite the best efforts of the UN to support the two leaders, the strain began to show by 1992. Rauf and Vassiliou pressed on but the UN acknowledged there was a 'lack of trust' preventing the leaders from ever moving forward. The lack of confidence was enough to prompt the newly-appointed Secretary-General Boutros Ghali, in 1992, to write a report expressing his concerns that any successful outcome was 'difficult to envisage' between the two sides. Ghali sought to remedy the situation with a series of 'Confidence Building Measures' but failed to secure a signature from either side.

Ghali would later be accused of having failed to get the leaders ever to agree as previous proposals of his had also fallen to the wayside. Whilst his lack of skill and inexperience were often cited as reasons for the failures, it appears the situation was made worse by the decision of the European Court of Justice to cut off the TRNC's export to

UK markets. Additional embargoes deepened the crisis for Rauf and his community and served to sour relations between the two sides even further.

Rauf's popular status and relationship with his community also suffered as a result of more embargoes being heaped on the Turkish Cypriots. The TRNC's economy was already in difficulties but now threatened further by the persistent embargoes and would go on to have devastating repercussions for a growing generation. Over time, the restrictions placed on the TRNC prevented Turkish Cypriots from trading, denied them participation in any political forum and even prevented them from entering sporting events. The social embargoes had a hugely negative impact on young Turkish Cypriots in particular who resented being denied opportunities and access to an international community that could have provided them with the benefits of trade and education.

Rauf was aware of the need to secure a future for the TRNC and willingly agreed to meet with his old adversary, Glafkos Clerides (who had succeeded Vassiliou in 1993). Clerides and Rauf had a long history together which everyone hoped would be a useful advantage that could benefit all Cypriots in the talks. Although the contact between the two leaders was considered extremely important, it unfortunately coincided with the EU decision to open accession negotiations with the Greek Cypriot-administered Republic of Cyprus.

Rauf and Clerides had not seen each other for four years but it was the EU that provided most of the challenges which contributed to a strained atmosphere. The initial meeting had been organised by the UN for the two leaders to meet in New York in July, 1997 with follow-up meetings scheduled in Geneva the next month. However, before Rauf left Cyprus for New York, he stopped in İstanbul and gave a brief press conference where he expressed his 'tempered optimism' and his upset regarding the EU.

In his address to the press Rauf explained the ramifications of the EU's actions spelt disaster for the TRNC. The application for membership into the EU had been made by the Greek Cypriot Republic of Cyprus on behalf of the entire island. He was furious that the 'so-called government of Cyprus' could be deemed as the 'sole interlocutor' and able to speak on behalf of the Turkish Cypriots. In his opinion, the EU had committed the 'gravest injustice' by accepting Cyprus' application. It would have a biased affect on the talks and create discord: "We are seeking impartiality," he complained during an interview "[but] the EU has already convicted us."

His rendition of the EU and its failings became a familiar song but Rauf had no intention of restricting his opinions solely based on the EU's actions. He also expressed his dismay at the actions of the UN and appeared to be tired of their involvement. He could not fathom why he was expected to go to New York, some 3000 miles away, when he and Clerides held offices just 15 minutes apart and needed only cross the Green Line in a matter of minutes to come face-to-face.

Rauf was adept at making his feelings known and always used his own particular brand of irony to punctuate his point — in this case at the expense of the UN. In media interviews with the Turkish press he expressed his dismay at just how 'ridiculous' he found the situation; he mockingly queried his own diplomatic skills — or rather the lack of them, in the presence of superior diplomats who could obviously teach him a thing or two: "For world diplomats to agree to this sort of scenario, as if it will be better if you talk there and not here, indicates that there are still in the diplomatic world a lot of things which I have to learn and I will learn whether or not this will be helpful for a negotiated settlement. By going through this experience anew because in the past we have again met thousands of miles away and it didn't help at all. So we'll see this time whether it will help."

After his brief conference in İstanbul, Rauf took time to visit family and indulge himself by putting in an attendance at a concert before visiting his friend, and President of Turkey, Süleyman Demirel. Although Rauf had always been consistent in his interviews that had demonstrated his concerns over the handling of the Cyprus issue, he could always expect an honest evaluation from his closest friends; Demirel was no exception.

It was important for Turkey, Demirel explained, not to have a positive atmosphere 'spoiled' which had been created by the announcement of the candidacy of Turkey to the EU. Demirel advised Rauf to take a 'conciliatory approach' which Rauf tried in earnest to adopt. He took on board the necessity to keep the peace for Turkey's sake but struggled in the meetings. Negotiations with Clerides were frustrating and later described by him as an exercise of 'playing hide and seek' as neither men were forthcoming. His quietly simmering anger at the lack of progress remained contained but rushed to the surface when he saw the UN Secretary-General's submitted paper had not included the Turkish Cypriots' proposal of confederation, contributing to the lack of sincerity he had felt from the meetings. Rauf declared 'there was no reason to remain' and walked away from the negotiating table.

The next meeting between Rauf and Clerides, was a tentative affair and would take place in the UN home of Alvaro de Soto, the special advisor to the UN's Secretary

General, in 2001 with plenty of media in attendance. Rauf was no stranger to playing up to the media in order to obtain the best advantage but found himself upstaged by Clerides who had already planned how to gain the best advantage from the arrangement.

The initial first few minutes began with plenty of pleasantries until Rauf asked de Soto, as a formal request, where he wanted him to sit. Despite de Soto's polite protestations that he should feel comfortable to sit where he pleased, Rauf admitted to hovering near de Soto's right side in the hope he would be waved gracefully in that direction. However, Clerides was quick to interject with the suggestion that he should sit on de Soto's right as he had been sitting there before the media had been allowed to enter the room. Rauf knew this would set the tone of the meeting and procure international recognition for Clerides' position as the righteous representative of the Republic of Cyprus. "Glafkos has the media photos in mind," Rauf wryly noted during the recorded exchange. "By being on the right hand side of the United Nations special representative, it is obvious that he wants to underline once again that he is the Government of Cyprus..."

Clerides was able to successfully plant himself on de Soto's right which caused an uncomfortable beginning to the discussions. Rauf had always used humour to alleviate uncomfortable silences and his dialogue with Clerides would be no exception. With a broad smile aimed towards his counterpart's direction, Rauf hinted at Clerides' venerable age by suggesting they both should 'stop the dialogue of the deaf.' Clerides snorted in defence at Rauf that, despite being 82-years-old, his 'hearing was not too bad.'

Rauf's humorous jibes were a welcome distraction but never enough to lighten the heated discussions. The talks were dominated by the EU and Cyprus' intentions to join it which would exclude the unrecognised TRNC. Rauf insisted the EU declare that a political solution should be found before Cyprus entered the EU. Clerides disagreed and claimed it was not in his control of what action the EU might decide to take. It was a red rag to a bull for Rauf who refused to be sidelined and informed Clerides of how time was needed to organise a new political structure. His angry retort also included very colourful, metaphorical language that referenced the devil as he sat glaring at his opponent.

De Soto attempted to defuse the situation by offering refreshments to the two men. Clerides asked for a 'Greek coffee' with sugar prompting Rauf to ask for a coffee without sugar but he added that he wanted his beverage to be a 'Turkish coffee.' De Soto looked at both men questioningly. "I was under the impression," he stated, "that there was a useful *tour d'horizon* on generalities, but on the definition of a cup of coffee, how quickly can you disagree?"

De Soto had aptly managed to sum up the difficulties between the two leaders, who struggled to agree on anything. Rauf, who was not prepared to accept the unfavourable impression, made his own attempts to explain the issue. He reminded Clerides that the 'whole world' recognised Turkish coffee but Greece and Greek Cyprus insisted on calling it Greek coffee as a demonstration of 'anti-Turkish sentiments'. Clerides looked pointedly at Rauf before stating he had changed his mind and now wanted tea instead causing all the men to erupt with laughter.

Whilst the meeting had managed to raise a few smiles, there were assurances for the UN that the two leaders were intent on meeting again. Rauf did not want to appear too optimistic but was able to contend that the atmosphere had been 'friendly' with a 'useful exchange of views.' He also appeared to enjoy the company and easy-going demeanour of the UN's representative de Soto later joking about their shared problem of hair loss: "I knew we would get along," he declared to de Soto, whilst smoothing his hand over his bald pate, "as we both visit the same barber."

The meetings between the two leaders continued with the friendly atmosphere still intact. Meanwhile, the Secretary-General Kofi Annan had been busy forging a comprehensive settlement which he hoped the two sides would agree to. A series of drafts presented to the two leaders were the most detailed solution offered to date and became known as the Annan Plan*.

The Annan Plan had been tabled several times by the Secretary-General until the finalised plan was submitted in March 2004. Clerides had already left the negotiation table by then and was replaced as President by Tassos Papadopoulos (he had been elected in February 2003). Neither Rauf nor Papadopoulos were impressed with the Annan Plan. Rauf suggested in his book, *The Cyprus Problem*, the Greek Cypriot side had refused to come to the table toward the end of negotiations as they did not want to 'sit around a table in terms of equality.' The empty chair, designated for a Greek Cypriot representative, meant, according to Rauf, a decision was made to have 'separate votes of the two sides and presumably leave them to fight about it later'.

The 'separate votes' was a reference to the Referendum held on 24 April 2004 to put the Annan Plan to the Cypriot people for their approval. Both Papadopoulos and Rauf

---

*The Annan Plan proposed by the United Nations was designed to resolve the Cyprus issue with a restructuring of the Republic of Cyprus to become a federation of two states. It was eventually put to a referendum for the people of Cyprus to decide upon. The referenda saw an overwhelming support of 65% from Turkish Cypriots voting in favour and only 24% of Greek Cypriots in support.

campaigned vigorously in their respective communities to encourage a 'no' vote. Papadopoulos appealed to his compatriots' sense of nationalism and 'dignity' to 'defend the Republic of Cyprus', and urged them not to destroy its abolition. Rauf, however, reminded his community of the unsavoury deeds and rumours that were linked to the Greek Cypriot leader and his predecessors — Papadopoulos, along with Clerides, had been named as one of the architects of the *Akritas Plan*. Mr. Never and Mr. No, as they were nicknamed respectively by the Turkish Cypriot opposition leader, Mustafa Akıncı, would both be granted their wishes.

The Annan Plan failed with interesting results: the Greek Cypriot community voted strongly against the plan whilst Turkish Cypriots (led by Mehmet Ali Talat), to Rauf's surprise, voted in favour for the plan. It was a crushing blow for many who had thought the Annan Plan would be the answer to the island's historic dilemma. De Soto couldn't mask his own disappointment when he stated how he believed a 'unique and historic chance to resolve the Cyprus problem has been missed...Cyprus will remain divided and militarised as it accedes to the European Union and the benefits of a settlement will not be realised.' The Secretary-General Kofi Annan, the man behind the plan, echoed de Soto's sentiments feeling strongly that the island's 30-year division would remain.

However, the outcome gave Turkish Cypriots the opportunity to demonstrate to the outside world their willingness to live as an integrated society with Greek Cypriots under the auspices of the European Union. For Rauf, the voting results would have far more serious consequences.

Rauf knew from the losses he suffered in the December 2003 legislative elections that his days as the unchallenged leader were numbered; the referendum results in 2004 only serving to prove he was no longer needed. Turkish Cypriots, the younger generation in particular, had made their feelings clear. Prior to the referendum, demonstrations had been held in 2002 demanding reunification of the island in the belief it would lead to EU citizenship. The desire for Cyprus to enter the EU in 2004 meant shaping the future for many Turkish Cypriots and allowing for greater freedom — including the lifting of the embargoes.

Rauf disagreed and wanted to convince his community that they were looking in the wrong direction, via the EU, for a solution. He held a deep mistrust of the Greek Cypriots and its governing body and issued a publication, *The Cyprus Problem*, just seven months after the decision was made that had allowed Cyprus to enter the EU. He launched an attack on the Annan Plan claiming a 'very long list' of reasons existed at to why the plan should have been rejected that was apparent 'in each and every Turkish Cypriot' as well as the leadership.

However, Rauf's discussion of Cyprus' entrance to the EU, in the same publication, took a disturbing turn and also revealed a petty side to him. In his attempt to silence his critics and prove his motives were right, he resorted to mocking Papadopoulos. His derision of Papadopoulos suggested the Greek Cypriot President was weak-minded with a problem that all Cypriots needed to be aware of. Using bold headlines, Rauf suggested Papadopoulos was suffering memory loss; and failing the assertion of memory loss, he was 'suffering from an illness' or possibly was 'a liar.' Although Rauf conceded it was not 'the remit of this column to investigate and find out what is wrong with the President' he made sure the reader was aware of his concerns about the President's sanity.

The publication did little to sway the voting public and

Rauf knew he had reached the end as his community's unchallenged leader. He didn't wait to be ousted and announced he would not stand as President for a fifth term. His tenure as President of the TRNC came to an end on 17th April 2005 — the day of the elections.

He was succeeded by Mehmet Ali Talat who had promoted a 'yes' vote for the Annan Plan which that day received an overwhelming endorsement from Turkish Cypriots keen for change.

Left to right Javier Peréz de Cuéllar, George Vassiliou and Rauf in
New York between 26th February and 2nd March 1990

Above left to right, Secretary-General's Special Advisor Alvaro
de Soto, Vassiliou's successor President Glafkos Clerides, UN
Secretary-General Kofi Annan and Rauf at the UNFICYP
Chief of Mission's residence, where Mr. Annan hosted a dinner
for the two leaders. The photo was taken prior to Clerides
leaving office in 2003

CHAPTER EIGHTEEN

The Copenhagen Files

Retirement from politics was not something Rauf had planned upon. Cyprus' complicated nature and uncertain future had consumed his career and life but he had never envisaged an alternative for himself. It was to be his community that instigated his resignation and the severance package offered by the United Nations, known as the Annan Plan, did little in the way of compensation.

The Annan Plan that had been presented to all Cypriots left Rauf wholly dissatisfied. He had had grave concerns that matched his political advisors misgivings: Çavlan Süerdem, had been a senior advisor to Rauf and made it clear the plan fell 'way behind the agreements as provided for by the 1960 constitution for the Turkish Cypriots.' Despite the apprehension felt by Rauf and his team, it went to Referendum on 24 April 2004 to the people of Cyprus.

Mehmet Ali Talat, backed by Turkey, had led the campaign to encourage Turkish Cypriots to vote for the Annan Plan that clinched a majority vote in favour. The support shown toward Talat had a considerable effect on Rauf. Less than a month after the referendum results, Rauf announced he would not stand in the next elections set for the following year.

Bitterly disappointed, Rauf pulled on a brave public mask and used his venerable age as an escape into retirement.

However, the reality was quite different as he continued to work, writing volumes and attending public forums that enabled him to continue as an outspoken individual against any form of reunification with Greek Cyprus.

With Mehmet Ali Talat replacing him as President, Rauf's status as a private citizen also afforded him some advantages. No longer an active politician Rauf was quick to realise he could 'be more trouble' with a rare opportunity to convey his opinions to a wider audience. He was not restricted by convention or the political requirements as demanded by Turkey; he even relished the idea that he was not expected to be 'polite' and could say what he really felt about the Cyprus issue without fear of impunity. No longer held by any restraints, Rauf's deep-seated convictions were now unfurled.

The Annan Plan, his last major involvement in the future of the TRNC, came under fire as it epitomised the international community's poor handling of the 'Cyprus problem'. The proposal to solve Cyprus' issues, crafted by the UN, was a little-understood document and unlikely to have been read. "It's 9,000 pages long. Tell me how many people actually read and understood the thing?" Rauf pointed out critically. He also added that it would have been 'impossible for most people, let alone local people, to really understand the implications of the Annan Plan and what it meant for them'.

Rauf, openly unhappy with the long-winded and complicated document, also believed Turkish Cypriots were being duped into accepting a solution. He had advised Ankara the plan was still only in its infancy and the invitation to start the talks, prior to the plan's consideration, in 1999 was to hurry the Turkish Cypriots into accepting it before a decision was made regarding the

Greek Cypriot application to join the EU. Whilst the talks were still underway, the Greek Cypriot administration, seen as the legitimate government, had pressed on with their application for membership. Rauf was furious with the UN for not cautioning the Greek Cypriot side at any time, during their efforts to obtain entry into the EU, that the application would reduce hopes of a settlement. His anger did little to influence the UN who responded by putting pressure on the weaker Turkish side to accept the plan.

He railed against the UN for manipulating and threatening Turkish Cypriots with the prospect of not having a voice once the decision was made for the Greek Cypriot side to enter the EU, which now appeared imminent. The UN had wanted a quick solution to suit the EU timetable and encouraged the Turkish Cypriot side to accept the plan as de Soto explained that 'when the Greek Cypriot side joins the EU then the Turkish Cypriot side will lose its bargaining powers.'

In the early stages of the ill-fated Annan Plan* in 2002, Rauf had been seriously ill in a New York hospital recovering from heart surgery when he was first presented with the document. The timing was not the only issue for Rauf who, still in a weakened state post surgery, was unhappy at the pressure being heaped upon him. Although Rauf (and another source close to him) refused to name the aide, he maintained the representative placed the paperwork in front of him, as he lay in his hospital bed, and stressed the need for him to sign an agreement which would allow the plan as a consideration at the negotiation table.

Rauf's ill-health had prevented him from attending the

The Annan Plan had undergone five revisions in total between 2002 and 2004. However, by Annan Plan II (presented 10th December 2002) intense pressure was being applied on both sides to reach an agreement before the Copenhagen Summit talks in person and most of his opinions and signatures had to be retrieved from his hospital bed. He received Turkey's newly-appointed foreign minister, Yaşar Yakış, with grace but continued to make clear he was not prepared to accept the plan causing the leader of Turkey's new governing party, Recep Tayyip Erdoğan, to express his own frustrations at the delays. Erdoğan had found the plan acceptable enough to base negotiations upon and even predicted 'a deal could be reached by the middle of next year'.

Although Rauf made public statements citing his ill-health as an issue preventing the talks from reaching a conclusion that included the EU plan, he did not elicit a great deal of sympathy from his community. They held him, and his absence, during the early negotiations, from the table as being responsible for losing the opportunity to be taken into the EU. Erdoğan took a further swipe at Rauf suggesting the delays had become a personal issue. In his view, the problem was not "Mr. Denktaş' personal business...[and he] should pay more attention to what Turkish Cypriots think and the growing protest against his rule".

Despite coming under immense criticism for his handling of the talks, which included raised questions on his health, Rauf noted with concern that the talks were still 'gaining momentum.' Turkey was acutely aware of Rauf's hospitalisation but ploughed on regardless insisting that the TRNC's Foreign Minister, Tahsin Ertuğruloğlu be sent in his place. Rauf was angered by Turkey's actions but he did at least have the support of Ertuğruloğlu who expounded the views belonging to him.

The discussions took place with a familiar face — Alvaro

*Recep Tayyip Erdoğan (born 1954) became Turkey's 25th Prime Minister on 14th March 2003. He is also the chairman of the ruling Justice and Development Party (in Turkish: *Adelet ve Kalkınma Partisi*) developed from the tradition of Islamism.

de Soto, who was the Special Advisor to the Secretary-General and very informed on the issues pertaining to Cyprus along with Rauf's concerns.

Ertuğruloğlu argued admirably on behalf of the TRNC President and also drew de Soto's attention to the multitude of problems that plagued Turkish Cypriots which were leaving them 'cornered': their President was ill; Greek Cypriots were going into the EU under a 'false identity' as the Republic of Cyprus; Turkey was distracted whilst it underwent a change of government and under these circumstances, the UN were trying to impose a time-frame on them. Other issues also left the TRNC in doubt as to the genuine intentions of the Annan Plan — notably land, population and demilitarisation issues.

Rauf had suspected the Greek Cypriot side had 'excellent input' into the preparation of the plan with his suspicions confirmed by the Turkish military who had viewed the diagrams provided on the map of Cyprus. The map delineated redrawn borders in anticipation of resettling Cypriots and land control but appeared to be in favour of Greek Cypriots. Its carefully-drawn borders were specific enough to make sure Turkish occupation and protection would be rendered virtually impossible.

Rauf did his best to highlight his unease of the Annan Plan and refused to remain neutral despite Mehmet Ali Talat's request to do so during the referendum process. At every opportunity he used the media to reveal as much as he could about the plan's contents and its failings.

When questioned about his biased approach Rauf pointed out he had taken an oath to protect the state and its 'sovereignty' and was under no obligation to advise Turkish Cypriots to accept the Annan Plan. To reiterate his point, Rauf declared his own vote at the referendum 'in view of the negative aspects in the Annan Plan' would be given a resounding 'no'.

Rauf's efforts were not enough to persuade the voting majority of Turkish Cypriots to reject the plan. Despite Rauf publicly declaring the plan excessively pro-Greek, they were willing to accept it on the grounds that their prolonged isolation and exclusion from Europe would end, both the EU and UN having promised sanctions and embargoes would be lifted.

Although Turkish Cypriots had complied with the international community's wishes, the voting outcome sent shockwaves through both the EU and the UN with the unexpected vote against the plan by the Greek Cypriot community. A variety of reasons were claimed, including that the plan had not been 'well balanced' and disregarded Greek Cypriot views, as a reason for their rejections. However, it did not affect Greek Cyprus' accession to the European Union as Greece its sponsor had considerable influence. They had the single veto against the enlargement of the EU by the remaining nine candidates*, which had pushed the EU into taking the Republic of Cyprus in.

RAUF knew his Presidential signature being omitted from any of the documents relating to the Annan plan would not change the outcome but refused to consign himself to its fate. The aftermath of the plan saw Rauf campaign vigorously to remind Turkish Cypriots of their losses, and what they could expect from the Republic of Cyprus. He

*British conservative politician, Chris Patten, also confirmed in a statement that the EU had to accept Greek Cyprus' accession 'because Greece would have otherwise blocked the membership of other countries'. His comments were noted during a meeting with officials from the US Embassy in Brussels.

had absolutely no trust in the Greek Cypriots' commitment to abiding by an agreement that would safeguard Turkish Cypriot rights; and he was of the opinion the Annan Plan had not even attempted to offer those rights.

LESS than a year before he died, Rauf reiterated his staunch belief that it was impossible for Greek Cypriots to commit themselves to any agreement as they would never change their agenda of becoming unified with Greece: "I really believe that the Greek Cypriots will do it again. Any new agreement will be used by them as they used the 1960 agreement, in the words of Makarios, 'as a springboard for *enosis*'. This time they don't have to declare *enosis* because they have indirectly achieved it by EU membership."

Rauf's regard for the Annan Plan did not lessen despite its failure. He was determined to explain to his community why it should never have reached them in the first place. Throughout Rauf's career, both as a public and private person, he had kept meticulous notes and filed copies of all paperwork in his private library. His official and private office housed several files that included transcripts and office memos of all the meetings he had held or attended. The detailed conversations that had occurred between the parties involved in the development of the Annan Plan were no exception. Using his copious notes and transcripts, he wrote a damning book he had titled, *The Copenhagen Files,* detailing the failings of the Annan Plan and purporting to tell the tale of 'deceit and dirty tricks' played on the Turkish Cypriots in the international community's pursuit of a solution for Cyprus.

The manuscript was not published during his lifetime but Rauf appeared keen to leave a last comment behind as a warning to all. His frustrations over the Annan Plan leapt out from every page but were also coupled with his regrets that he had not achieved his goal of legitimizing the TRNC. He deplored the situation of Turkish Cypriots living in stateless limbo and gave an insight into his desperation by frequently stating that he wished to 'have seen the TRNC recognised – even if it was for just 24 hours.'

Although feeling that he had failed in his endeavours to provide a state for his people, his efforts to do so were at least recognised by some members of his own community and international friends and supporters. An influential collective decided to honour his contributions by recommending his name for the Nobel Peace Prize 2011*. On learning of the intentions to nominate him, Rauf politely refused the suggestion — adamant he did not deserve the accolade citing he had not succeeded in his aim of legalizing the TRNC.

Undeterred by Rauf's modest protestations, the nomination was still presented and accepted by the Oslo committee. Although Rauf never learned the fate of the Prize, it was a testament of his commitment to Turkish Cypriots that his nomination was deemed worthy for consideration.

His tireless campaign and work on behalf of his community had been noted: he had served several decades as a guardian for his community and throughout his tenure as their leader had been unchallenged. He hadn't waited to be ousted by his successor Talat — who had promoted the idea that a bright future awaited Turkish Cypriots under the terms of the Annan Plan. Rauf had been under no such illusion and was proved right when it failed to deliver on its

*Rauf's nomination for the Nobel Peace Prize was submitted by Lord Maginnis on behalf of all its signatories to the Nobel Peace Prize Committee in Oslo, January 2011. See Appendix D for full citation.

promises of lifting embargoes in exchange for a 'yes' vote by the Turkish Cypriot side.

The bitter disappointment felt by his community was evident as Turkish Cypriots struggled to accept they would still be excluded from the world market and stateless. However, they had not lost their foundations and right to be known as Turkish Cypriots. Rauf died on 13th January, 2012 leaving an important legacy for his people: they had a homeland and were at least free to fight for their rights without fear and the threat of violence.

In retirement: Rauf surrounded by some of his beloved pets. Boncuk, his favourite dog, is the recipient of special attention

In retirement: Rauf at the unveiling of the British Cyprus Memorial, 14th November 2009

ACKNOWLEDGEMENTS

I could not have written this book without the immense help and guidance I got from a great many people who knew Rauf Denktaş personally, who lived through his times, and often shared his experiences of the troubled years which dominated his adult life.

I should begin by thanking Altan Houssein for his introduction to Rauf Denktaş and his steadfast support throughout the many months I spent in research and writing.

I would like to thank Corinna Phillips for taking the time to proofread my work, sift through endless hours of taped recordings and put pen to paper to transcribe verbatim everything she heard. Her help was invaluable. My thanks also to Tom Roche for the work and design of the cover for this book.

I was very fortunate to have been introduced to many of Rauf Denktaş's friends and colleagues who all willingly gave their time to relate the experiences they shared with Rauf. Two people in particular who gave me tremendous support are worth a special mention: Vedat Çelik who always made himself available at short notice to answer my questions with honesty, humour and warmth. And Çavlan Süerdem who also gave up much of his time as well as working hard to procure an interview with the very elusive President Demirel. I'm indebted to both.

Many thanks must go to the Denktaş family who kindly allowed me into their home and to take up the time of their beloved husband and father and for giving me their own personal time to share their experiences of Rauf.

A very big thank you to Martina Cole for her advice and backing with this project.My thanks also to Osman Saffetoğlu.

I would also like to express my gratitude for the services of the various Public Offices and Government Departments in the TRNC. They were always helpful and kept meticulous records to which I was given access.

Lastly, I would like to thank all at Okman Printing for their help and support to make sure this book happened. Special thanks to Orhan Akbulut for his patience and editing skills.

Appendix A

THE AKRITAS PLAN

*The secret document written in 1963 setting out
the Greek Cypriot process for rewriting the 1960
Constitution and clearing the way to enosis
— union with Greece*

THE recent public statements of His Beatitude have outlined the course which our national issue will follow. As we have stressed in the past, national struggles are neither judged nor solved from day to day, nor is it possible to fix time limits for the achievement of the various stages of their development. Our national cause must always be examined and judged in the light of the conditions and developments of the moment, and the measures which will be taken, the tactics, and the time of implementing each measure must be determined by the conditions existing at the time, both internationally, and internally. The entire effort is trying and must necessarily pass through various stages, because the factors which influence the final result are many and varied. It is sufficient, however, that all should understand that the measures which are prescribed now constitute only the first step, one simple stage towards the final and unalterable national objective, i.e., to the full and unfettered exercise of the right of self-determination of the people.

Since the purpose remains unalterable, what remains is to examine the subject of tactics. It is necessary to divide the subject of tactics under two headings, that is: internal tactics and external, since in each case both the presentation and the handling of our cause will be different.

A. EXTERNAL TACTICS (*international*).

During the recent stages of our national struggle the Cyprus problem has been presented to diplomatic circles as a demand for the exercise of the right of self-determination by the people of Cyprus. In securing the right of self-determination obstacles have been created by the well-known conditions, the existence of a Turkish minority, by the inter-communal conflict and the attempts to show that co-existence of both communities under one government was impossible. Finally, for many international circles the problem was solved by the London and Zurich Agreements, a solution which was presented as the result of negotiations and agreement between the two sides.

a) Consequently, our first target has been to cultivate internationally the impression that the Cyprus problem has not really been solved an the solution requires revision.

b) Our first objective was our endeavour to be vindicated as the Greek majority and to create the impression that:

(i) The solution given is neither satisfactory not fair;

(ii) The agreement reached was not the result of a free and voluntary acceptance of a compromise of the conflicting views;

(iii) That the revision of the agreements constitutes a compelling necessity for survival, and not an effort of the Greeks to repudiate their signature;

(iv) That the co-existence of the two communities is possible, and

(v) That the strong element on which foreign states ought to rely is the Greek majority and not the Turkish Cypriots.

c) All the above has required very difficult effort, and has been achieved to a satisfactory degree. Most of the foreign representatives have been convinced that the solution given was neither fair nor satisfactory, that it was signed under pressure and without real negotiations and that it was imposed under various threats. It is significant argument that the solution achieved has not been ratified by the people, because our leadership, acting wisely, avoided calling the people to ratify it by a plebiscite, which the people, in the 1959 spirit, would have done if called upon.

Generally, it has been established that the administration of Cyprus up to now has been carried out by the Greeks and that the Turks have confined themselves to a negative role.

d) *Second objective.* The first stage having been completed, we mus programme the second stage of our activities and objectives on the international level. These objectives in general can be outlined as follows:

(i) The Greek efforts are directed towards removing unreasonable and unfair provisions of administration and not to oppress the Turkish Cypriots;

(ii) The removal of these oppressive provisions must take place now because tomorrow it will be too late;

(iii) The removal of these provisions, despite the fact that this is reasonable and necessary, because of the unreasonable attitude of the Turks is not possible by agreement, and therefore unilateral action is justified;

(iv) The issue of revision is an internal affair of the Cypriots and does not give the right of military or other intervention;

(v) The proposed amendments are reasonable, just, and safeguard the reasonable rights of the minority.

e) Today it has been generally demonstrated that the international climate is against every type of oppression and, more specifically, against the oppression of minorities. The Turks have already succeeded in persuading international opinion that union of Cyprus with Greece amounts to an attempt to enslave them. Further, it is estimated that we have better chances of succeeding in our efforts to influence international public opinion in our favour if we present our demand, as we did during the struggle, as a demand to exercise the right of self-determination, rather than as a demand for union with Greece (*enosis*).

In order, however, to secure the exercise of complete and free self-determination, we must get free of all those provisions of the constitution and of the agreements (Treaty of Guarantee, Treaty of Alliance) which prevent the free and unfettered expression and implementation of the wishes of our people and which create dangers of external intervention. It is for this reason that the first target of attack has been the Treaty of Guarantee, which was the first that was stated to be no longer recognised by the Greek Cypriots.

When this is achieved no legal or moral power can prevent us from deciding our future alone and freely and exercising the right of self-determination by a plebiscite.

From the above, the conclusion can be drawn that for the success of our plan a chain of actions is needed, each of which is necessary, otherwise, future actions will remain legally unjustified and politically unachieved, while at the same time we will expose our people and the country to serious consequences. *The actions to be taken can be summed up as follows:*

a) Amendment of the negative elements of the agreements and parallel abandonment of the Treaties of Guarantee and Alliance. This step is necessary because the need for amendments of the negative aspects of the treaties is generally accepted internationally and is considered justified (we can even justify unilateral action), while at the same time intervention from outside to prevent us amending them is unjustified and inapplicable;

b) As a result of our above actions, the Treaty of Guarantee (right of unilateral intervention) becomes legally and substantively inapplicable;

c) The people, once Cyprus is not bound by the restrictions of the Treaties of Guarantee and Alliance regarding the exercise of the right of self-determination, will be able to give expression to and implement their desire.

d) Legal confrontation by the forces of State of every internal or external intervention.

It is therefore obvious that if we hope to have any chance of success internationally in our above actions, we cannot and must not reveal or declare the various stages of the struggle before the previous one is completed. For instance, if it is accepted that the above four stages are necessary, then it is unthinkable to speak of amendments in stage (a) if stage (d) is revealed. How can it be possible to aim at the amendment of the negative aspects of the constitution by arguing that this is necessary for the functioning of the State if stage (d) is revealed?

The above relate to targets, aims and tactics in the international field. *And now on the internal front:*

B. INTERNAL FRONT.

1. The only danger which could be described as insurmountable is the possibility of external intervention, by

force, not so much because of the material damage, nor because of the danger itself (which, in the last analysis, it is possible for us to deal with partly or totally by force), but mainly because of the possible political consequences. Intervention is threatened or implemented before stage (c), then such intervention would be legally debatable, if not justified. This fact has a lot of weight both internationally and in the United Nations.

From the history of many recent instances we have learnt that in not a single case of intervention, whether legally justified or not, has either the United Nations or any other power succeeded in evicting the invader without serious concessions detrimental to the victim. Even in the case of the Israeli attack against Suez, which was condemned by almost all nations, and on which Soviet intervention was threatened, Israel withdrew, but received as a concession the port of Eilat on the Red Sea. Naturally, more serious dangers exist for Cyprus.

If, on the other hand, we consider and justify our action under (a) above well, on the one hand, intervention is not justified and, on the other, it cannot be carried out before consultations between the guarantors Greece, Turkey and the UK. It is at this stage of consultations (before intervention) that we need international support. We shall have it if the proposed amendments by us appear reasonable and justifiable.

Hence, the first objective is to avoid intervention by the choice of the amendments we would request in the first stage.

Tactics: We shall attempt to justify unilateral action for constitutional amendments once the efforts for a common agreement are excluded. As this stage the provisions in (ii) and (in) are applicable in parallel.

2. It is obvious that in order to justify intervention, a more serious reason must exist and a more immediate danger than a simple constitutional amendment. Such a reason could be an immediate declaration of *Enosis* before stages (a)-(c) or serious inter-communal violence which would be presented as massacres of the Turks.

Reason (a) has already been dealt with in the first part and, consequently, it remains only to consider the danger of inter-communal violence. Since we do not intend, without provocation, to attack or kill Turks, the possibility remains that the Turkish Cypriots, as soon as we proceed to the unilateral amendment of any article of the constitution, will react instinctively, creating incidents and clashes or stage, under orders, killings, atrocities or bomb attacks on Turks, in order to create the impression that the Greeks have indeed attacked the Turks, in which case intervention would be justified, for their protection.

TACTICS. Our actions for constitutional amendments will be in the open and we will always appear ready for peaceful negotiations. Our actions will not be of a provocative or violent nature.

Should clashes occur, they will be dealt with in the initial stages legally by the legally-established security forces, in accordance with a plan. All actions will be clothed in legal form.

3. Before the right of unilateral amendments of the constitution is established, decisions and actions which require positive violent acts, such as, for example, the use of force to unify the separate municipalities, must be avoided. Such a decision compels the Government to intervene by force to bring about the unification of municipal properties, which will probably compel the Turks to react violently. On the contrary, it is easier for us, using legal methods, to amend, for instance, the provision of the 70 to 30 ratio in the public service, when it is the Turks who will have to take positive violent action, while for us this procedure will not amount to action, but to refusal to act (to implement).

The same applies to the issue of the separate majorities with regard to taxation legislation. These measures have already been considered and a series of similar measures have been chosen for implementation. Once our right of unilateral amendments to the constitution is established *de facto* by such actions, then we shall be able to advance using our judgment and our strength more decidedly.

4. It is, however, naive to believe that it is possible to proceed to substantive acts of amendment of the constitution, as a first step of our general plan, as has been described above, without the Turks attempting to create or to stage violent clashes. For this reason, the existence of our organisation is an imperative necessity because:

a) In the event of instinctive violent Turkish reactions, if our counter-attacks are not immediate, we run the risk effacing panic in the Greeks in the towns and thus losing substantial vital areas, while, on the other hand, an immediate show of our strength may bring the Turks to their senses and confine their actions to sporadic insignificant acts, and

b) In the event of a planned or staged Turkish attack, it is imperative to overcome it by force in the shortest possible time, because if we succeed in gaining command of the situation (in one or two days), no outside, intervention would be either justified or possible.

c) In either of the above cases, effective use of force in dealing with the Turks will facilitate to a great extent our subsequent actions for further amendments. It would then be possible for unilateral amendments to be made, without any Turkish reaction, because they will know that their reaction will be weak or seriously harmful for their community, and

d) In the event of the clashes becoming more general or general we must be ready to proceed with the actions described in (a) to (b), including the immediate declaration of *Enosis*, because then there would be no reason to wait nor room for diplomatic action.

5. At no stage should we neglect the need to enlighten, and to face the propaganda and the reactions of those who cannot or should not know our plans. It has been shown that our struggle must pass through four stages and that we must not reveal publicly and at improper times our plans and intentions.

Complete secrecy is more than a national duty. IT IS A VITAL NECESSITY FOR SURVIVAL AND SUCCESS. This will not prevent the reactionaries and the irresponsible demagogues from indulging in an orgy of exploitation of patriotism and provocations. The plan provides them with fertile ground, because it gives them the opportunity to allege that the efforts of the leadership are confined to the objective of constitutional amendments and not to pure national objectives. Our task becomes more difficult because by necessity, and depending on the prevailing circumstances, even the constitutional amendments must be made in stages. However, all this must not draw us into irresponsible demagogy nor to bidding higher in the stakes of nationalism. Our acts will be our most truthful defenders. In any event, because the above task must make substantial progress and yield results long before the next elections, for obvious reasons, in the relatively short time in between we must show self-restraint and remain cool.

At the same time, however, we must not only maintain the present unity and discipline of the patriotic forces, but increase it. This can only be done by the necessary briefing of our members and through them of our people.

In the first instance, we must uncover what the reactionaries stand for. Some of them are opportunist and irresponsible, as their recent past has shown. They are negative and aimless reactionaries who fanatically oppose our leadership, but without at the same time offering a substantive and practical solution. We need a steady and strong government in order to promote our plans up to the last moment. These opponents are verbalists and sloganists, but unwilling to proceed to concrete acts or to suffer sacrifices. For example, even at the present stage they offer nothing more concrete than recourse to the United Nations, that is, words again without cost to themselves. They must, therefore, be isolated. In parallel, we shall brief our members only ORALLY about our intentions. Our sub-headquarters must, in gatherings of our members, analyse and explain fully

310

and continuously the above, until each one of our members understands fully and is in a position to brief others.

NO WRITTEN REPORT IS PERMITTED. THE LOSS OF ANY DOCUMENT ON THE ABOVE AMOUNTS TO TREASON AGAINST THE NATION.

No act can damage our struggle as vitally and decisively as the revealing of the present document or its publication by our opponents. With the exception of word-of-mouth briefing, all our other actions, i.e., publications in the Press, resolutions, etc., must be very restrained and no mention of the above should be made. Similarly, in public speeches and gatherings, only responsible persons may make, under the personal responsibility of the Leader or Deputy Leaders, references in general terms to the plan. They must also have the authorisation of either the Leader or the Deputy Leader who must approve the text. ON NO ACCOUNT ARE REFERENCES IN THE PRESS OR ANY OTHER PUBLICATION PERMITTED.

Tactics. Complete briefing of our people and of the public by word of mouth. Publicly we shall endeavour to appear as moderates. Projection of or reference to our plans in the Press or in writing is strictly prohibited. Officials and other responsible persons will continue to brief and to raise the morale and the desire for the struggle of our people, but such briefing excludes making our plans public knowledge by the Press or otherwise.

NOTES: This document will be destroyed by fire on the personal responsibility of the Leader and the Deputy Leader in the presence of all the members of the General Staff within 10 days from its receipt. Copies or part copies are prohibited: members of the staff of the Office of the Deputy Leader may have copies on the personal responsibility of the Leader, but may not remove them from the Office of the Deputy Leader.

The Leader
AKRITAS

APPENDIX B

The Thirteen Amendments to the 1960 Constitution designed by Archbishop Makarios III To diminish Turkish Cypriot rights

1. The right of veto of the President and the Vice-President of the Republic to be abolished.

2. The Vice-President of the Republic to deputise for or replace the President of the Republic in case of his temporary absence or incapacity to perform his duties. In consequence, therefore, all the constitutional provisions in respect of joint action by the President and the Vice-President of the Republic to be modified accordingly.

3. The Greek President of the House of Representatives and its Turkish Vice-President to be elected by the House as a whole and not as at present the President by the Greek Members of the House and the Vice-President by the Turkish Members of the House.

4. The Vice-President of the House of Representatives to deputise for or replace the President of the House in case of his temporary absence or incapacity to perform his duties.

5. The constitutional provisions regarding separate majority for enactment of Laws by the House of Representatives to be abolished.

6. The constitutional provision regarding the establishment of separate Municipalities in the five main towns to be abolished. Provision should be made so that: (a) The Municipal Council in each of the aforesaid five towns shall consist of

Greek and Turkish Councillors in proportion to the number of the Greek and Turkish inhabitants of such town by whom they shall be elected respectively. (b) In the Budget of each of such aforesaid towns, after deducting any expenditure required for common services, a percentage of the balance proportionate to the number of the Turkish inhabitants of such town shall be earmarked and disposed of in accordance with the wishes of the Turkish Councillors.

7. The constitutional provision regarding Courts consisting of Greek Judges to try Greeks and of Turkish Judges to try Turks and of mixed Courts consisting of Greek and Turkish Judges to try cases where the litigants are Greeks and Turks to be abolished.

8. The division of the Security Forces into Police and Gendarmerie to be abolished, (Provision to be made in case the Head of the Police is a Greek,the Deputy Head to be a Turk and *vice versa*).

9. The numerical strength of the Security Forces and of the Army to be determined by Law and not by agreement between the President and the Vice-President of the Republic.

10. The proportion of the participation of Greek and Turkish Cypriots in the composition of the Public Service and of the Forces of the Republic, i.e. the Police and the Army, to be modified in proportion to the ratio of the population of Greek and Turkish Cypriots.

11. The number of the members of the Public Service Commission to be reduced from ten to either five or seven.

12. All the decisions of the Public Service Commission to be taken by simple majority. If there is an allegation of discrimination on the unanimous request either of the Greek or of the Turkish members of the Commission, its Chairman to be bound to refer the matter to the Supreme Constitutional Court.

13. The Greek Communal Chamber to be abolished.

APPENDIX C

Rauf Denktaş' speech to the
UN Security Council
February 28, 1964 — the first of his eleven
speeches to the UN between 1964 and 1996

'MR PRESIDENT, I thank you and I thank all the representatives for having given me the opportunity to address you on the tragic events in Cyprus. My community, which has suffered more than 800 dead or wounded in a matter of two months, will be most grateful. Twenty thousand of them have been rendered homeless or workless and rely upon charity for their living. The whole Turkish community has been living under virtual Greek siege since 21 December, 1963. All these people have been following the deliberations of your Council with anxiety. The fact that you have consented to hear their side of the story will be a great relief to them and I thank you once again on their behalf.

I have followed the long deliberations here with some anguish because every hour which has passed in argument has meant to my community either another lost life or more people rendered homeless. Each day for them has been another day under siege and under terror. But I was relieved to find that the consensus of opinion in this Council is to bring the bloodshed in Cyprus to an immediate end, to find means of doing so quickly and effectively. On this point, may I say that the guarantor Powers, under the treaty which has been the subject of attack in this Council, could have done this conjointly, quickly and effectively, but the Greek Cypriots did not want it as this would be a disservice to their cause. They wanted to do away with the treaties and with the Constitution.

While innocent Turkish women and children were being killed or wounded, Archbishop Makarios, in complete disregard of all that was going on in Cyprus, refused to have an immediate peacekeeping force in Cyprus offered by the United States, by the United Kingdom and by Greece and Turkey. While all this was going on in Cyprus, the representative of Archbishop Makarios in the United Nations tried twice, under the smokescreen of invasion by Turkey, to get a resolution from the Security Council in general terms on the inviolability of the integrity and independence of Cyprus. The intention was to get such a resolution hurriedly and then to interpret it in their own way and be able to declare that the treaties were dead and of no effect and that the guarantor Powers could do nothing while the Greeks destroyed the Constitution and annihilated the Turkish [Cypriot] community.

Mr Kyprianou has asked the Council: "Is it conceivable, is it possible, that the Greeks should contemplate the annihilation of a hundred thousand Turks?" Well, it will take some time to complete the extermination of a hundred thousand Turks, but may I say that it is not necessary that all of us should be killed. It is sufficient if life is made impossible for us in Cyprus and that is the object of the attack on us. I have listened very carefully to the speeches delivered several times by Mr Kyprianou. My conviction is that they do not want a peacekeeping force in Cyprus. This conviction has been confirmed by the speeches I have heard from him. Mr Kyprianou has confined his endeavours to leaving the killing of Turks in Cyprus by what he called the 'security forces' out of focus and to blaming others for those events, while attempting to get the very resolution which Mr Rossides twice before attempted to get from the Council under a false alarm.

Mr. Kyprianou has said that if the shadow of the Treaties which brought about the Republic of Cyprus was removed, then tension would be eliminated in the island and all would be well. To prove his point he mentioned that since the day this matter has been before the Council, the fear of invasion by Turkey has diminished, and, therefore, the tension has been reduced and there have been only isolated incidents in the island.

For persons who have absolute control over the Greek Cypriot gunmen, be they called "security forces" or not, such statements are easy to make. It shows that they have given orders to their gunmen to lie in wait while these proceedings go on.

Under the guise of isolated incidents, Turkish villagers have, however, been under constant threat and isolation. Turks have continued to die and mysteriously vanish. Guns and ammunition are still rolling in. Turks are still stranded and under siege. We know the pattern of these machinations. We saw them in the years 1955 and 1958. Each time the Cyprus case came before the United Nations, the Greek terrorists, under the same leaders, either pulled the trigger or waited, according to orders. Mr Kyprianou has said that if the resolution which he seeks is not forthcoming then the root of evil will continue to be there, meaning that tension will rise and bloodshed continue. I feel sure that this Council will not be blackmailed into an irresponsible action or one-sided resolution. I have absolute faith as to that.

It is very significant that Archbishop Makarios on 18 February, 1964 had this to say to a correspondent of UPI: 'I do not think a larger peacekeeping force on Cyprus is necessary. If the Greek Cypriot resolution demanding guarantees against aggression is adopted by the United Nations Security Council, the need for a peacekeeping force will be eliminated. The main question now is to abrogate the Cyprus Treaties that give Britain, Greece and Turkey the right to intervene in Cyprus affairs.'

This statement by Makarios and the manoeuvres by his representatives here in this Council are sufficient proof of the fact that the Greek Cypriots are trying to abuse the authority of this Council. While the only urgent need in Cyprus is the taking of such active measures as would ensure a cessation of violence and return to normality by moving in a peacekeeping force, the Greeks maintain that unless they get the resolution they want, nothing can be done in or for Cyprus.

This attitude and these declarations are also absolute proof of the already well-known fact that the attack on the Turks was an organised one for political reasons, and that such murder and violence as we have witnessed in the last few months is a tool in the hands of the Greek Cypriot authorities for getting their political ends. Had this not been so, how could the Archbishop so forcefully and categorically say that 'if the resolution I ask for is given, no peacekeeping force will be necessary'?

He will get his resolution: he will interpret it as having abrogated the Treaties; he will defy the guaranteeing powers; and then under the umbrella of your resolution, he will deal with the Turks the way he thinks best. If violence is necessary during this process, he will resort to violence and tell the world, as he did in December last, that his 'security forces' are dealing with some Turkish rebels.

This is the pattern of Greek mentality. I repeat my utmost faith in your Council's wisdom not to fall in with such mentality. Permit me, therefore, to tackle the problem in its essence and essentials. To understand these, it is necessary to understand the basis of the Republic of Cyprus and the reasons for the *sui generis* provisions in its Constitution, as well as the absolute necessity for the Treaties which brought it about.

Each country, each state, has its own peculiar and individual characteristics. That is why it is dangerous to apply general principles in complete disregard of such peculiarities. On the principle of each case to be decided on its own merits, I am sure that you will decide the issue before you on the merits, peculiarities and inherent characteristics of Cyprus. Otherwise, the result will be chaotic.

Very briefly, these are the facts.

Turks and Greeks have lived in Cyprus together since 1571. They have so lived always as Greeks or Turks. They have each stuck to their separate culture, religion, tradition and national heritage. They are in effect Turkey and Greece projected into Cyprus for the Turkish and Greek populations respectively. Any attempts to make them anything but Greeks or Turks have met with strong opposition from these groups in Cyprus. They each lived as autonomous communities together, yet always separate. Down to the smallest village there have always been and there are, Greek and Turkish authorities looking after the affairs of their communities separately.

As long as they enjoyed equality and justice, they lived together happily. As soon as one side attempted to dominate the other politically, trouble brewed and their relations were momentarily estranged. Greeks started this attempt to dominate the Turks after the British rule. Petitions for union with Greece met with counter petitions from the Turks opposing it. Demonstrations for union with Greece met with counter demonstrations by the Turks.

When the Greeks took up arms in 1955, not for independence — that is very important for the Security Council and for the United Nations, not for independence but for the union of Cyprus with Greece — it was inevitable that the Turks would oppose them, because the Turks were thus being put from the rule of one colonial power to another. This opposition brought violence. Turks reacted, inter-communal relations became estranged, bitter and full of mistrust and enmity. The Cyprus question came before the United Nations several times during 1955 and 1958.

The Greek Cypriots tried to get a resolution in complete disregard of the Turkish Cypriot factor. The United Nations refused to fall into this trap, and advised the parties, that is to say Greek and Turkish Cypriots who were warring against each other for different political aims, and Greece and Turkey, their recognized and avowed motherlands, to find a just and peaceful solution by negotiation. That is how the Zürich Agreement was reached in 1959. Archbishop Makarios and Dr. Küçük representing the two communities, were in constant touch with their respective motherlands during this time. At all stages they consented to what was being agreed to as a compromise solution. There should be no victors and no vanquished. Peaceful settlement necessitated that the two sides should make mutual sacrifices.

The fight arose because the Greeks wanted union and offered the Turkish Cypriots the position of a minority. The Turkish Cypriots refused this and demanded union with Turkey, or at least partition. We would never accept to live at the mercy of the Greek Cypriots. We had good examples of what life would be under them. The EOKA gunmen had repeatedly declared that once the fight against the British was brought to a victorious end, the fight against the Turks would be sharp and short.

Our struggle on the island was a constant danger to peace

between Turkey and Greece. So the compromise was reached in 1959 fairly and responsibly. A government of partnership was born. The two communities sat at a conference table and agreed upon the terms and conditions of this partnership. An eminent jurist of international law from Switzerland presided over our deliberations. Greece and Turkey I repeat, the two motherlands had their representatives there and we, the two communities, had ours. It was a settlement between equals, not between the majority and the minority.

The notion of majority and minority would have arisen had there been a Cypriot nation. There was not even the slightest notion of such a nation. Out of this partnership this notion might arise by a process of evolution when, in time, mutual goodwill, trust and friendship became the rule rather than the exception.

This notion of unity of Cypriotism could have arisen if the larger community had wanted it and had worked for it. But that has not been the case. From the beginning we were told in no uncertain terms that what we believed to be an honourable compromise was for the Greek Cypriots the beginning of a new struggle for achieving union with Greece. In other words, they had tied us down by international treaties and now want to use parts of the treaties for their own ends.

I would like to quote some statements repeatedly made by the Archbishop as from 1 April, 1960. He said: "These achievements are not, of course, absolute, but the present reality does not completely close the circle of our pursuits." He continues as follows: "The realisation of our hopes and aspirations is not complete under the Zürich and London Agreements. We have acquired a bastion and a starting point for peaceful campaigns. From these bastions we shall continue to struggle with a view to consummating victory."

This was a public statement from a responsible man who was becoming the head of a newly-born state.

Then, on 20 December, 1961, he said: "Taking into consideration the general interest of the people of Cyprus, I shall disregard any constitutional provision which, if abused, may obstruct the regular functioning of the state."

There was a constitutional court created under our Constitution for abuses and for other matters in Cyprus. An eminent German jurist was at the head of it, with Greek Cypriot and Turkish Cypriot participation. And in spite of that, this was an open declaration that he (Makarios) would disregard any constitutional provisions. This is from the head of a state newly born.

On 5 January 1962, he said: "The noble struggles of the people never come to an end. These struggles, although they undergo transformation are never terminated. The struggle of the people of Cyprus, too will go on. The Zürich and London Agreements form a landmark in the course of this struggle, but at the same time, are a starting point and bastion for further struggles, with the object of capitalizing on what has been achieved for further conquests."

On 12 February, 1963, he said the following: "Even if the Constitutional Court says that what I am doing on municipalities is unconstitutional, I will not respect anything of these things."

On 1 April, 1963, he said: "As we kneel before the graves of our martyrs, we hear them shout: 'Forward, beyond the graves'... The armed struggle ended, but it is continuing in a different form so that the present may be appraised and the future conquered."

On 27 July, 1963 he said: "The agreements do not form the goal; they are the present but not the future. The Greek Cypriot people will continue their national course and shape their future in accordance with their will. The Zürich and London Agreements have a number of positive elements, but also negative ones, and that Greeks will work to take advantage of the positive elements and get rid of the negative ones."

There are numerous other quotations, but I shall not delay the Council by reading them.

Will the United Nations endorse such conduct? Can a man,

a party to a simple transaction, take advantage of the 'positive' elements and refuse to abide by the 'negative' elements? Even in private life this is not allowed. How can the Security Council help Archbishop Makarios, if, in his own words, the Greeks are going to work to take advantage of the positive elements and get rid of the negative ones by completely disregarding the Turks and their rights in Cyprus? What will the fate of other international treaties be if governments which sign them freely are allowed to advance the excuses which the Greek Cypriots are now advancing for abrogating these treaties?

Archbishop Makarios having agreed to the independent Republic solely for the purpose of using this Republic as a springboard for *enosis* union of Cyprus with Greece his administration could do nothing but serve his purpose. All Turkish rights were denied or refused under humiliating accusations. All government organs set about doing nothing but eliminating all Turkish rights. In spite of the guarantees and the special rights worked into the Constitution, everything possible was done to reduce us and treat us as a mere minority. Nothing was done to stop the rising tide towards the condemnation of the [1960] Agreements by the Greeks. Churches and schools became a training ground for anti-Turkish, anti-Constitution upbringing of youth. A police state was clamped down upon us. Human rights and constitutional safeguards were completely disregarded. Turkish Cypriots, while necessarily doing their utmost to keep up the morale of their people, bent all their energies to bringing the Greek leadership to reason.

Dr. Küçük's message to Archbishop Makarios gives a good picture of the Turkish stand. It is dated 19 February, 1964. This was an open letter addressed to Archbishop Makarios. It says:

"Your broadcast last night reminded me of the constant efforts which were made during the short life of the Republic to create conditions in which the two communities could live together in peace and prosperity and co operate in a spirit of friendship, with goodwill and understanding. Lest you have forgotten my concrete appeals to you and the negative and evasive attitude which you always showed toward them, may I list below a few instances of this and the response with which they were met by you?

"You will no doubt recollect that I had to appeal to you many times, both orally and in writing, that you and certain Greek Cypriot ministers should refrain from taking leading parts in the campaign for *enosis* and against the Zürich and London Agreements and the Constitution. You refused to entertain my appeals and on the contrary continued to direct and even intensify the campaign."

"Three major constitutional crises occurred during the life of the Republic: taxation legislation, municipalities, and the Cyprus Army. [Dr. Küçük]then deals with these separately. I can give this letter to the secretariat, to be incorporated in my speech, because it is a long letter. It ends this way: "I cannot conclude this letter without stressing the difference of attitude which you and I adopted in our approach to the problems which have confronted us since the independence of Cyprus. As illustrated above, while you did your best to maintain a world of hatred toward Turks and thus destroy all hopes of coexistence in peace and friendship. I, on the other hand, as you well know, toiled hard to keep alive our Constitution and to create conditions in which the two communities could live and prosper together.

"It is most fitting to quote here from a letter which I sent to you on 22 August, 1963 in an effort to bring you to the path of reason and goodwill:

'Your Beatitude is no doubt aware that the campaign for the abrogation of the [1960] Agreements and for the amendment of our Constitution by unilateral action has recently assumed such proportions that it is no longer possible to accept the rapid spread of the feeling of uneasiness, insecurity, distrust, and enmity. As a result, we have been dragged to the verge of a constitutional crisis, from which runs the risk of falling into an abyss of calamity and devastation'.

"In the circumstances. I found myself compelled to appeal

again to Your Beatitude and to request you to end such a campaign. In that letter I also said: 'I wish to express the view that, despite what has so far been done, reason will prevail and in the end it will be possible to save Cyprus from plunging headlong into a state of chaos, anarchy, and disaster. I sincerely hope that Your Beatitude will rise to the occasion and abandon such plans and intentions which are against the establishment of constitutional order, and thus avert the danger which is looming over Cyprus.

For our part, I wish to emphasize here also that Turks are in favour of the solution of certain inter-communal disputes entirely in accordance with the provisions of the agreement and the Constitution.'

All those things which we thought were done away with under the [1960] Agreements in order to reach a compromise agreement were thus carried out and carried on by the most 'responsible' people. How could we feel secure? How could we feel happy?"

About March 1963, Archbishop Makarios openly declared that 1964 would be a decisive year. In 1963 he had forced the German President of the Constitutional Court to resign because this professor of international law had refused to give judgment against the Turks at Greek dictation. He chose his law and his conscience. That was not good enough for the Greeks. Circumstances were created, and he was forced to resign. In an interview given on 27 December, 1963 by Professor Forsthoff to an Associated Press correspondent in Heidelberg this is what he said, very briefly and to the point.

He said that he himself was convinced that if the government of Cyprus had been able to stick to the Constitution for five years most of the problems would have been mastered. 'I have told Makarios that time and again,' he said. But the Cyprus government had no intention of sticking to the Constitution because sticking to the Constitution would bring about trust and confidence, understanding and friendship, and people would settle down to a normal life. That was not what he

[Makarios] wanted. He wanted the people to be separated; he wanted people to doubt each other so that he could guide his own policy of abrogating the Agreements.

It is a result of this predetermined policy that the police pressure on the Turks of Cyprus increased from day to day. Illegal searches became a rule of the day. Resentment arose, naturally. In the last three years they had tried several times, by deliberate provocation, to make the Turks come out with an attack on the Greeks so that they would find the excuse to hit us back with all their might. We did not fall into that trap, and they knew we would not do so.

So, on the night of 21 December, 1963, they found the excuse. A Turkish family going to its house was stopped on the way by armed Greek youngsters. They pretended to be policemen.

They never disclosed their identity. They said 'we are the men of the Ministry of the Interior.' At gun point they tried to search the Turkish women and men. The women refused. They said: 'You must take us to the police station if we are to be searched.' Then people, hearing this altercation, gathered round. It is said that about fifteen persons gathered round, and while the altercation was going on, two Greek officers, this time in uniform, came to the scene, shooting their way in and killing a Turkish women and man and wounding five other Turks.

We did our best to keep this as a police affair, and we tried to localise the matter, but again that was not good enough for the government of Cyprus. When this event happened all Greek policemen were called to the police stations and fully armed. No arms were issued to the Turks, and the following day, when we issued the statement by Dr. Küçük calling upon the people to remain quiet and calm, the Cyprus Broadcasting service, which again was under the same Ministry, refused to publish it. They said, 'we shall publish only police bulletins', and we soon began to see what those bulletins were to be. By the evening they started telling the world that there was rebellion going on in the Nicosia area and that the security forces were dealing with the rebels.

In fact we were all surrounded by Greek policemen, held in by private Greek armies of whose existence we did not know until then, and we were attacked with automatic rifles. The next day Dr. Küçük was made to record an appeal to the Turkish community again to keep calm, and telling them that there was a ceasefire. This tape was taken away used by the Cyprus Broadcasting Corporation repeatedly making the Turks believe that there was nothing going on, while shooting in fact was going on in the Nicosia area and any Turk who dared to approach Nicosia was either killed or taken as a hostage.

I shall not elaborate on the horror which we suffered. For five days we were cut off from the world. Our telephones, including the telephone of the Vce-President, were disconnected. The radio was in the hands of the Greeks, and they issued bulletins continuously saying that a rebellion was going on and that they were dealing with the rebels. The wireless telegraph service was in their hands and no foreign correspondent could come to our side as we were completely surrounded and cut off.

It was after the fifth day, after a last appeal had been made by the Turks to all the guarantor Powers calling for help for the last time — previously they had not heeded our appeal at all — telling them that we had received an ultimatum from Mr Pandelidis, the police officer who had started the whole thing and who had told his number two on the Turkish side that if we did not all surrender they would smash us out from our homes with mortar bombs by next morning.

It was thereafter that the Turkish contingent moved out of its barracks and took a position as the result of which the Greeks who were attacking us had to leave unfinished a work which they were doing thoroughly. It was only then that we were saved.

I understand the resentment of Mr Kyprianou as a result of the moving out of the Turkish contingent. It prevented them [the Greek Cypriots] from completing a very thorough job, and our insistence on the Treaty of Guarantee must be appreciated because it has saved us. That is why I am here. That is why so many thousands of Turks can still look to this Council with hope.

A great deal of complaint has been centred around the moving of this contingent, which did not fire even one shot, but it is on record that at the time the Turkish contingent moved out, the Greek contingent also moved out from the other side, taking over charge of the airfields and other parts of the Greek town. These people were there to maintain law and order, and they had done so without firing a single shot. In the meantime the British forces came and took over the control and command of these two contingents. They are doing an admirable job. I think they deserve thanks.

It is these Powers which have needed further help from their other allies in order to maintain peace in Cyprus and bring sanity and reason to all of us. I think that is the reason we are all here — not to change Treaties, not to insist on conditions which we shall later use for our own ends.

That is the urgent work before this Council, and that is why all Cypriots in Cyprus, Turks or Greeks, who want peace and who want a cessation of bloodshed look to the Council for a decision on that particular issue.

There is one very important factor which I should like the Security Council to understand. Innocent and unarmed people may die in a fight: that may be the result of any fight and it can be explained. But in our case, women and children have been killed deliberately and brutally in their houses. Seven hundred people were taken as hostages by the so-called security forces. I have before me a Greek publication, *Cyprus Today,* supplement No. 2, November December 1963; the actual date of the issue is 3 January 1964. This is a publication of the Greek Communal Chamber. I shall read out part of paragraph 13, as follows:

'On the question of hostages, [Mr Yorgadjis] said the Turkish leaders have been informed officially by the President of the Republic that approximately 700 Turkish citizens have been evacuated from areas in which fierce fighting was taking place and have been removed and housed in Greek schools in safe areas....'

Now, the information came to us officially after the cease-fire that they had approximately 700 people. When we demanded the release of these people, we were told that they had been taken for safety purposes. Only 534 were returned to us. We asked what had happened to the others. The answer was: we have no others; that is the number we had. But there were British eyewitnesses who saw some of these hostages lined up and shot. Later we saw several of them buried in mass graves, fully clothed, women and children included. As I have said, the information came to us officially that the number was approximately 700.

In any case, a responsible security force should have known the number of people they had removed: we should not have been given an approximate number. We have asked what happened to the missing. It is no use insisting that the total number was delivered to us. We want to know what happened to the missing, the people who did not return to their homes, who have not been found, who have vanished. Their families are entitled, in the name of humanity, to know at least where the graves of these people are.

Turks that were ill have been removed from the hospitals. They have vanished. We want to know where they are, or at least where their graves are. In all humanity, we are entitled to know. Of course, this is not one of the Security Council's tasks, but it is material to the issue before the Council. It helps the Council to understand why we insist on these treaties, why we insist on these rights. Without them we shall just vanish.

After the ceasefire and after foreign correspondents came into our sector and the horror was disclosed, there was no more fighting in Nicosia. But it is very significant that the houses of the 700 people and of other persons who had fled from the Greek sectors were completely destroyed, either gutted by fire or pulled down by bulldozers. This happened all over Cyprus. Wherever the Turks had to leave their homes, those homes were gutted or pulled down.

The message which this teaches us is: you have to bow to our will or to die if you defy us — or you have to leave Cyprus for good. There is no room for us in Cyprus. I cannot say who is behind this, but this is the mentality of the people who hold the power and have the guns in their hands today, and stand there to do so for a long time to come. Will the Security Council, then, adopt a resolution which will leave us completely at the mercy of these people? It is held that in order to achieve a resolution which will be acceptable to the Cyprus government something must be said about the integrity and independence of Cyprus. They say: in order to make the Turks feel secure, let us have a United Nations force in Cyprus, but the resolution must state that the independence and integrity of Cyprus are to be maintained by the Security Council.

As we see it, the trick in such a position is the following. The United Nations force will go to Cyprus for a matter of three months. But they [the Greeks] have made no secret of the fact that they will immediately interpret the resolution as rendering the Treaty of Guarantee invalid, and that resolution will be in their hands for good. Thus for three months they will tell their gunmen: do not shoot. Then the United Nations Force will go away, and with the Security Council resolution in their hands, they will defy the guarantor Powers and argue that the Treaty of Guarantee is invalid because the Security Council has adopted this resolution. And on that basis they will deal with us as they please.

It may be said that I am a very suspicious Turk. I may have been suspicious before the incidents, but now the facts have confirmed what I have just told the Council.

The other day Mr Kyprianou said that there is now little or no activity in Cyprus, that everything is normal, that in some parts Greeks and Turks have signed declarations that they will keep the peace. Well, my information from Dr. Küçük is that

Turks continue to be under a state of siege. In some places they are running short of food. In some places they cannot get medicine. No one can go to work. Life is at a standstill as far as the Turks are concerned.

In some small places, there may be Turks working. But that is not the question. The question is: are we entitled to live in human dignity as free people in a land where we have lived for 400 years, or are we to be put at the mercy of the Greek Cypriots and to be treated as a mere minority when we have never had that status in 400 years?

Are we to be tricked out of our right to bargain equally just because they have killed some of us? That is the main issue before the Security Council today. It must not be forgotten that it was because Greeks feared partition and Turks feared Greek discrimination and eventual union with Greece that these guarantees had to be worked into the Constitution. If these guarantees are now removed, there will be no authority whatever to rule out the union of Cyprus with Greece. They may say, 'Let us enter into another treaty'. But the assurances of people who have defied treaties within a few days of signing them certainly cannot satisfy us.

In spite of these guarantees we have suffered discrimination, we have suffered indignity, and finally we have suffered the killings and the destruction of property. They now want you to tell them, 'Bravo for all this, you have done well!'; and they want you to honour them by giving them a free licence to argue that the treaties are invalid and, under this illusion, continue to subjugate the Turks, take away our constitutional rights and, if necessary, resort to further violence.

We all stand for the rule of law; there is a rule of law in Cyprus that is the Constitution. If it is necessary that it should be changed it can be changed only by argument and by making the other side see your point of view. It cannot be changed by killing, by massacre; it cannot be changed in this way.

Before I conclude I should like to deal with one or two points which Mr Kyprianou dealt with. He has shaken in his hand since the London meeting some secret and mysterious documents stating that the Turkish leadership has put its signature to certain documents which prove beyond any doubt that there was a plot between the Turkish leadership and Turkish government in order to partition the island and he has read parts of this document.

In London I challenged him to produce these documents for the public to read as a whole and to prove in whose custody they were at the time they came into their hands who gave it to them, when they got them, who signed them. All these things must be proved before documents can be discussed. I challenged this; nothing was produced.

Now I challenge again. If they got these documents before these incidents, then they should have done their duty as a responsible government and taken some action against these people. If they got them after the incidents and I think that was their case in London then they must tell us where and how they got them. They must produce proof and then rest on it. But the facts disprove the documents.

If the Turkish leadership in Cyprus was involved in such a plot for partition in conjunction with the leaders in Turkey, the two months' fight in Cyprus would not have ended in the way it did; the facts in Cyprus would not be as they are today: some Turks armed mostly with shotguns and all Greeks armed thoroughly; Turks shrieking for help from Turkey and Turkey, adamant [not] to come in without being sure that a massacre is taking place and then all it does is to give warning and nothing more; it is a call to the guarantor Powers to take a hand.

Do these facts prove the existence of a plot between the Turkish leadership and the Turkish government? Do they prove that we were ready for such a plot? There was one side in Cyprus which wanted to abrogate the Agreements by hook or by crook, by murder if necessary, and that side has proved its case. That is the case before you.

Today no Constitution is in effect in Cyprus. None of the provisions of the Constitution are being complied with or applied. In the circumstances which have been created it cannot be applied. So the two communities have fallen apart. It is not the fault of Mr Kyprianou that he has not been able to get full instructions from Dr. Küçük and the Turkish Ministers to have this discussed fully in the Ministerial Council. The Greek gunmen will not let the Turks go to the other side and the ministerial function is finished. But with due respect to him, I do not think he can say nor that he can claim in justice and fairness and humanity that he can represent the Turkish [Cypriot] voice, that he can fully represent the Turkish [Cypriot] side in this Council. He cannot.

Mr President, I thank you most sincerely for giving me this hearing, I have done my best to tell you our side of the story. I thank you for your patience and I thank you for your kindness. It has been a great help to me and it will be a great help to my community, as I hope what I have just told you may be a help to you in your deliberating and in reaching your decisions.'

Following this speech on 4th March 1964 the Security Council passed the landmark — and disastrous — Resolution 186 recognising the Greek Cypriot regime as the lawful government of Cyprus.

APPENDIX D

The Citation which supported the nomination of Rauf Denktaş to the Nobel Peace Prize Committee in Oslo, January 2011

This Citation has been prepared with the assistance of
MICHAEL STEPHEN LLM, a Barrister and international lawyer and who
was a Conservative member of the UK
Parliament 1992-97. He held a Harkness Fellowship in International
Law at Stanford and Harvard, and was Assistant Legal Adviser to the
UK Ambassador to the UN for the 25th General Assembly . He is the
author of *The Cyprus Question* (London, July 2001)

A TRAGEDY UNFOLDS

RAUf Raif Denktaş, the son of a District Court judge honoured by the British with the award of the MBE, trained as a barrister in London; he returned to Cyprus in 1947, aged 23, and set out on building a legal practice, assuming that this would be his career and that perhaps, like his father, he would one day become a judge.

It was not to be. The end of the second world war was to prove also the beginning of the end of a world in which countries such as Britain could rule as they once did. Anti-imperialism was the cry across its colonies, as it was for the French and Dutch, and indeed within the year the British would grant independence to and divide the Indian sub-continent. As elsewhere, this mood affected Cyprus, where the Greek Cypriots dreamed again of *enosis* — union with Greece — and the removal of their British masters, willingly or unwillingly.

Britain's retreat from Palestine in 1948, and the founding of the independent state of Israel, came after the Jewish Stern gang mounted a bloody terrorist campaign; it would be the model for a similar terrorist campaign in Cyprus seven years later, though the outcome would be different. The British would not give up Cyprus as easily. Its strategic value was too great for that. Even so, across the imperial world — in French Indo-China, in Dutch Indonesia, in British Malaya, and elsewhere, terror was seen as a legitimate weapon by extremist groups bent on ending colonial rule.

For the Greek Cypriots, or at least for large numbers of them, *enosis* was the dream, and as the majority people on the island, union with Greece would mean that the Turkish Cypriots — 18% of the population — would simply exchange one colonial master for another, and one far less agreeable than the British. There would be no place for them in a Greek island, save as second-class citizens; the equality they enjoyed under the British would be no more.

Cyprus, taken by the Turks in 1571, had been leased to the British in 1878; after the First World War, in which Turkey had been defeated along with Germany, the British had annexed the island as a Crown Colony. In the hopes of uniting the two communities there they banned their identification as 'Greek' or 'Turk', describing them instead by their religion — 'Turkish Cypriots were 'the Moslem Community' and Greek Cypriots 'the Orthodox Christian Community'. It was forbidden to campaign for *enosis*, and those who openly did so were sent away to Greece. Although neither community liked these restrictions, they did protect the Turkish Cypriots, until 1945 from feeling threatened by *enosis* extremists. Denktaş remembers these as the golden years of intercommunal contact.

'When I came back to Cyprus I found the atmosphere completely different' he recalls. 'Relations between the two peoples of Cyprus had been soured by talk of *enosis*, which Turkish Cypriots knew would lead to domination and eventual death or expulsion of us all from Cyprus, as had already happened in Crete. So when people ask me whether my struggle has been religious, or nationalist, or whatever, I reply that it is, and always has been, against domination by anyone. For us, colonisation by Greeks or Greek Cypriots would be much worse than by the British.'

Yet in those first years after the war the Turkish Cypriots could take comfort from the fact that the British gave no sign of departing. Indeed they made clear that Cyprus was one colony they intended to keep, though with a general promise that its two peoples might have more say in their affairs in the future — but no more than that. The island would not become Greek, however great the clamour. The Turkish Cypriots need have no fear of that.

What was to change that comfortable view of Cyprus

came with the terrorist campaign led by the Greek colonel Grivas in April 1955. Calling itself EOKA, and dedicated to *enosis*, it would bomb and kill its way across Cyprus for the next four years . The price of that would be the lives of 371 British servicemen, 69 policemen from both communities, and almost 300 civilians, 29 of them British.

The campaign in the event would fail in its central purpose — *enosis* — for neither Britain nor Turkey would accept that. In particular, if Greek Cypriots were to join themselves to Greece, Turkey for its part made clear that it would demand partition.

In 1958 Turkish Foreign Minister Zorlu invited the acknowledged Turkish Cypriot leader Dr. Küçük to his suite at the Waldorf-Astoria in New York, and Denktaş went with him. Zorlu told them what was in the mind of the British, Greek and Turkish governments — a kind of federal set-up, a partnership. The Greek Cypriot Archbishop Makarios would be the president and Küçük his deputy. The outline of a future agreement was put before the two men. Denktaş gave his legal opinion — that it did not look like a federation to him and that the rights were only on paper — worthless if the Greek Cypriots chose subsequently to tear them up. The minimum guarantee they needed was at least a token Turkish military presence on the island.

Zorlu doubted that, believing that the Greek Cypriots would never agree to Turkish troops on the island. Denktaş persisted, as he would persist again when he and Küçük met Zorlu next, this time in Ankara. A token force would suffice, he argued, just to show Makarios that any attempt to destroy the agreed partnership would automatically involve the two Motherlands as co-guarantors of the agreement.

Equally distrustful of Makarios, Dr. Küçük fully supported him. Both were sure he would destroy any agreement for the sake of *enosis* and they were not going to leave their people at his mercy just because the Turkish government had signed a piece of paper making them guarantors. Physical presence, they insisted, was essential. A week later a surprised Zorlu reported to them that Greece in fact had agreed that the guarantors could station troops in Cyprus — and that Makarios had consented. It was a major step forward. On the face of it, the proposed agreement was no long a paper tiger.

In 1959, following agreement between the Turkish and Greek Prime Ministers in Zurich, Küçük represented the Turkish Cypriots at the London Conference in February and signed the agreement on their behalf. On August 16, 1960 the Republic of Cyprus came into existence. Küçük was elected unopposed as vice-President and served until December 1963 when, after just three years, the new Republic disintegrated. Out of office, he continued to serve as leader of the Turkish Cypriots until on February 18, 1973 he retired, having been diagnosed with cancer, and was succeeded by Rauf Denktaş.

WITH the British gone — though they retained two sovereign Bases on the south coast, which satisfied their strategic interest in the island — it had soon became worryingly clear that the Greek Cypriots did not intend to abide by the Constitution, and that their entry into that solemn legal obligation with the Turkish Cypriots in 1960 had been a deception. Swift evidence of that had come on July 28,1960 when President Makarios said in a speech that 'the agreements do not form the goal — they are the present and not the future. The Greek Cypriot people will continue their national cause and shape their future in accordance with *THEIR* will.'

Denktaş was rightly alarmed, and there were more warnings ahead for in a speech on September 4, 1962 Makarios told an applauding crowd of Greek Cypriots that '*until this Turkish community forming part of the Turkish race which has been the terrible enemy of Hellenism is expelled, the duty of the heroes of EOKA can never be considered as terminated.*'

This ominous and inflammatory statement seemed to confirm to Denktaş that his fears for the future were not misplaced. Yet the complacent answer of the outside world was that he and the Turkish Cypriots should 'take no notice of it'. They were told that it was just rhetoric, for internal consumption within the Greek Cypriot community. However, the Turkish Cypriots were to discover that when Greek Cypriot leaders make statements of that kind they should be taken seriously — as an anxious Denktaş had thought they should from the beginning.

Article 173 of the Cyprus Constitution provided for separate municipalities for Turkish Cypriots in the five main towns. The Greek Cypriots refused to implement this mandatory provision and in order to pressure them to do so the Turkish Cypriots said that unless they did they would not vote for the government's taxation proposals. The Greek Cypriots remained intransigent, so the Turkish Cypriots took the matter to the supreme Constitutional Court of Cyprus. The court comprised one Greek Cypriot judge, one Turkish Cypriot judge, and a neutral President — Dr. Ernst Forsthoff, a German.

In February 1963 Archbishop Makarios declared on behalf of the Greek Cypriots that if the Court ruled against them they would ignore it. On April 25, 1963 the Court did rule against them *(Turkish Communal Chamber v Council of Ministers 5 CLR (1963) 59, 77, 78)*— but, as Makarios had said they would, the Greek Cypriots simply dismissed that as binding.

The German president resigned in protest and with that the rule of law in Cyprus collapsed. A furious Dr. Forsthoff had gone to Dr. Küçük and Denktaş the previous evening to prepare them for his resignation, explaining that 'I cannot work like this'. He went on to say that if Turkey were minded to exercise its right as a guarantor to intervene there could be no better reason than this blatant disregard for the law.

'I don't think he was thinking of military intervention' says Denktaş, 'but he was certainly of the view that Turkey could and should do something.' Turkey did indeed protest the action of the Greek Cypriots, and so did the British, but neither did anything further.

Given this weak signal from the two guarantor powers, the Greek Cypriots went further in November 1963, and demanded the abolition of eight of the basic articles which had been included in the 1960 Agreement for the protection of the Turkish Cypriots. Their aim was manifestly to reduce the Turkish Cypriot people to the status of a mere minority, wholly subject to the control of the Greek Cypriots. They would be masters of the island.

Glafcos Clerides, later to succeed Makarios as president, has admitted in his memoirs, *Cyprus — My Deposition*, that there was no need for constitutional amendments. As he wrote, 'Makarios, at the head of the bi-communal state of Cyprus, had decided to proceed, stage by stage, to the unilateral abrogation of the rights granted to the Turkish community by the Zurich and London Agreements and to reduce its political status to a minority, using prematurely the excuse of the unworkability of certain provisions of the constitution.'

He goes on to say that 'an honest evaluation of the situation during the period 1960-63, divorced from propaganda tendencies, would lead to the conclusion that there was no need to press for constitutional amendments'. Nevertheless, according to Clerides, Makarios 'refused to accept practical solutions failing short of constitutional amendments' in spite of the fact that Clerides had himself 'reached an agreement with the Turkish Cypriot side for a series of practical solutions'.

Clerides admits that 'the delicate period of 1960-63, when both communities were questioning the sincerity of the other over their real commitment to independence, was not the proper time to request constitutional amendments on the grounds that the constitution was unworkable, when in fact unworkability could not be established.'

Despite that frank admission by Clerides, Greek Cypriots today often claim that constitutional amendments were inevitable on the grounds that the Turkish Cypriots abused their veto power. Yet here again Clerides shows that not to be true: 'The veto powers were not used either by the President

or the vice-President on any law or decision of the House of
Representatives. The vice-President used once, I believe, his
veto power on a decision of the Council of Ministers relating
to the composition of the units of the army of the Republic.
The Greek Cypriot side was actually pleased the vice- President
used his veto on defence because it happily prevented the
planned implementation of an army consisting of 60% Greek
Cypriots and 40% Turkish Cypriots.' Instead, there would be
no Turkish Cypriots at all.

However, none of this was by chance. Makarios, even as he
was signing the 1960 independence settlement, had secretly
ordered the preparation of what would be called the *Akritas*
plan — its existence known only when the whole plan was
published in the Greek Cypriot newspaper *Patris* on April 21,
1966 — and which was designed to ensure that as soon as
the moment was right the Greek Cypriots would begin the
removal of Turkish Cypriots from government, and their
progressive elimination from the island.

That moment came when Makarios put forward his 13
amendments to the constitution to remove the basic terms of
the 1960 Agreement. His excuse to the world would be that
he had no choice in the face of Turkish Cypriot 'manipulation'
of the Constitution. With that, he then gave the order for
battle.

For Denktaş and those around him, the terrible events
which were to begin in December 1963 were not unexpected.
Although he then had no knowledge of the *Akritas* plan he
had become convinced that Makarios was set on destroying
the 1960 Republic, and in his reports to the Turkish
government he predicted a campaign of violence against the
Turkish Cypriots, judging that it would commence after New
Year 1964, though to his lasting regret Ankara discounted his
warnings.

He was to be proved right save on the date: the violence
began a week earlier — at Christmas. As he would say later,
'the *Akritas* plan destroyed the only compromise ever reached

between Greece and Turkey and between Greek and Turkish Cypriots about Cyprus. It revived bloodshed and hatred. It thrust Cyprus and its peoples back into the extremes of *enosis* and partition. It was bound sooner or later to bring some kind of intervention from Turkey.

'This rash, wicked, conspiracy was an act of supreme folly by the Greek Cypriot leaders, who still refuse to admit their wrongdoing. They continue to accuse others of bringing undeserved disasters upon them, but the truth is that it was they who broke up the bi-communal state and separated the Greeks and Turks from one another.'

The distinguished philosopher Professor Michael Moran of Sussex University, England, in his masterly work *Sovereignty Divided* (1998) gave this explanation for the way that the Greek Cypriots perceived themselves as 'the master race' and the Turkish Cypriots as of no consequence:

'It was because they were under a kind of ideological spell, a collective mental condition similar to what Marxists used to call false-consciousness, that the Greek Cypriots could embark upon their particular course of action in December 1963 with all the zeal and confidence they did.

'Brainwashed through at least a hundred years of school-teaching and sermonising into a set of beliefs pathologically at odds with any plausible account of historical and political realities; lacking contact with a counterbalancing tradition of rational criticism; for the most part incapable of ironic scepticism towards theological obfuscation — the Greek Cypriot leaders were effectively de-sensitised to the equally important rights of the Turkish Cypriots. In this way they were able to treat their Turkish compatriots with such consistent and irrational abuse, hardly noticing that this was in fact what they were doing.'

THE KILLING BEGINS

THE massacre of Turkish Cypriots which began at Christmas 1963 was on such a scale that it could not be hidden from the world, notwithstanding Greek Cypriot claims that it was not they who had started the slaughter — which they would later dub 'The Turkish Revolt'.

Professor Ernst Forsthoff, the German 'neutral' who had resigned in disgust eight months earlier from the presidency of the supreme Constitutional Court of Cyprus, told *Die Welt* on December 27, 1963: 'Makarios bears on his shoulders the sole responsibility of the recent tragic events. His aim is to deprive the Turkish community of their rights.' In an interview with UPI press agency three days later he said: 'All this happened because Makarios wanted to remove all constitutional rights from the Turkish Cypriots.'

On December 28,1963 the London *Daily Express* carried the following report from Cyprus: 'We went tonight into the sealed-off Turkish Cypriot Quarter of Nicosia in which 200 to 300 people had been slaughtered in the last five days. We were the first western reporters there and we have seen sights too frightful to be described in print. Horror so extreme that the people seemed stunned and in tears'.

Three days later another British newspaper, *The Guardian*, reported: 'It is nonsense to claim, as the Greek Cypriots do, that all casualties were caused by fighting between armed men of both sides. On Christmas Eve many Turkish Cypriot people were brutally attacked and murdered in their suburban homes, including the wife and children of the Turkish Cypriot head of army medical services, allegedly by a group of forty men, many in army boots and greatcoats.' Although the Turkish Cypriots fought back as best they could, there were no massacres of Greek Cypriot civilians.

On New Year's Day 1964 the London *Daily Herald* reported in a despatch from Cyprus: 'When I came across the

Turkish homes they were an appalling sight. Apart from the walls they just did not exist. I doubt if a napalm attack could have created more devastation. Under roofs which had caved in I found a twisted mass of bed springs, children's cots, and grey ashes of what had once been tables, chairs and wardrobes. In the neighbouring village of Ayios Vasilios I counted 16 wrecked and burnt-out homes. They were all Turkish Cypriot. In neither village did I find a scrap of damage to any Greek Cypriot house.'

On January 12, 1964 official confirmation of all this came from the British High Commission in Nicosia, which told London *(Telegram no. 162)*: 'The Greek (Cypriot) police are led by extremists who provoked the fighting and deliberately engaged in atrocities. They have recruited into their ranks as 'special constables' gun-happy young thugs...Makarios assured Sir Arthur Clark [the High Commissioner] that there will be no attack. His assurance is as worthless as previous assurances have proved.'

On January14, 1964 the London *Daily Telegraph* reported that the Turkish Cypriot inhabitants of Ayios Vasilios had been massacred three weeks earlier, on December 26,1963, and reported their exhumation from a mass grave in the presence of the Red Cross and British paratroops.

Many harrowing stories from that period and 1974 are recounted by the Chief Matron of the Nicosia Hospital, Nurse Türkan Aziz MBE, in her memoirs *The Death of Friendship*. She recalls (*Chapter 9*) how Greek Cypriots roamed the hospital wards killing the Turkish Cypriot patients, and found the bodies of two Turkish Cypriot boys who had taken refuge in her own apartments.

'The two sat on chairs exactly where I had left them, but this time they did not rise to greet me with smiles. Dark blood welled through the tattered remnants of their shirts and dripped on the carpet. Their Greek Cypriot 'guard' had vanished, spraying the staircase senselessly with bullets as he left'. *(page 84)*.

Matron Aziz describes the horror of Ayios Vasilios as follows: 'A few feet down they found the first bodies, three

343

men thrown on top of each other, then a boy whose hands had been tied behind his knees, then a little girl, then an old man dressed in his peasant-style baggy trousers, then some women. There were 21 bodies, almost all dressed, but not in hospital garb. These were Turkish Cypriot families who had lived in Ayios Vasilios.'

The relevance of 'hospital garb' is that the Greek Cypriots, in a Press statement headed *Turks distort the truth,* had insisted that the bodies were of patients in the hospital who had died of natural causes. *(page 90).*

On February 13, 1964 the Greeks and Greek Cypriots attacked the Turkish Cypriot quarter of Limassol with tanks, killing 16 and injuring 35. Two days later the *Daily Telegraph* reported: 'It is a real military operation which the Greek Cypriots launched against the 6,000 inhabitants of the Turkish Cypriot Quarter yesterday morning. A spokesman for the Greek Cypriot government has recognised this officially. It is hard to conceive how Greek and Turkish Cypriots may seriously contemplate working together after all that has happened.'

A further massacre of Turkish Cypriots, at Limassol, was reported by the London Sunday newspaper *The Observer* the following day, February 16, 1964, and there were many more such appalling stories. In the United States, on February 17, 1964 the *Washington Post* judged that 'Greek Cypriot fanatics appear bent on a policy of genocide'.

MORE than300TurkishCypriots went missing without trace from these massacres of 1963/64, and their bodies are even now being exhumed by the Joint Committee on Missing Persons. These dreadful events were not the responsibility of 'the Greek Colonels' of 1974, or an unrepresentative handful of Greek Cypriot extremists. The persecution of the Turkish Cypriots was an act of policy on the part of the Greek Cypriot political and religious leadership, which has to this day made no serious attempt to bring the murderers to justice. And the world knew that.

The UK Commons Foreign Affairs Select Committee found that 'there is little doubt that much of the violence which the Turkish Cypriots claim led to the total or partial destruction of 103 Turkish villages and the displacement of about a quarter of the total Turkish Cypriot population, was either directly inspired by, or certainly connived at, by the Greek Cypriot leadership'.

In his memoirs, the American Under-Secretary of State, George Ball, said that the Greek Cypriot leader's 'central interest was to block off Turkish intervention so that he and his Greek Cypriots could go on happily massacring Turkish Cypriots. Obviously we would never permit that.'

The fact is, however, that neither the US, the UK, the UN, nor anyone other than Turkey eleven years later, took effective action to prevent it. In the same book *(page 340)* George Ball quotes Adlai Stevenson as saying that Makarios was a wicked, unreliable conniver, who concealed his venality under the sanctimonious vestments of a religious leader and comments that 'in the years I had known Adlai I had never heard him speak of anyone with such vitriol.'

Ball also recalls *(page 345)* that during his visit to Cyprus in the spring of 1964, Sir Cyril Pickard, the British Under-Secretary of State for Commonwealth Relations, 'denounced the Archbishop in devastating language for the outrages inflicted on the Turkish Cypriots.' Ball himself told the Greek Cypriot leader that 'if he persisted in his cruel and reckless conduct Turkey would inevitably invade, and neither the Us nor any other western power would raise a finger to stop them.'

He further recalls that 'a massacre took place in Limassol on the south coast in which as I recall about 50 Turkish Cypriots were killed, in some cases by bulldozers crushing their flimsy homes. I said to Makarios sharply that such beastly actions had to stop.'

On his visit to Athens at that time he also records *(page 353)* that 'Greek Prime Minister [George] Papandreou contended that the 'turbulence' over Cyprus resulted only from Turkey's invasion threats. I told him that although I had heard all that before it simply was not true.'

The British government recorded (*FO doc. 1057 of 15.2.1964*) that George Ball 'thought that Makarios' aim was to get the Cyprus problem into the UN orbit where the slogan of self-determination, supported by the Communist bloc and the neutralists, could exert pressure towards the establishment of an independent unitary state, where he could do what he liked with the Turkish Cypriots.' On that he was to be proved wholly right.

Professor J. D. Bowers of the Department of Genocide Studies at Illinois University in the United States has openly concluded *(research report 2009)* that the murders of Turkish Cypriots between 1963 and 1974 met the UN definition of attempted genocide.

BLUNDER AT THE UN

THE immediate question for the international community was how to stop the killing. The British, sallying out from their two sovereign bases on the island, attempted to protect the Turkish Cypriots as best they could, but deeply conscious that they were the ex-colonial masters, and as such bound not to favour one side or another, it was obvious that what was urgently needed was that peacekeeping should become the responsibility of the United Nations. But therein lay a problem.

The UN could not impose a peacekeeping force on a sovereign nation, it could intervene only by invitation. But an invitation from whom? On any constitutional analysis the government of the Republic of Cyprus, a member of the UN, was no longer in being since the Greek Cypriots had in forcing the Turkish Cypriots out of office and parliament fatally breached the 1960 constitution. They could claim to be the *de facto* government of the Greek Cypriots but not of the island. The Republic of Cyprus as defined in 1960 was no more.

Yet, since they occupied all the government offices, and controlled the courts, the police and the National Guard, reality obliged at least their temporary recognition if UN troops were to sent in. By terrible irony therefore the UN Security Council would find itself having to ask a government without legal standing for permission to intervene to stop that same regime from killing the citizens of the lawful government they themselves had brought down.

However, the imperative was that the Turkish Cypriots should be protected. Turning a blind eye to the niceties of international law was therefore the necessary price for the greater good — of lives that must be saved — or so it seemed to the Security Council. The Greek Cypriots had not wanted the UN on the island but in the end, in their eagerness to stop the killings, the UN made an offer the Greek Cypriots could not refuse: in return for their acceptance of a peacekeeping force, they would be recognised as the legal government — until, that is, the two communities could somehow resolve their differences and the 1960 Agreement could be restored The future would have to sort itself out.

The man who was chosen to represent the Turkish Cypriot case, and thereby challenge the legitimacy of a government the Greek Cypriots in fact had hijacked, was 40-year-old Rauf Denktaş who went to New York in February 1964, a few weeks after the massacres had begun. Unfortunately he would find himself an outsider in the corridors of the UN. The Greek Cypriots had made sure of that.

In the three years before the killings began, and even before that, Makarios — flying his anti-imperial banner and parading his credentials as a champion of independence — had been assiduously courting the 'Non-Aligned Movement' of which the Burmese UN Secretary-General, U Thant, was an enthusiastic supporter. He had also been wooing the Soviet

Union and its satellites. When therefore the Cyprus question came before the Security Council in February 1964 he was in a strong position in the UN as a whole.

While the Greek Cypriots were duly treated by the UN as the 'government of Cyprus' and accorded full rights as the representatives of a member-state — as if it were still the same Republic of Cyprus established in 1960 — Denktaş was obliged to apply as 'an interested person' under Rule 39 of the Security Council's Rules of Procedure.

He could speak, as he would do on February 28, but how powerful and persuasive his speech, and it succeeded on both counts, his great weakness was its own contradiction — that in order to stop the killings, the Security Council needed a lawful government in place, and that issue having been settled behind doors, he was effectively wasting his time.

Nevertheless his speech remains of historic importance — as a contemporary record of the human disaster which had overtaken the island, and as a damning indictment of the way in which the Greek Cypriots had played fast-and-loose with the Constitution — and the international community. *It is therefore quoted in full in Citation 2 hereafter.*

Four days later, on March 4, 1964, the Council passed — and disastrously so for the Turkish Cypriots — the landmark Resolution 186. The Greek Cypriots were jubilant. Next day, as the *Cyprus Mail* reported, Makarios declared that 'we have secured a resolution in the first phase of our struggle in the international field' —and claiming that by the UN recognition Turkey could no longer intervene under the Treaty of Guarantee.

DENKTAŞ had protested the mention of 'the government of Cyprus' in the draft resolution. The Turkish representative also protested, and the passing of the final resolution was delayed because of that. The British and Americans insisted to Denktaş that he should not concern himself about the recognition of Makarios — it would be sorted out later. Meanwhile the imperative was to get the UN troops into place to stop the killing and destruction. 'Don't worry, we will not interpret it as you fear' was the message. 'There is blood flowing in Cyprus, it is your blood Mr. Denktaş and you are delaying the arrival of UN peacekeepers — is it not a pity?'

Turkey took the same view. The Turkish Prime Minister İnönü told Ankara's UN representative that he was satisfied that in the resolution the term 'Cyprus government' referred to that originally set up and guaranteed to both communities in 1960 — and not the Greek Cypriot regime which had subverted it. Britain had agreed with this definition.

The real issue was that UN troops got to Cyprus without delay — and for that, Turkey would back Britain and the US, both key members of the Security Council and whose support for the resolution was critical to its success.

Denktaş left the Security Council in tears. He later recalled that 'Sinan Korle, a Turk who was Deputy Director of Protocol at the UN, invited me to his office, and said "why are you worrying about Security Council Resolutions, Nobody listens to them." I was surprised, I was shocked.

'Despite all our efforts to prevent the Greek Cypriot regime being described as the Government of Cyprus it was done,' recalls Denktaş. 'We were assured that it referred only to the legitimate Makarios-Küçük government under the 1960 Constitution'. Yet, as he would swiftly realise, that was not the view held within the General Assembly: what had been solely intended as a means of deploying UN peacekeepers became, once the resolution was passed, a fact in the eyes of most member states.

Nothing was done to correct the record in the horse-trading world of the UN and its General Assembly where, lobbied by the Greek Cypriots, the majority interpreted 'government of Cyprus' as the opposite of that intended in the Security Council resolution — that the Greek Cypriot regime not the 1960 government was the lawful government of the Republic of Cyprus.

Denktaş was not alone in his dismay. A few weeks later, on May 2, the British Prime Minister, Sir Alec Douglas-Home in querying *Despatch 911* pointedly asked: Why doesn't the Secretary-General deal jointly with Makarios and Küçük? That is what he should do. Makarios is not the Government of Cyprus. However, with a diplomatic fiction having translated itself into fact, the British government, as with every other government except Turkey, lazily accepted thenceforth the UN consensus that the Greek Cypriot administration was and is the lawful government of Cyprus. For the British the reason for going 'along with the crowd' was in part that there was a General Election later that year which ousted the Conservative prime minister Douglas-Home and his replacement by a Labour prime minister, Harold Wilson.

Cyprus got lost in the process. The unintended consequence of that has enabled the Greek Cypriots ever since to treat the Turkish Cypriots as a mere community, to take most of the international aid for themselves, to embargo Turkish Cypriot trade and communications with the outside world, to occupy the Cyprus chair in all international institutions, and to convince the world that they, and not the Turkish Cypriots are the injured party.

The immediate consequence in March 1964 was that, having been given recognition at the UN as the lawful government, the Greek Cypriot leaders took that to mean they now had a free hand to drive out the Turkish Cypriots as and when they liked. The Greek Cypriots would lose no time in showing how true that would seem to be.

Three days after the passing of Resolution 186 the killings started again.

SO MUCH FOR PEACE

RAUF Denktaş was still in New York and due to give a lecture in a room below the Turkish Embassy when the news came in that the Greek Cypriots had attacked the crowded market place in Paphos — his birthplace — on Saturday March 7, 1964 — just 72 hours after Resolution 186 had been passed in the belief that all would now be well in Cyprus.

British troops in Paphos, acting as mediators, had extracted a promise from the Greek Cypriots that there would be no violence in the port, and reassured by this local Turkish Cypriots in the nearby villages had gone into Paphos that day to shop in the market, located between the Greek and Turkish quarters.

The killing began when a Turkish Cypriot postman, on his way to deliver letters, was shot dead by a Greek Cypriot. A panic ensued as other Greek Cypriots started firing from their quarter. Nobody knew what to do or where to go for safety. The scene of the attack was nearer to the Turkish Cypriot side, so the people there took everyone — Greek as well as Turkish — into their homes to shelter from the bullets as Turkish Cypriots defending the quarter fired back. Next day, after the shooting had stopped, all the Greek Cypriots who had taken refuge in the Turkish Cypriot houses, returned home to their own quarter.

With their own people back, the Greek Cypriots then surrounded the Turkish Cypriot Quarter with armed men and began to fire with bazookas, heavy machine guns, and mortars. Hundreds of mortar bombs were falling on the houses. They then brought up armoured bulldozers— some eight of them in all — to try to break down what little defences there were, but they turned back after Turkish Cypriot defenders fired on them. The Greek Cypriots continued shooting and throwing mortar bombs all that day and then again until around noon the following day.

In New York, as he was shown the telegrams coming into

351

the Turkish Embassy about the attack — including one which read 'the situation is desperate for the Turkish Cypriots, they cannot survive' — he broke down, tears flowing from his eyes. 'I cannot go on', he wept. 'These people who are dying trusted me to protect them.'

Later he was to hear that the Turkish Air Force had flown over Paphos and with that warning the Greek Cypriots had accordingly proposed a truce. A green line was drawn there by the British commander, and in that tiny area the Turkish Cypriots of Paphos would have to survive for the next eleven years, their homes destroyed around them.

STILL not confident that they could eliminate the Turkish Cypriots without help from Greece, the Greek Cypriots began to augment their forces soon afterwards. In his book *Democracy at Gunpoint* Andreas Papandreou recalls that in 1964 'a clandestine operation began on a huge scale; of nightly shipments of arms and 'volunteers' who arrive in Cyprus in civilian clothes and then join their Greek Cypriot units.'

Newsweek likewise reported on July 27, 1964: 'Before dawn each day the great iron doors of the port of Limassol are slammed shut... UN troops are barred. A few hours later the doors swing open and covered lorries, weaving on overloaded springs, roar out of the port and head toward the Troodos mountains.'

In September 1964 the Secretary-General reported to the Security Council *(UN doc. 5950)*: 'In addition to losses incurred in agriculture and in industry during the first part of the year, the Turkish Cypriot community had lost other sources of its income including the salaries of over 4,000 persons who were employed by the Cyprus government.' The trade of the Turkish Cypriot community had considerably declined during the period, and unemployment reached a very high level of approximately 25,000 breadwinners.

Turkish Cypriots had become refugees in their own land.

Expenditure of the Turkish Communal Chamber had dropped considerably, as a yearly subsidy formerly received from the government had ceased in 1964. Furthermore, a large part of its remaining resources had to be used for unemployment relief and other forms of compensation as approximately half the entire Turkish Cypriot population came to be on relief.

During the period 1963 to 1974 the freedom of movement of Turkish Cypriots was severely restricted *(UN docs. S/5764, S/5950, S/7350)*; they were denied postal services *(UN docs. S/5950. S/7001)*; their access to building materials, electrical equipment, motor parts, fuel, chemicals and many other commodities was severely restricted *(UN docs. S/5950, S/7350)*; and Turkish Cypriot refugees had to live in tents and caves.

On September 10, 1964 the UN Secretary-General reported that 'the economic restrictions being imposed against the Turkish Cypriot communities, which in some instances has been so severe as to amount to veritable siege, indicated that the government of Cyprus seeks to force a potential solution by economic pressure.' *(UN doc. S/5950).*

They would still be trying to do that four decades later.

DESPITE the withdrawal of Turkish Cypriots into defended enclaves, they were subjected to a further massacre of civilians in 1967 when, on March 27 the Greeks and Greek Cypriots shelled the village of Mari for four hours. On November 15,1967 some 2,000 armed men with artillery and armoured forces attacked the Turkish Cypriot quarter of Ayios Theodoros. At the same time the village of Getcikale (Kophinou) was assaulted.

During these attacks UN soldiers watched helplessly as women, children, and old men were killed — many burned alive in their own homes — and 50 houses were destroyed. Only further warning flights by the Turkish Air Force prevented more massacres at this time, and forced the withdrawal of some of the mainland Greek forces which had been illegally built-up in Cyprus.

And what was the reaction of the international community?

They did not launch air attacks against the Greek Cypriots, as they later did against the Serbs — they did not complain about ethnic cleansing, or 'attempts to change the demographic character of Cyprus'. They expressed no concern for Turkish Cypriot missing persons, nor for the homes, farms and businesses they had lost, and they did not complain about the 20,000 Greek troops on the island.

Makarios, it seemed, had won.

In the world at large the only voice to be heard pleading the cause of the Turkish Cypriots was that of Rauf Denktaş. And the only reason he was still able to do that was because after his UN speech a furious Makarios had ordered his arrest if he ever set foot in Cyprus again. Turkey had asked the British to provide security for him when he went back but they had said that was not practical since their authority did not extend beyond their two sovereign bases. Accordingly he was advised to remain in Turkey until the arrival of the UN peacekeepers — to be known as UNFICYP — who would provide him with protection and security. That would prove a wildly optimistic hope. His stay in Ankara would last four-and-a-half years.

However, it also gave Denktaş a freedom Makarios had not intended — that of continuing to speak out as he travelled from London to Brussels, to Paris, to Bonn, to New York, and anywhere else he needed to go to argue the Turkish Cypriot case. Had he returned to Cyprus he would have been silenced, almost certainly confined with Dr. Küçük for eleven years in that small area of Nicosia into which the Turkish Cypriots had been squeezed. Indeed, he might not have survived what was to come given the threat he posed to the claims of the Greek Cypriots that they alone ruled the island.

As it was, one lone voice was better than none. Even so

by 1967 and in his fifth year of exile in Ankara, he knew that whatever the risks he had to get back to Cyprus and rally his people to believe that all was not yet lost.

But how? Ankara was against such an idea, believing it was doomed to failure since the Greek Cypriots would arrest him on sight. The Turkish navy could hardly take him there in a warship; nor could he be parachuted into the night. Surely he was of more value as a roving ambassador, a missionary preaching the cause? Even if as yet it had yielded no positive results, he was a thorn in the side of the Greek Cypriots.

Denktaş would not be dissuaded. If he could not get help, then he would smuggle himself back to the island. He would sail home himself. Unfortunately it would be a bold step doomed from the beginning. After an arduous crossing with two companions in a fishing boat and then their transfer to a speedboat in which in heavy seas they were almost drowned, they eventually landed — only to be almost immediately arrested. Even after his long exile he was too well known a figure to avoid instant recognition. His mission had ended even before it had started.

Taken under guard to the central police station in Nicosia he was blindfolded and interrogated by Greek Army officers before being handed over to the Greek Cypriots and put in prison — in a cell which he remembered from his days as a practising barrister was on Death Row.

What should happen to him? There had been hot-headed talk of killing him, with the excuse that he had been shot dead while trying to escape. Wiser heads prevailed. His death would provoke an international outcry; it would infuriate the Turks. Yet setting him free was unthinkable while confining him in some Turkish Cypriot enclave was dangerous, for that would be to give his people a leader. The only answer, it seemed, and Makarios agreed, was to send him back where he had come from — to Turkey. The decision taken, he was flown back next day.

Nevertheless it had not been entirely a wasted adventure.

355

Denktaş at large was a man to reckon with. A year later Makarios would offer to talk to him, to discuss some means of reconciling the Turkish Cypriots to their minority status in an island controlled by the majority. Makarios was not in retreat for what he now wanted from the Turkish Cypriots, wrapped up as concession, was their surrender.

IN the Spring of 1968 an emissary was despatched to Ankara to talk to Denktaş and propose a meeting on neutral ground. Attorney-General Kriton Tornarides, who was not only the legal adviser of Makarios, but a man in whom Makarios had great confidence, would represent the Greek Cypriots.

For Denktaş the order for his arrest was the first immediate signal that Makarios was now a law unto himself. He learned of it on arriving in Ankara *en route* from New York to his home in Nicosia. There was no specified or alleged 'offence', simply a presidential order that if he ever went back to Cyprus he did so at his peril. The real reason for this was the fury of Makarios that Denktaş in his powerful speech in New York had exposed him to the world for what he was and what he had done. For that, and not least the threat he posed to the 'legitimacy claim' of the Greek Cypriots, he had to be punished. But that having failed, now he was to be wooed.

Denktaş discussed this offer with the Turkish foreign minister. He agreed. Something might come of it, and that something might be better than nothing. Denktaş flew to London. Tornarides, whom he knew when they worked as law officers under the British, was staying at the Cumberland Hotel at Marble Arch, and they met there with no one else present.

Tornarides asked: *'What can we do? How can we put matters right?'* Denktaş was very blunt in response. 'We were partners, but your people have destroyed the partnership. We have to re-establish it, having regard to what has happened. We need to be sure that *enosis* has really been abandoned, and the guarantee system has to continue.'

That talks might in fact yield some result, the Makarios regime opened the door by restoring his passport, taken away five years earlier. Denktaş was free at last to return to Cyprus which he did, arriving on April 13,1968. Soon afterwards Makarios appointed Gafcos Clerides — a future president and a former legal colleague and friend of Denktaş — to handle negotiations. Some ten weeks later they met together in July in private for three days in Beirut and discussed the agenda for substantive talks.

The Greek constitutional expert Michael Dekleris, who took part in the negotiations as an advisor to the Greek Cypriot side, recorded that 'in July of 1968 the best opportunity appeared for dialogue. Denktaş played the most energetic role and made dramatic concessions on practically all constitutional issues. What he offered must be considered as the maximum of Turkish concessions which represented a big improvement on the Zurich regime.'

Proposals, counter-proposals, concessions, constructive suggestions — one round of talks would be followed by another, with very little real progress in fact. For to Denktaş there could be no compromise which involved his acceptance that the 1960 agreement was dead and buried, that the Greek Cypriot regime was the lawful government, and that his people were other than political equals.

What none of them could foresee, of course, was that the Greek Cypriots who would actually change the course of events had their own very different ambitions for the future — and that the issue would not be settled by negotiations but by war.

IN 1971 Grivas — the former Greek colonel who had launched the terrorist campaign 1955-1959 — returned to Cyprus to form EOKA-B, committed to making Cyprus a wholly Greek island and annexing it to Greece. In a speech to the Greek Cypriot armed forces he made clear his purpose:

357

'The Greek forces from Greece have come to Cyprus in order to impose the will of the Greeks of Cyprus upon the Turks.

By July 15, 1974 mainland Greek troops assembled in Cyprus represented a powerful force and with their backing the Greek Cypriot National Guard overthrew Makarios and installed former EOKA gunman Nicos Sampson as 'President.' They immediately began to murder Greek Cypriots opposed to them as well as Turkish Cypriots.

On July 22 the *Washington Star News* reported: 'Bodies littered the streets and there were mass burials.... People who were told by Makarios to lay down their guns were shot by the National Guard.'

Even Greek Cypriots sought Turkey's help. In her memoirs, Greek Cypriot MP Rina Katsellis, writes:'*16th July 1974.* Is Makarios alive? Is he dead? The Makarios supporters arrested, the EOKA-B supporters freed .... I did not shed a tear, why should I? Did the stupidity and fanaticism deserve a tear? There are some who beg Turkey to intervene... *18th July 1974* — 'My God!...Everyone is frozen with fear...everyone is frozen with horror...my brother said that in brutality they have surpassed the Germans of the second world war... Nothing is sacred to these people, and they call themselves Greeks! ...we must not keep that name any longer.'

That help came two days later when Turkey at last intervened. No one else lifted a finger.

As the *Daily Telegraph* recalled on August 15, 1996, 'Turkish Cypriots, who had suffered from physical attacks since 1963, called on the guarantor powers to prevent a Greek conquest of the island. When Britain did nothing Turkey invaded Cyprus and occupied its northern part.'

The Greek newspaper *Eleftherotipia* published an interview with Nicos Sampson on February 26, 1981 in which he said: 'Had Turkey not intervened I would not only have proclaimed *enosis* — I would have annihilated the Turks in Cyprus.' He would have done so in accordance with the second ethnic-cleansing blueprint, *The Iphestos Plan*.

The 1976 UK House of Commons Select Committee on Cyprus found that Turkey had proposed joint Anglo-Turkish action under the Treaty of Guarantee and, as reported in the London *Daily Telegraph*, this was confirmed by Prime Minister Ecevit on August 14,1974. However, the Labour government in Britain refused to take any effective action, even though they had troops and aircraft in the Sovereign Bases in Cyprus. They argued that Britain was under no duty to take military action, but Article II of the Treaty provided that Britain would guarantee the state of affairs established by the basic articles of the 1960 Constitution, which it manifestly failed to do.

The Select Committee concluded that 'Britain had a legal right to intervene, she had a moral obligation to intervene. She did not intervene for reasons which the (Labour) government refuses to give.'

'On 20th July 1974 Turkey intervened under Article Iv of the Treaty of Guarantee' *(UK Foreign & Commonwealth Office doc. CPS/75, Jan., 1987)*. 'Turkey exercised its right of intervention in accordance with Article Iv of the Guarantee Treaty of 1960.' *(Resolution 573, Standing Committee of the Consultative Assembly of the Council of Europe, 29th July 1974)*.

TURKEY ENDS THE MURDERS

FIVE days after the Greek-led coup had deposed Makarios — he escaped in a British helicopter — and replaced him with the EOKA terrorist Nicos Sampson, Turkey struck back. With hundreds of civilians already murdered, Makarios supporters among them, Turkey, with British approval, set out to stop the slaughter. They would have to fight hard before that was possible.

That day and the next 132 Turkish Cypriot enclaves on the island, including Turkish villages, Turkish quarters in mixed villages as well as Turkish quarters in Limassol, Larnaca, Baf

(Paphos) and Magosa (Famagusta) were attacked and largely overrun by heavily-armed Greek forces, and the Greek Cypriot National Guard.

Thousands of male Turkish Cypriot inhabitants were rounded up, and either arrested and detained as hostages in detention centres under inhuman conditions, or killed in cold blood. As a result of the rounding up of the male population, Turkish Cypriot women and children in these areas were completely deprived of any protection and were left in fear of their lives at the mercy of Greek and Greek Cypriot gunmen.

As of July 20, the Old City of Magosa (Famagusta) and the three Turkish suburbs of Baykal, Sakarya and Karakol, came under heavy fire. Around 6,000 Turkish Cypriots lived in the Old City and another 6,000 in the three suburbs. They were hammered by heavy artillery, mortars, rifles and even Russian T34 tanks.

During that night Turkish Cypriots living in the suburbs were quietly evacuated into the Old City through a tunnel under the walls, leaving behind their homes and everything in them.

Next morning, when the Greeks discovered what had happened, they resumed their attacks against the Old City, now crammed with 12,000 people. It was to go on for nearly a month — the besieged Turkish Cypriot quarter of Magosa would not finally be liberated until August 15.

On July 23, 1974 the *Washington Post* reported: 'In a Greek raid on a small Turkish village near Limassol 36 people out of a population of 200 were killed. The Greeks said that they had been given orders to kill the inhabitants of the Turkish villages before the Turkish forces arrived.'

On July 24, 1974 *France Soir* reported: 'The Greeks burned Turkish mosques and set fire to Turkish homes in the villages around Famagusta. Defenceless Turkish villagers who have no weapons live in an atmosphere of terror and they evacuate their homes and go and live in tents in the forests. The Greeks' actions are a shame to humanity.'

On July 28 the *New York Times* reported that 14 Turkish Cypriot men had been shot in Alaminos. They would report worse to come. 'On the morning of August 14, a group of National Guardsmen and EOKA-B terrorists entered the village of Aloa (Atillar), west of Famagusta, and rounded up all the men, women and children they could find. They took the 57 villagers in question to a nearby field and shot them with automatic weapons. Afterwards, they dug a ditch and buried the victims in it by bulldozing earth over them. When the corpses were unearthed a few days later, they were almost beyond recognition, for the bulldozer, while running over the dead villagers, had dismembered them. Arms and heads had been torn off, and the victims had been reduced to a heap of bones and flesh. Only three of the inhabitants of Aloa survived the massacre.

'Meanwhile, a few miles away, another group of Greek Cypriot armed men made their way into the village of Maratha (Murataga) and slaughtered its inhabitants. They then took the inhabitants of the nearby village of Sandalaris (Sandallar) to Maratha and executed them too. As in Aloa, the victims were buried in a ditch by means of a bulldozer. When the mutilated bodies of the inhabitants of Maratha and Sandalaris were unearthed from the common grave on September 1, as many as 88 corpses were counted.'

TURKEY'S obligation under the Treaty of Guarantee was to re-establish the state of affairs established by the basic articles of the 1960 Constitution. That was a state of affairs in which the Turkish Cypriots could at the very least stay alive and play their part as political equals in the government of the island.

On July 30, 1974, after the first phase of the Turkish intervention, an international conference had been held in Geneva between Turkey, Greece and Britain. The Geneva Declaration of the guarantor powers recognised: *(a)* that Constitutional government no longer existed in Cyprus; *(b)* the existence in Cyprus of two autonomous administrations; one Turkish Cypriot and the other Greek Cypriot.

It was agreed that Greek and Greek Cypriot forces would leave all the Turkish Cypriot enclaves, but instead, in savage contradiction, they proceeded to murder almost the entire civilian population of six Turkish Cypriot enclaves in both the north and south of the island, and despite the presence in Cyprus of UN troops.

Denktaş realised that neither of these general objectives could be achieved by returning the Turkish Cypriots to the *status quo ante*, and Turkey could not possibly have done so. That status was not the one envisaged by the 1960 Constitution, and Makarios who had been restored to office after the coup was himself responsible for the massacres of 1963, 1964, and 1967. He had also been responsible for expelling the Turkish Cypriots from all their positions in the state, and for squeezing them into less than 3% of the island with only the basic necessities for life.

The Greek Cypriot journalist Stavros Angelides wrote as follows in *Fileleftheros* on September 16, 1990: 'Did we really have constitutional order before the invasion and even before the coup? Was this the constitutional order we had signed with Turkey, Greece, Britain, and the Turkish Cypriots? Such an argument is absolutely baseless. We, the Greek Cypriot side, started to overthrow the constitution soon after Zurich [in 1959].'

Turkey's action in 1974 —though condemned as an unlawful invasion by today's Greek Cypriot leadership and the start of all the island's problems — created a safe haven for the Turkish Cypriots, just as 17 years later the western powers, with Turkey's help, created a safe haven for the Kurdish people in Northern Iraq, and 25 years later — again with Turkey's help — created a safe haven in Kosovo.

However, although the island was now physically divided and there would be no more killings of Turkish Cypriots from that time on, the UN continued to treat the Greek Cypriot

Makarios regime as the lawful government of Cyprus. The Turkish Cypriots would find themselves free and safe for the first time in eleven years — and for that the world would punish them.

As soon as Sampson had been deposed Glafcos Clerides took over from him as acting President, in the enforced absence of Makarios. He contacted Denktaş and asked if he might come to the north to visit Greek Cypriots who were being kept in the *Dome Hotel* in Kyrenia and in the village of Bellapais a few miles away. This was agreed, and Denktaş accompanied him.

Clerides assured the people that he would settle with Denktaş and all would be well for the future. It was obvious to Denktaş that the Greek Cypriots wanted to go south to be with their own people, and that they blamed their misfortune on Makarios and the obsession of their leadership with *enosis*.

In Famagusta all the Greek Cypriots moved to the south as soon as they heard that the Turkish army was coming. About 20,000 Greek Cypriots were not allowed by their own government to go to the south until after the exchange of populations agreement which Denktaş made with Clerides in 1975, and by 2001 there were still about 500 left in the Karpas peninsula in the north, who were given financial incentives by the Greek Cypriot Administration to stay there.

Denktaş recalls that the humanitarian work went reasonably well because Clerides was the Greek Cypriot leader at the time He remembers it as a process of give and take — if one side wanted something then they had to give something in return.

It was also agreed that Denktaş should be allowed to visit Turkish Cypriots who were being kept in the south, and while he was there the people begged him to persuade the Greek Cypriots to let them go to the north. At first Clerides said no, but eventually he agreed to allow people who were elderly or in need of medical care, and students who needed to attend Turkish schools, to leave. Later, Denktaş was to be grateful to Clerides on a personal level for allowing the body of his long-dead mother to be brought to the North for reburial next to his father.

The 1960 Agreements having been repudiated by the conduct of the Greek Cypriots, and expressly abrogated by the Greek Cypriot leaders, Turkish Cypriots could not live for long in a political limbo. At the end of January 1975 Denktaş received a phone call from Turkish Foreign Minister, Mehit Esenbel. He told him that the Americans and the British wanted to send Makarios back to Cyprus. They had told Esenbel that they regarded Makarios as a strong leader who could command the support of the Greek Cypriots, and that if he returned to Cyprus he would realise that *enosis* was now impossible and would have to lead them towards a sensible arrangement with the Turkish Cypriots. They had asked for Turkey's agreement, and Esenbel wanted to know Denktaş' views. He then astonished Denktaş by saying that Turkey had already agreed.

Denktaş told him that Turkey had made a serious mistake. Makarios was a man who could not be trusted. He had already led a coup against the 1960 Republic and thrown the Turkish Cypriots out of all their positions and tried to kill them all. If he now returned, especially with Turkey's consent, the world would see him as the legitimate President of Cyprus, which he had ceased to be when he overthrew the constitution in December 1963. He would be able to use that status to demand the withdrawal of Turkey from Cyprus. 'Is that what you want?' said Denktaş.

'So what can we do now?' asked Esenbel.

'We have no alternative' replied Denktaş 'but to declare our own independence in the North on the day he comes back, so as to make it clear to the world that we the Turkish Cypriots do not accept him as the President of all Cyprus.'

'Yes, you are right, something has to be done, I will ring you back in an hour or so.' About two hours later he called again. 'We agree that you should declare your own state, but call it a federated state'

'But Mehit, how can we have a federated state without a federation?'

'Declare your federated state on the basis that you are inviting the Greek Cypriots to form their own federated state, and if they don't do it within a reasonable time then you should declare a Republic.'

Denktaş said it wouldn't work, but Esenbel replied 'all you have now is a Turkish Cypriot Administration — accept my suggestion and you will then be a state, albeit a federated state. We can't keep Makarios out forever and you will at least be getting something out of his return.' He then added gravely: 'At this time Turkey cannot take responsibility for the declaration of full independence. We have enough difficulties already with Cyprus'.

Denktaş saw it as his duty to advance the cause of the Turkish Cypriot people and knew he could do it only if he could keep Turkey with them. He agreed to commend a federated state to his people, and it was declared on February 13, 1975 with the expressed intention that it should one day form part of a federation for the whole of Cyprus.

Once more the UN showed its partiality, and in Security Council Resolution 367 of March 12, 1975 'regretted' the decision of the Turkish Cypriots, while continuing to reward the unilateral decision of the Greek Cypriots in 1963 to impose their own autonomous administration on Cyprus.

There is an inherent contradiction in this resolution, which stresses negotiations between the two communities on an equal footing and on the other hand regrets the assertion by the Turkish Cypriots of the statehood that they needed in order to possess equal standing with the Greek Cypriots.

IN 1974/75 Many Turkish Cypriots left their homes in the south with such possessions as they could carry, and struggled through the Troodos mountains on foot to get away from the Greeks and Greek Cypriots. In one dreadful case a Greek

Cypriot taxi driver killed his passengers. The registration number of the taxi had been recorded by the Turkish Cypriot leaders in the south before the unfortunate family set out, so the driver was eventually convicted of murdering the two Turkish Cypriot women, one girl, and two small children. The most significant feature of this case is that when arrested he claimed in his defence that 'they were only Turks' having been led to believe for most of his life that Turks were not entitled to the rights of ordinary human beings.

In July 1975, just before the third Vienna meeting, Denktaş received news that 34 people had been caught trying to escape to the north. They were savagely beaten with rifle butts and marched with broken ribs into the town of Ktima. They were lined up in the square where the Greek Cypriot townspeople spat in their faces. The UN were there but could not,or would not do anything about it. The news broke whilst Denktaş was addressing a rally at the Kyrenia stadium in the presence of Turkish Minister, Fezioglu, to celebrate the first anniversary of the liberation.

An old woman stood up in the crowd holding a bundle of clothes and shouted: 'Denktaş, you know who I am, you know what I had in Paphos, but this bundle is all I have now — our people left in the south are suffering every day, and now we hear of this outrage we must get them out.' The crowd roared its approval.

Denktaş told them that the Greek Cypriot refusal to allow the Turkish Cypriots to leave was a violation of human rights and of common humanity, and was against everything he was trying to do to make a reconciliation with the Greek Cypriots. He promised them that within a short time he would get the Turkish Cypriots out.

As soon as he landed in Vienna for the talks Denktaş made a statement that he could not and would not allow talks to go on for weeks whilst Turkish Cypriot people in the south were being abused, attacked, and humiliated. He demanded an urgent solution. He met immediately with Kurt Waldheim, the newly-elected UN Secretary-General, and told him that there were so many thousands of people in Northern Cyprus outraged by what had happened that it would be impossible to prevent very serious trouble if he, Waldheim, could not get Clerides to see the necessity for releasing the Turkish Cypriots immediately.

The meeting started the next morning but Denktaş was not called in until about midday. Waldheim had been talking with Clerides for at least three hours, and was able to tell Denktaş that he had agreed to release the Turkish Cypriots. This was put into a formal agreement, and published in the Vienna III Communiqué on 2nd August 1975. Following this Exchange of Populations Agreement Turkish Cypriots moved to the North and Greek Cypriots moved to the south under arrangements made by the UN.

For the first year after the Turkish intervention Rauf Denktaş' priority had been the enormous humanitarian task of resettling those in the north who had been confined in the enclaves, bringing the Turkish Cypriots to the north and finding them homes and if possible jobs, and starting to rebuild the Turkish Cypriot economy which the Greek Cypriots had wrecked in 1963.

Later he turned his attention to the long-term political future of the Turkish Cypriot people. It had become clear to him that it was not possible for the Turkish Cypriots and the Greek Cypriots to live together in peace, and that their future on the island if not as two separate states had to be within a bi-zonal, bi-communal structure in which each of the two peoples could live securely in its own geographical area.

He has however believed since 1963 that it is not possible to negotiate a new structure with a Greek Cypriot side which regards itself, and is regarded by the world, and now by the European Union, as the government of Cyprus, but he has responded to the entreaties of successive Turkish governments, who in turn were influenced by America, Britain and the EU.

Until Bulent Ecevit returned to government Turkey would

always tell Denktaş: 'Don't worry, the Americans will solve this problem for us, you have nothing to lose by carrying on the talks indefinitely.' Denktaş has always believed this to be a mistake, as it has enabled the Greek Cypriots to keep the issue on the international agenda and consolidate their position over the years as 'government of Cyprus.'

Denktaş wrote a letter to Makarios on January 9, 1977 saying that unless the two of them met it would not be possible to make any progress. He copied this letter to the UN, and he believed the Americans had a talk with Makarios, as a result of which a meeting was arranged for January 27, 1977 in the presence of the retiring UN Secretary-General Perez de Cuéllar,. They met briefly at the airport, and then met again on February 12, 1977, in the presence of the new Secretary-General Kurt Waldheim. Denktaş reminded Makarios that he himself was the author of geographical separation when he threw the Turkish Cypriots out of the Republic in 1963 and confined them in ghettos comprising less than 3% of the island, and said 'unless you and your people accept what you have done to us and learn the lessons of the past you will never understand us and be able to work with us for the future.'

Denktaş knew that Makarios remembered very well what had happened, and had no intention of working with Turkish Cypriots in the future except to manoeuvre them back into a position of weakness in Cyprus. He also knew that it was vital to Makarios' strategy that the world should not be reminded of what had happened — still the case today, since the Greek Cypriots will happily talk about events after 20th July 20, 1974 but not what went before. Makarios therefore replied, as all his successors, and some well-meaning international commentators, have done, 'Let us forget the past and look to the future.'

'No', responded Denktaş 'I am not trying to embarrass you, but I want you and the Secretary-General to acknowledge what has happened and to listen to how we Turkish Cypriots feel.'

He then spoke for about 90 minutes, detailing all the

massacres and other illegal actions for which Makarios and his associates had been responsible, and going through the *Akritas* plan and the *Iphestos* plan, which were the Greek Cypriot plans for the elimination of the Turkish Cypriots in 1963 and 1974 respectively, of which Makarios knew and had approved.

Denktaş could see that Makarios was very uncomfortable, to have to listen to the details of these crimes in the presence of the Secretary-General, who was recording what was said. At length he tried to divert the conversation to generalised, irrelevant, subjects, but Denktaş said 'No, we are both here to settle the future of our peoples, are you willing to agree to a bi-zonal, bi-communal structure?'

Much to Denktaş' surprise he said 'Yes'. Having stated so adamantly and so publicly for so long that he would never contemplate such a solution, and having reprimanded Clerides when he discussed the idea with Denktaş in February the previous year, Denktaş doubted that answer. Nevertheless Makarios and Denktaş then started to draft what became the High Level Agreement of February 12, 1977. Its terms were as follows:

•We are seeking an independent, non-aligned, bi-communal federal republic.

• The territory under the administration of each community should be discussed in the light of economic viability or productivity and land ownership

•Questions of principles like freedom of movement, freedom of settlement, the right of property and other specific matters are open for discussion taking into consideration the fundamental basis of a bi-communal federal system and certain practical difficulties which may arise for the Turkish Cypriot community.

•The powers and functions of the central federal government will be such as to safeguard the unity of the country, having regard to the bi-communal character of the state.

Nothing came of it.

MAKARIOS died on August 3, 1977 and was replaced by Kyprianou. Denktaş did not regard Kyprianou as a strong leader. He thought he was not a man of decision, and was imprisoned by the policy of Makarios. Denktaş saw in him no humour and no vision, and believes he was obsessed by the idea of making Cyprus a Greek island. Denktaş found him very difficult to deal with.

No progress toward settlement having been made in the six years that followed — and with no prospect of further talks getting anywhere either — the Turkish Cypriots declared independence as the Turkish Republic of Northern Cyprus on November 15, 1983, and elected Rauf Denktaş as their first President. However, they expressly declared that they wished to work towards a new Constitution for the whole of Cyprus.

The Turkish Republic of Northern Cyprus remains today, thanks to Denktaş a multi-party democracy, with a free judiciary, a free press, and free trade unions. It is sometimes described as a 'breakaway state,' but there was nothing to break away from. As Denktaş repeatedly reminded the world, it was not they but the Greek Cypriots who broke away from the 1960 Republic in 1963 and set up a wholly Greek Cypriot Republic which they continued, and still continue, to call the Republic of Cyprus. They have usurped even the name of the bi-communal Republic.

Yet again Britain, the United Nations, and the world in general deplored this claim to self-government. The Security Council, by Resolutions 541 and 550, purported to declare the Declaration of Independence 'legally invalid,' and called upon states not to recognise the TRNC. However, it has never specified whether the constitutional law of Cyprus or international law is said to be the basis of such illegality. If constitutional law, it has never explained how the 1960 constitution, having been repudiated and expressly abrogated by the Greek Cypriot side as long ago as 1963, could still be binding upon the Turkish Cypriot side in 1983.

In November 1984, after lengthy discussions with both

sides the then UN Secretary-General, Perez de Cuéllar, put forward a draft framework agreement for a comprehensive solution of the problem through the establishment of a federal republic. On December 1, 1984 *The Times* wrote: 'In a dramatic move which would break the diplomatic impasse on efforts to end the division of Cyprus, the Turkish Cypriot community has offered important concessions and effectively left the ball in the Greek Cypriot court. Rauf Denktaş, the leader of the Turkish Cypriots announced on Thursday that his side was in complete agreement with the peace plan put forward by the UN Secretary-General.'

Kyprianou said he could accept the plan only as a basis for discussion. This announcement surprised even his own people, and a motion of censure upon him was passed in the Greek Cypriot House of Representatives. During the debate Ezekias Papaioannou, leader of the AKEL Party said: 'Kyprianou never adopted the basis of federation which was agreed upon by Makarios and Denktaş, and he never exerted any effort for the solution of the Cyprus problem on the basis of a federation. He never respected the summit agreements.'

Glafcos Clerides, then leader of the Democratic Rally Party said: 'Kyprianou asked for the renegotiation of everything from A to Z. He should not have brought forth again issues which had already been debated and agreed upon with Denktaş.'

On 21st January 1985 the Associated Press wrote: 'All points of the draft agreement, which set basic guidelines for the reunification of the Mediterranean island under a loose federation, were accepted by the Turkish Cypriot side. Mr. Kyprianou wanted to renegotiate almost all 14 points of the agreement.' According to *The Washington Times* (22nd January 1985) 'the blame for the breakdown of the Cyprus talks at the UN on Sunday lies with Greek Cypriot President Spyros Kyprianou ... according to a consensus of western diplomats and UN officials. These sources concede that Turkey and the Turkish Cypriot leadership have been more than conciliatory and reasonable in their approach to a plan for a two-zone

371

Cypriot federation drafted by UN Secretary- General Perez de Cuéllar, formerly the UN mediator in Cyprus and an expert on the issue.'

The Times on 21st January 1985 wrote that UN officials said that Kyprianou even questioned the basic tenets and principles of an accommodation with the Turkish Cypriots, including the concept of bi-zonality and equal political status for the two communities. In April 1985, the Secretary-General put forward an amended version of his plan, which was accepted by the Greek Cypriots. This document had not however been discussed with both sides and the Turkish Cypriots rejected it. In March 1986, after further discussions, this time with both sides, the Secretary-General put forward a new draft framework agreement, which again envisaged a federal solution. This document was again accepted by the Turkish Cypriots in its entirety, but rejected by the Greek Cypriots.

When he had presented his plan the Secretary-General made it clear (*UN doc. S/18102/Add.1, para. 6*) that it 'preserved all the points on which agreement had been achieved since August 1984...suggested solutions to the remaining divergencies in a manner that in my judgement protected the interests of both communities, and proposed procedures for negotiation of the outstanding issues which remained to be tackled, including withdrawal of non-Cypriot forces, guarantees, and freedom of movement, freedom of settlement, and the right to property'.

On October 23, 1987 in the British House of Commons the Minister of State for Foreign & Commonwealth Affairs said that 'we continue to believe that the proposals form a good basis for settlement and we urge their acceptance even now. We believe that the proposals took account of both the internal and international aspects of the Cyprus problem. They were put forward on the basis that acceptance of each part depended on the acceptance of the whole'.

However, the Greek Cypriots persisted in their demand that the issues which were important to them be isolated and dealt with as a precondition. They were thereby seeking to take the benefits of the Secretary-General's initiative without making any concessions. Even Constantine Mitsotakis, later to be Prime Minister of Greece, said that withdrawal of Turkish troops should be seen as the result of a settlement not the precondition for one.

On June 14, 1986 *The Times* reported that 'the UN Secretary-General had cast his usual diplomatic discretion aside to blame the Greek Cypriot community for obstructing his attempts at a negotiated solution to the Cyprus dispute ... The warning was a rare concerted public effort to bring home the message to the Greek Cypriots that time was not on their side. With the Turkish Cypriots having firmly placed themselves in the right by accepting the UN package the door was open for further consolidation of their Turkish Republic of Northern Cyprus'. That was 24 years ago, and nothing has happened.

In all the years that followed, Denktaş tried many times to negotiate a settlement. On November 21, 1994 he wrote to the UN Secretary-General: 'I wish to confirm that I am prepared and willing to sign the confidence-building measures agreement; that I believe that the implementation of the confidence-building measures agreement would help in facilitating an overall solution; that we are fully committed to a bi-communal and bi-zonal federal solution; and that I am always available and prepared to engage in face-to-face negotiations with Mr. Clerides. The Turkish Cypriot side does have the political will and readiness to reach a negotiated settlement with the Greek Cypriot side and to bring an equitable solution and lasting peace to both peoples of our beautiful island.'

Seven years later with no progress to show for all the discussions under UN auspices he decided in November 2000 that there was no point in further UN talks until the international community and the UN itself became willing to treat the two sides as equals. He nevertheless invited the

Greek Cypriot leader for direct talks with him in 2001. Again, it came to nothing.

Denktaş, although still President, stepped aside during the referenda on the UN Annan Plan in 2004 and he was right to do so, given his own conviction that the Greek Cypriots would veto it as they had always done with every other initiative; however, he did not want to dash the hopes of his own people by telling them that. So he remained silent as they overwhelmingly voted 'Yes' — only to find that the Greek Cypriots yet again had flatly rejected a plan which would have given them the rights lost a generation earlier.

It may be said that the man least surprised by that was Rauf Denktaş. As he recognised, though few others did, the Greek Cypriots had already been guaranteed entry into the EU, whatever the outcome, and therefore were under no pressure to compromise, and without compromise — as he had argued throughout his political life — there could be no solution. The EU had been hoodwinked, as the UN had been over the years, and the complaints in Brussels that the Greek Cypriots had 'cheated' their way into Europe came too late to matter.

Nevertheless, the Greek Cypriots were now the Republic of Cyprus in the European Union as they had been confirmed as such in the UN in 1964. As for the Turkish Cypriots their rewards for having supported the UN plan were to be promises but nothing else. At the behest of the Greek Cypriots they would remain economically embargoed, denied direct flights, or even to take part in international sport, and their government branded as 'pseudo' and 'illegal'.

Fifty years on from the establishment of the Republic of Cyprus, designed to ensure that political equality and rights, all that is left is a Constitution which as Denktaş warned at the time might not be worth the paper it was written on. And so it has proved.

In April 2005 Rauf Denktaş retired as the Leader of the Turkish Cypriots at the age of 81, after a lifetime of service to his people and to the cause of peace. He was awarded

374

Turkey's state Medal of Honour, and there can be few more deserving recipients of this high mark of the Turkish nation's esteem. President Sezer was right to say that under his skilful leadership the Turkish Cypriot people were able to overcome many difficulties and live in freedom and honour under the principles of equality and peace.

Select Bibliography

ATAKOL, Kenan, T*urkish & Greek Cypriots. Is Their Separation Permanent?* Metu Press, 2003

BEŞIR, Özkul, *Sessiz gidişin, Sessiz dönüşü, 1. Kitap,* ATEŞ MATBAACILIK LTD, 2010
— *Sessiz gidişin, Sessiz dönüşü, 2. Kitap,* ATEŞ MATBAACILIK LTD, 2010

BOZKURT, Umut and TRIMIKLINIOTIS Nicos (Editors), *Beyond a Divided Cyprus: A State and Society in Transformation,* Palgrave Macmillan publisher, 2012

BÖLÜKBAŞI, Süha, *Turkish-American Relations and Cyprus,* University Press of America, 1989

Chronology of Cyprus Conflict 1878- 1978, Historical Research Group, Cyprus, 1978

CRAIG, Ian and O'MALLEY Brendan, *The Cyprus Conspiracy: America, Espionage and the Turkish Invasion,* I. B. Tauris,2001

CRAWSHAW, Nancy, *The Cyprus Revolt,* Unwin Hyman, 1978

DENKTAŞ, Rauf, T*he Cyprus Problem, What it is — How can it be solved?* CYREP Cyprus Research and Publishing Centre, 2004
— *Karkot River,* 7th edition, Remzi Kitabevi, 2005

DENKTAŞ, Rauf R., and MORAN Michael, *Cyprus: Unity and Difference,* İstanbul Kültür University Publications No: 96, 2009

DÜNYA Kıbrıs Türkleri Vakfı et al, 1 *Dünya Kıbrıs Türkleri Kongresi,* Dünya Kıbrıs Türkleri Vakfı, 2009

GAZIOĞLU, Ahmet C., *ENOSIS ÇEMBERİNDEN KIBRIS CUMHURİYETİNE, CYREP* Cyprus Research and Publishing Centre, 2000
— *Cyprus, The Island of Sustained Crisis, Volume 1* (15 May

1963 -13 March 1964), CYREP Cyprus Research and
Publishing Centre, 1998
— *The Island of Sustained Crisis, Volume 2* (March 1964-
August 1964), CYREP Cyprus Research and Publishing
Centre, 2002

KORKMAZ, Haktanır, *The Grand Deception*, AbeBooks

LAPTALI, Hüseyin, *Erenköy Sürüngeni*, UFUK MATBAASI

MATTHEWS, David, *The Cyprus Tapes*, Downlow Productions,
1999

MORAN, Michael, *Cyprus: A European Anomaly*, İstanbul Kültür
University Publications No: 137, 2010
— *Sovereignty Divided, Essays on the international dimensions
of the Cyprus problem*, CYREP Cyprus Research and
Publishing Centre, 1999

MORGAN, Tabitha, *Sweet and Bitter Island, A History of the
British in Cyprus,* I. B. Tauris & Co Ltd, 2010

OBERLING, Pierre, *Negotiating for Survival: The Turkish Cypriot
quest for a solution to the Cyprus problem,* Aldington Press,
1991

ORTEGA, A., *The Ortega Report*, July 1964, Dünya Kıbrıs
Türkleri Vakfı, 2011

PLÜMER, Aytuğ, *Cyprus, 1963-64: The Fateful Years,* CYREP
Cyprus Research and Publishing Centre, 2003
— *Kıbrıs Ekonomi Tarihi, Sarsıntılı Bir Devrin Anatomisi
(1960-1974),* Rüstem Kitabevi, 2008

REDDAWAY, John, *Burdened with Cyprus, The British Connection,*
Published jointly by K. Rüstem & Bro., and Weidenfeld &
Nicolson, 1986

SONYEL R., Salahi, *Cyprus: The Destruction of a Republic.* British
Documents 1960-65, The Eothen Press; 1 edition, 1997

STEPHEN, Michael, *The Cyprus Question,* Northgate
Publications, London, 2001

VANEZIS, P. N., *Cyprus The Unfinished Agony,* Abelord--
Schuman, 1977

Cyprus Gazette, 1941
Cyprus Mail, MITA Alex, 26 November 2002
Hürriyet Daily News, 7 July 1997
Hürriyet Daily News, 13 October 2011
Le Monde Diplomatique, May 2004
New York Times, 21 July 1974
Special News Bulletin, Turkish Communal Chamber, issue
    No.11, 6 January 1964
The Observer, London 22 December 1963
Vatan Gündem, 23 November 2004

WENZKE Caroline and LINDLEY Dan, *Dismantling the
    Cyprus Conspiracy: The US role in the Cypriot Crises of 1963,
    1967 and 1974,* www.nd.edu/~dindley/handouts
FALLACI, Oriana, *An Interview with Archbishop Makarios III :*
    November 1974, http://www.cyprus-conflict.net/
DIRVANA Emin, interview with *Cyprus, Britain's Grim Legacy,
    End of Empire*, ITV documentary, 22 July 1984
www.europeanvoice.com
www.keeptalkinggreece.com
www.britains-smallwars.com/cyprus
www.topix.com/forum/world/cyprus/
www.kpros.org/documents

Index